AF541319

Global Marketing Management

Global Marketing Management

Dr. Atul Mathur

Dr. Sandeep Sharma

Global Marketing Management

ISBN 978-93-5111-238-9
© Reserved

All Rights Reserved. No Part of this book may be reproduced in any manner without written permission.

Published in 2014 in India by

RANDOM PUBLICATIONS

4376-A/4B, Gali Murari Lal, Ansari Road
New Delhi-110 002
Phone: +9111-43580356, 23289044
E-mail: randomexports@gmail.com; sales@randompublications.com;
info@randompublications.com

Reprinted 2023

Type Setting by : Keystoneprintads, Delhi-110051
Digitally Printed at: Replika Press Pvt. Ltd.

Acknowledgement

It is a matter of great honor for me to place on record my gratitudes towards those who were of great help during the completion of this book.

Firstly I would like to pay my regards and reverence at the holy feet of Radhasoami Dayal, who showered all his grace, mercy and blessings on me during the completion of this book. To my revered father professor Dr. Agam Prasad Mathur popularly known as Dadaji, I express my sincere thanks and regards, it is he who has nurtured me and has made me whatever I am today. I bow before him and pray to almighty that he keeps showering his love and affection on me always.

For my wife Smt. Deepa Mathur I have no words to express my deep sense of gratitude for the unconditional support and encouragement, to my children Ms. Sureeti, Ms. Suhani and Saras, I am thankful for their constant support and suggestions. For my grandson Deep I wish to convey all my love and affection.

To the publisher of this book Mr. Sushil Mehra and Mr. Atul Mehra and to Mr. Rahul Singhal, I have no words to express my thanks as it would not have possible without them to publish this book.

Last but not the least I wish to dedicate this book to my brother late Dr. Achint Kumar, for it is he who always had been a guiding force behind me, I miss you a lot dada.

Dr. Atul Mathur

Preface

As global competition increases, multinational companies must change how they manage and alter their organizational structures accordingly. The ultimate goal is to enhance their current position to take advantage of opportunities existing in the global marketplace. Whether your company is already multinational, or you are domestic company looking into foreign expansion, there are many strategic decisions involved with planning, implementing and maintaining appropriate business processes. For instance, will you use a standardized or adapted marketing approach, expand in a concentrated vs. dispersed manner, or have integrated vs. independent operations? It makes no difference what industry you are involved with or the size of your organization. Marketers must fully understand the nature of competition, planning requirements and market-entry options from a global perspective. This post will identify elements that are present in the most successful international and global organizations.

Throughout the past few decades, there has been much debate over whether global homogenization of consumer tastes allows for standardization of the marketing mix. To refresh, understand that there are differences between global marketing and international marketing. Global marketing implies that your organization standardizes its marketing programs, coordinates across markets and practices global integration. Today, many companies have trouble deciding whether using a truly global marketing strategy is right for them. There is a slight trend back toward localization due to new efficiencies of customization made possible by technology, the Internet, and new manufacturing processes. "Mass Customization" has now taken the place of "Mass Production." In today's world, the customer does not always respond to a "one size fits all" approach.

If your company chooses to go global, planning is essential and is one area that business-owners are often not disciplined enough to do. As previously discussed, international business can be much more complex than doing business domestically. Planning is a tool that allows you to relate to the future. It is an attempt to control the effects of the internal, external and customer environments in such a way that the firm can set and meet goals. When goals are solidified and a commitment is made to specific resources, growth is more likely.

I thank all members of my team who have helped in the preparation of the book. My special thanks go to "Random Publications" who have published the book.

– *Dr. Sandeep Sharma*

Contents

1

Introduction

DEFINITION

Management process through which goods and services move from concept to the customer. As a philosophy, it is based on thinking about the business in terms of customer needs and their satisfaction.

As a practice, it consists in coordination of four elements called 4P's:

1. Identification, selection, and development of a product,
2. Determination of its price,
3. Selection of a distribution channel to reach the customer's place, and
4. Development and implementation of a promotional strategy.

Marketing differs from selling because "Selling concerns itself with the tricks and techniques of getting people to exchange their cash for your product. It is not concerned with the values that the exchange is all about. And it does not, as marketing invariably does, view the entire business process as consisting of a tightly integrated effort to discover, create, arouse, and satisfy customer needs."

CONCEPT OF MARKETING

BACKGROUND

Several definitions have been proposed for the term marketing. Each tends to emphasize different issues. Memorizing a definition is unlikely to be useful; ultimately, it makes more sense to thinking of ways to benefit from creating customer value in the most effective way, subject to ethical and other constraints that one may have. The 2006 and 2007 definitions offered by the American Marketing Association are relatively similar, with the 2007 appearing a bit more concise.

Note that the definitions make several points:

- A main objective of marketing is to create customer value.
- Marketing usually involves an exchange between buyers and sellers or between other parties.

- Marketing has an impact on the firm, its suppliers, its customers, and others affected by the firm's choices.
- Marketing frequently involves enduring relationships between buyers, sellers, and other parties.
- Processes involved include "creating, communicating, delivering, and exchanging offerings."

Delivering Customer Value

The central idea behind marketing is the idea that a firm or other entity will create something of value to one or more customers who, in turn, are willing to pay enough to make the venture worthwhile considering opportunity costs. Value can be created in a number of different ways. Some firms manufacture basic products but provide relatively little value above that. Other firms make products whose tangible value is supplemented by services.

It is not necessary for a firm to physically handle a product to add value—e.g., online airline reservation systems add value by compiling information about available flight connections and fares, allowing the customer to buy a ticket, forwarding billing information to the airline, and forwarding reservation information to the customer. It should be noted that value must be examined from the point of view of the customer. Some customer segments value certain product attributes more than others. A very expensive product—relative to others in the category—may, in fact, represent great value to a particular customer segment because the benefits received are seen as even greater than the sacrifice made. Some segments have very unique and specific desires, and may value what—to some individuals—may seem a "lower quality" item—very highly.

Some Forms of Customer Value

The marketing process involves ways that value can be created for the customer. *Form utility* involves the idea that the product is made available to the consumer in some form that is more useful than any commodities that are used to create it. A customer buys a chair, for example, rather than the wood and other components used to create the chair. Thus, the customer benefits from the specialization that allows the manufacturer to more efficiently create a chair than the customer could do himself or herself.

Place utility refers to the idea that a product made available to the customer at a preferred location is worth more than one at the place of manufacture. It is much more convenient for the customer to be able to buy food items in a supermarket in his or her neighbourhood than it is to pick up these from the farmer. *Time utility* involves the idea of having the product made available when needed by the customer. The customer may buy a turkey a few days before Thanksgiving without having to plan to have it available.

Intermediaries take care of the logistics to have the turkeys—which are easily perishable and bulky to store in a freezer—available when customers demand them. *Possession utility* involves the idea that the consumer can go to one store and obtain a large assortment of goods from different manufacturers during one shopping occasion. Supermarkets combine food and other household items from a number of different suppliers in one place. Certain "superstores" such as the European *hypermarkets* and the Wal-Mart "super centres" combine even more items into one setting.

The Marketing vs. the Selling Concept

Two approaches to marketing exist. The traditional *selling* concept emphasizes selling existing products. The philosophy here is that if a product is not selling, more aggressive measures must be taken to sell it—e.g., cutting price, advertising more, or hiring more aggressive sales-people. When the railroads started to lose business due to the advent of more effective trucks that could deliver goods right to the customer's door, the railroads cut prices instead of recognizing that the customers ultimately wanted *transportation* of goods, *not* necessarily *railroad* transportation.

Smith Corona, a manufacturer of typewriters, was too slow to realise that consumers wanted the ability to process documents and *not* typewriters per se. The *marketing* concept, in contrast, focuses on getting consumers what they seek, *regardless of whether this entails coming up with entirely new products.* The 4 Ps—*product, place, promotion,* and *price*—represent the variables that are within the control of the firm. In contrast, the firm is faced with uncertainty from the environment.

THE MARKETING ENVIRONMENT

Elements of the Environment

The marketing *environment* involves factors that, for the most part, are beyond the control of the company. Thus, the company must *adapt* to these factors. It is important to observe how the environment changes so that a firm can adapt its strategies appropriately.

Consider these environmental forces:

- *Competition*: Competitors often "creep" in and threaten to take away markets from firms. For example, Japanese auto manufacturers became a serious threat to American car makers in the late 1970s and early 1980s. Similarly, the Lotus Corporation, maker of one of the first commercially successful spreadsheets, soon faced competition from other software firms. Note that while competition may be frustrating for the firm, it is good for consumers. Note that competition today is increasingly global in scope. It is important to recognize that competition can happen at different "levels." At the brand level, two firms compete in providing a very similar product or service. Coca Cola and Pepsi, for example, compete for the cola drink market, and United and American Airlines compete for the passenger air transportation market. Firms also face less direct—but frequently very serious—competition at the product level. For example, cola drinks compete against bottled water. Products or services can serve as substitutes for each other even though they are very different in form. Teleconferencing facilities, for example, are very different from airline passenger transportation, but both can "bring together" people for a "meeting." At the budget level, different products or services provide very different benefits, but buyers have to make choices as to what they will buy when they cannot afford—or are unwilling to spend on—both. For example, a family may decide between buying a new car or a high definition television set. The family may also have to choose between going on a foreign vacation or remodeling its kitchen. Firms, too, may have to make choices. The firm has the cash flow either to remodel its offices or install a more energy efficient climate control system; or the firm can choose either to invest in new product development or in a promotional campaign to increase awareness of its brand among consumers.

- *Economics*: Two economic forces strongly affect firms and their customers:
  - *Economic Cycles*: Some firms in particular are extremely vulnerable to changes in the economy. Consumers tend to put off buying a new car, going out to eat, or building new homes in bad times. In contrast, in good times, firms serving those needs may have difficulty keeping up with demand. One important point to realise is that different industries are affected to different degrees by changes in the economy. Although families can cut down on the quality of the food they buy—going with lower priced brands, for example—there are limits to the savings that can be made without greatly affecting the living standard of the family. On the other hand, it is often much easier to put off the purchase of a new car for a year or hold off on remodeling the family home. If need be, firms can keep the current computers—even though they are getting a bit slow—when sales are down. The economy goes through cycles. In the late 1990s, the U.S. economy was quite strong, and many luxury goods were sold. Currently, the economy fluctuates between increasing strength, stagnation, or slight decline. Many firms face consequences of economic downturns. Car makers, for example, have seen declining profit margins as they have had to cut prices and offer low interest rates on financing.

Generally, in good economic times, there is a great deal of demand, but this introduces a fear of possible inflation. In the U.S., the Federal Reserve will then try to prevent the economy from "overheating." This is usually done by raising interest rates. This makes businesses less willing to invest, and as a result, people tend to make less money. During a recession, unemployment tends to rise, causing consumers to spend less. This may result in a "bad circle," with more people losing their jobs due to lowered demands. Some businesses, however, may take this opportunity to invest in growth now that things can be bought more cheaply.

- *Inflation*: Over time, most economies experience some level of inflation. Therefore, it is useful to explicitly state whether a reference to money over time involves the actual dollar amount exchanged at any point or an "inflation adjusted" figure that "anchors" a given amount of money to the value of that money at some point in time. Suppose, for example, that cumulative inflation between 1960 and 2007 has been 1,000%—that is, on the average, it costs ten times as much to buy the same thing in 2007 as it did 47 years earlier. If the cumulative inflation between 1960 and 1984 had been 500%, we could talk about one 1984 dollar being worth fifty 1960 cents or two 2007 dollars. It is important to note that inflation is uneven. Some goods and services—such as health care and college tuition—are currently increasing in cost much higher than the average rate of inflation. Prices of computers, actually decline both in absolute numbers and in terms of the value for money paid once an adjustment has been made for the improvement in quality. That is, two years later, the computer has not only declined in price by 20%, but it may also be 30% better. In that case, then, there has actually been, over the period, a net deflation of 38.5% for the category.

- *Political*: Businesses are very vulnerable to changes in the political situation. For example, because consumer groups lobbied Congress, more stringent rules were made on the terms of car leases. The tobacco industry is currently the target of much negative attention from government and public interest groups. Currently, the desire to avoid aiding the enemy may result in laws that make it more difficult for American firms to export goods to other countries. Many industries have a strong economic interest in policies that benefit the industry may have a negative impact on the nation as a whole but enhance profits for the industry. For example, regulations that limit the amount of sugar that can be imported into the United States is estimated to cost each American approximately $10.00 a year. The total increase in profits to the sugar industry is difficult to estimate because many of the large producers of refined sugar are privately held corporations, but it is likely that the net gain to the industry is as much as the roughly $3 billion lost by Americans a whole. However, the interests of the industry are much more concentrated. The industry can rally its stockholders, unions and employees, and suppliers together to lobby for their special interests. In turn, the industry can join forces with other agricultural interests which each support each other's programmes.

- *Legal:* Firms are very vulnerable to changing laws and changing interpretations by the courts. Firms in the U.S. are very vulnerable to lawsuits. McDonald's, for example, is currently being sued by people who claim that eating the chain's hamburgers caused them to get fat. Firms are significantly limited in what they can do by various laws—some laws, for example, require that disclosures be made to consumers on the effective interest rates they pay on products bought on installment. A particularly interesting group of laws relate to antitrust. These laws basically exist to promote fair competition among firms. As suggested, consider such laws when we cover pricing later in the term.
- *Technological:* Changes in technology may significantly influence the demand for a product. For example, the advent of the fax machine was bad news for Federal Express. The Internet is a major threat to travel agents. Many record stores have been wiped out of business by the trend towards downloading songs. Although technological change eliminates or at least greatly diminishes some markets, it creates opportunities for others. For example, although Federal Express has lost a considerable amount of business from documents that can now be faxed or sent by the Internet rather than having to be physically shipped, there has been a large increase in demand for packages to be delivered overnight or "second day air." Just-in-time manufacturing techniques, in addition to online sales, have dramatically increased the market for such shipments. Online sites such as eBay now makes it possible to sell specialty products that, in the old days, would have been difficult to distribute. Although it has been possible for more than a hundred years to sell merchandise by catalog, buyers of these specialty products often had no easy access to the catalogs.
- *Social*: Changes in customs or demographics greatly influence firms. Fewer babies today are being born, resulting in a decreased demand for baby foods. More women work outside the home today, so there is a greater demand for prepared foods. There are more unmarried

singles today. This provides opportunities for some firms but creates problems for others. Today, there are more "blended" families that result as parents remarry after divorce. These families are often strapped for money but may require "duplicate" items for children at each parent's residence.

STRATEGIC PLANNING

Plans and Planning

Plans are needed to clarify what kinds of strategic objectives an organization would like to achieve and how this is to be done. Such plans must consider the amount of resources available. One critical resource is capital. Microsoft keeps a great deal of cash on hand to be able to "jump" on opportunities that come about. Small startup software firms, on the other hand, may have limited cash on hand. This means that they may have to forego what would have been a good investment because they do not have the cash to invest and cannot find a way to raise the capital.

Other resources that affect what a firm may be able to achieve include factors such as:

- *Trademarks/brand names*: It would be very difficult to compete against Coke and Pepsi in the cola market.
- *Patents*: It would be difficult to compete against Intel and AMD in the microprocessor market since both these firms have a number of patents that it is difficult to get around.
- *People*: Even with all of Microsoft's money available, it could not immediately hire the people needed to manufacture computer chips.
- *Distribution*: Stores have space for only a fraction of the products they are offered, so they must turn many away. A firm that does not have an established relationship with stores will be at a disadvantage in trying to introduce a new product.

Plans are subject to the choices and policies that the organization has made. Some firms have goals of social responsibility, for example. Some firms are willing to take a greater risk, which may result in a very large payoff but also involve the risk of a large loss, than others.

Strategic marketing is best seen as an *ongoing and never-ending process. Typically*:

- The organization will identify the *objectives* it wishes to achieve. This could involve profitability directly, but often profitability is a long term goal that may require some intermediate steps. The firm may seek to increase market share, achieve distribution in more outlets, have sales grow by a certain percentage, or have consumers evaluate the product more favourably. Some organizations have objectives that are not focused on monetary profit—e.g., promoting literacy or preventing breast cancer.

- An analysis is made, taking into consideration issues such as organizational resources, competitors, the competitors' strengths, different types of customers, changes in the market, or the impact of new technology.
- Based on this analysis, a plan is made based on *tradeoffs between the advantages and disadvantages* of different options available.
- This strategy is then carried out. The firm may design new products, revamp its advertising strategy, invest in getting more stores to carry the product, or decide to focus on a new customer segment.
- After implementation, the results or outcome are evaluated. If results are not as desired, a change may have to be made to the strategy. Even if results are satisfactory, the firm still needs to monitor the environment for changes.

Levels of Planning and Strategies

Plans for a firm can be made at several different levels. At the *corporate* level, the management considers the objectives of the *firm as a whole*. For example, Microsoft may want seek to grow by providing high quality software, hardware, and services to consumers. To achieve this goal, the firm may be willing to invest aggressively. Plans can also be made at the *business unit* level. For example, although Microsoft is best known for its operating systems and applications software, the firm also provides Internet access and makes video games.

Different managers will have responsibilities for different areas, and goals may best be made by those closest to the business area being considered. It is also more practical to hold managers accountable for performance if the plan is being made at a more specific level. Boeing has both commercial aircraft and defence divisions. Each is run by different managers, although there is some overlap in technology between the two. Therefore, plans are needed both at the corporate and at the business levels. Occasionally, plans will be made at the *functional* level, to allow managers to specialize and to increase managerial accountability.

Marketing, for example, may be charged with increasing awareness of Microsoft game consoles to 55% of the U.S. population or to increase the number of units of Microsoft Office sold. Finance may be charged with raising a given amount of capital at a given cost. Manufacturing may be charged with decreasing production costs by 5%.The firm needs to identify the business it is in. Here, a *balance* must be made so that the firm's *scope is not defined too narrowly or too broadly*. A firm may define its goal very narrowly and then miss opportunities in the market place.

For example, if Dell were to define itself only as a computer company, it might miss an opportunity to branch into PDAs or Internet service. Thus, they might instead define themselves as a provider of "information solutions." A company should not define itself too broadly, however, since this may result in loss of focus. For example, a manufacturer of baking soda should probably not see itself as a manufacturer of all types of chemicals. Sometimes, companies can define themselves in terms of a customer need. For example, 3M sees itself as being in the business of making products whose surfaces are bonded together. This accounts for both Post-It notes and computer disks. A firm's mission should generally include a discussion of the *customers served,* the kind of technology involved, and the markets served. Several issues are involved in selecting target customers.

As suggested, consider these in more detail within the context of segmentation, but for now, the firm needs to consider issues such as:

- The *size* of various market segments;
- How well these segments are being *served by existing firms;*
- *Changes* in the market—e.g., growth of segments or change in technology;
- How the firm should be *positioned,* or seen by customers. For example, Wal-Mart positions itself as providing value in retailing, while Nordstrom's defines itself more in terms of high levels of customer service.

The Boston Consulting Group matrix provides a firm an opportunity to assess *how well its business units work together.* Each business unit is evaluated in terms of two factors: *market share* and the *growth prospects* in the market. Generally, the larger a firm's share, the stronger its position, and the greater the growth in a market, the better future possibilities.

Four combinations emerge:

1. A *star* represents a business unit that has a high share in a growing market. For example, Motorola has a large share in the rapidly growing market for cellular phones.
2. A *question mark* results when a unit has a small share in a rapidly growing market. The firm's position, then, is not as strong as it would have been had its market share been greater, but there is an opportunity to grow. For example, Hewlett-Packard has a small share of the digital camera market, but this is a very rapidly growing market.
3. A *cash cow* results when a firm has a large share in a market that is not growing, and may even be shrinking. Brother has a large share of the typewriter market.
4. A *dog* results when a business unit has a small share in a market that is not growing. This is generally a somewhat unattractive situation, although dogs can still be profitable in the short run. For example, Smith Corona how has a small share of the typewriter market.

Firms are usually best of with a portfolio that has a *balance* of firms in each category. The cash cows tend to *generate cash but require little future investment*. On the other hand, stars generate some cash, but *even more cash is needed to invest in the future*—for research and development, marketing campaigns, and building new manufacturing facilities. Therefore, a firm may take excess cash from the cash cow and divert it to the star.

For example, Brother could "harvest" its profits from typewriters and invest this in the unit making colour laser printers, which will need the cash to grow. If a firm has cash cows that generate a lot of cash, this may be used to try to improve the market share of a question mark. A firm that has a number of promising stars in its portfolio may be in serious trouble if it does not have any cash cows to support it. If it is about to run out of cash—regardless of how profitable it is— is becomes vulnerable as a takeover target from a firm that has the cash to continue running it. A SWOT analysis is used to help the firm *identify effective strategies*. Successful firms such as Microsoft have certain strengths.

Microsoft, for example, has a great deal of technology, a huge staff of very talented engineers, a great deal of experience in designing software, a very large market share, a well respected brand name, and a great deal of cash. Microsoft also has some weaknesses, however: The game console and MSN units are currently running at a loss, and MSN has been unable to achieve desired levels of growth. Firms may face opportunities in the current market. Microsoft, for example, may have the opportunity to take advantage of its brand name to enter into the hardware market. Microsoft may also become a trusted source of consumer services.

Microsoft currently faces several threats, including the weak economy. Because fewer new computers are bough during a recession, fewer operating systems and software packages. Rather than merely listing strengths, weaknesses, opportunities, and threats, a SWOT analysis should suggest how the firm may use its strengths and opportunities to overcome weaknesses and threats. Decisions should also be made as to how resources should be allocated. For example, Microsoft could either decide to put more resources into MSN or to abandon this unit entirely.

Microsoft has a great deal of cash ready to spend, so the option to put resources towards MSN is available. Microsoft will also need to see how threats can be addressed. The firm can earn political good will by engaging in charitable acts, which it has money available to fund. For example, Microsoft has donated software and computers to schools. It can forego temporary profits by reducing prices temporarily to increase demand, or can "hold out" by maintaining current prices while not selling as many units. Criteria for effective marketing plans.

Marketing plans should meet several criteria:

- The plan must be *specific* enough so that it can be implemented and communicated to people in the firm. "Improving profitability" is usually too vague, but increasing net profits by 5%, increasing market share by 10%, gaining distribution in 2,000 more stores, and reducing manufacturing costs by 2% are all specific.

- The plan must be *measurable* so that one can see if it has been achieved. The plans involve specific numbers.
- The goal must be *achievable* or realistic. Plans that are unrealistic may result in poor use of resources or lowered morale within the firm.
- The goals must be *consistent*. For example, a firm cannot ordinarily simultaneously plan improve product features, increase profits, and reduce prices.

SOCIAL RESPONSIBILITY IN MARKETING

Ethical Responsibilities and Constraints

Businesses and people face some constraints on what can ethically be done to make money or to pursue other goals. Fraud and deception are not only morally wrong but also inhibit the efficient functioning of the economy. There are also behaviours that, even if they are not strictly illegal in a given jurisdiction, cannot be undertaken with a good conscience. There are a number of areas where an individual must consider his or her conscience to decide if a venture is acceptable. Some "paycheck advance" loan operators charge very high interest rates on small loans made in anticipation of a consumer's next paycheck.

Depending on state laws, effective interest rates may exceed 20% per *month*. In some cases, borrowers put up their automobiles as security, with many losing their only source of transportation through default. Although some consider this practice unconscionable, others assert that such loans may be the only way that a family can obtain cash to fill an immediate need.

Because of costs of administration are high, these costs, when spread over a small amount, will amount to a large percentage. Further, because the customer groups in question tend to have poor credit ratings with high anticipated rates of default, rates must be high enough to cover this.

Sustainability

Sustainability is a notion that proposes that socially responsible firms will somehow financially outperform other less responsible firms in the long run. This might result from customer loyalty, better employee morale, or public policy favouring ethical conduct. Empirical results testing this hypothesis are mixed, neither suggesting that more responsible firms, on the average, have a clear financial advantage nor a large burden. Thus, a useful approach may be to determine specific circumstances under which a firm may actually find the more responsible approach to be more profitable, under which circumstances responsible behaviour can be pursued without an overall significant downside, and the ethical responsibilities that a firm faces when a more responsible approach may be more costly.

The Individual, the Firm, and Society

Different individuals vary in their ethical convictions. Some are willing to work for the tobacco industry, for example, while others are not. Some are willing to mislead potential customers while others will normally not do this. There are, however, also broader societal and companywide values that may influence the individual business decision maker. Some religions, including Islam, disfavour the charging of interest. Although different groups differ somewhat in their interpretations of this issue, the Koran at the very least prohibits *usury*—charging excessive interest rates.

There is some disagreement as to whether more modest, fair interest rates are acceptable. In cultures where the stricter interpretation applies, a firm may be unwilling to set up an interest-based financing plan for customers who cannot pay cash. The firm might, instead, charge a higher price, with no additional charge for interest. Some firms also have their own ethical stands, either implicitly or explicitly. For example, Google has the motto "Do no evil." Other firms, on the other hand, may actively encourage lies, deception, and other reprehensible behaviour. Some firms elect to sell in less developed countries products that have been banned as unsafe in their own countries.

Making it Profitable for the Tobacco Industry to "Harvest"

Many see the tobacco industry as the "enemy" and may not want to do anything that can benefit the industry. However, in principle, it may actually be possible to make it profitable for the tobacco industry to "harvest"—to spend less money on brand building and gradually reduce the quantities sold. The tobacco industry is heavily concentrated, with three firms controlling most of the market. Some other industries are exempt from many antitrust law provisions. If the tobacco companies were allowed to collude and set prices, the equilibrium market price would probably go up, and the quantity of tobacco demanded would then go down.

It is been found that among teenagers, smoking rates are especially likely to decrease when prices increase. The tobacco companies could also be given some immediate tax breaks in return for giving up their trademarks some thirty years in the future. This would reduce the incentive to advertise, again leading to decreased demand in the future. The tax benefits needed might have to be very high, thus making the idea infeasible unless the nation is willing to trade off better health for such large revenue losses.

"Win-win" Marketing

In some cases, it may actually be profitable for companies to do good deeds. This may be the case, for example, when a firm receives a large amount of favourable publicity for its contributions, resulting in customer goodwill and an enhanced brand value. A pharmacy chain, for example, might pay for charitable good to develop information about treating diabetes. The chain could then make this information on its web site, paying for bandwidth and other hosting expenses that may be considerably less than the value of the positive publicity received.

Sponsored Fundraising

Non-profit groups often spend a large proportion of the money they take in on fundraising. This is problematic both because of the inefficiency of the process and the loss of potential proceeds that result and because potential donors who learn about or suspect high fundraising expenses may be less likely to donor.

This is an especially critical issue now that information on fundraising overhead for different organizations is readily available on the Internet. An alternative approach to fundraising that does not currently appear to be much in use is the idea of "sponsored" fundraising.

The idea here is that some firm might volunteer to send out fundraising appeals on behalf of the organization. For example, Microsoft might volunteer to send out letters asking people to donate to the American Red Cross. This may be a very cost effective method of promotion for the firm since the sponsor would benefit from both the positive publicity for its involvement and from the greater attention that would likely be given a fundraising appeal for a group of special interest than would be given to an ordinary advertisement or direct mail piece advertising the sponsor in a traditional way. One issue that comes up is the potential match between the sponsor and sponsee organization.

This may or may not be a critical issue since respondents are selected for the solicitation based on their predicted interest in the organization. Microsoft—directly or indirectly through the Bill and Melinda Gates Foundation—has been credited with a large number of charitable ventures and has the Congressional Black Caucus as one of its greatest supporters. In many cases, firms might volunteer for this fundraising effort in large part because of the spear heading efforts of high level executives whose families are affected by autism.

Commercial Comedy

Another win-win deal potential between industry and non-profit groups involves the idea of *commercial comedy*. Many non-profit groups are interested in finding low cost, high quality entertainment for fundraising events. After all, money spent on buying entertainment reduces the net proceeds available for the organization's programme. Firms, on the other hand, have difficulty getting current and potential customers to give attention to advertising in traditional media. If firms were able to create some high quality entertainment involving their mascotss—e.g., the Energizer Bunny, the Pillsbury Doughboy, and the AFLAC Duck—the audience at a fundraising event would give attention for an extended period of time. Good will would also be generated, and it is likely that the act would receive considerable media coverage.

SEGMENTATION, TARGETING, AND POSITIONING

Segmentation, targeting, and positioning together comprise a three stage process. We first determine which kinds of customers exist, then select which ones we are best off trying to serve and, finally, implement our segmentation by optimizing our products/services for that segment and communicating that we have made the choice to distinguish ourselves that way.

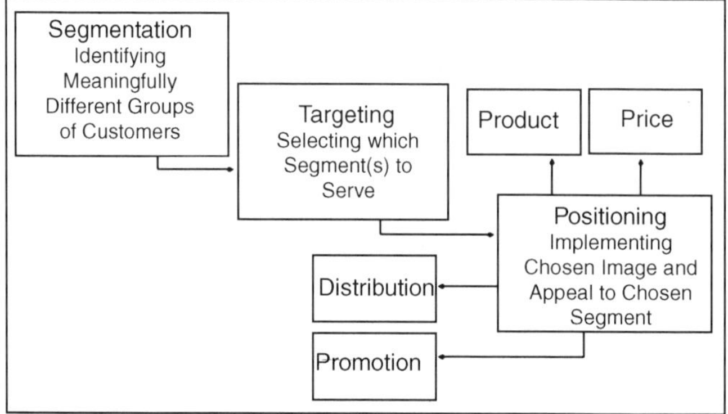

Segmentation involves finding out what kinds of consumers with different needs exist. In the auto market, for example, some consumers demand speed and performance, while others are much more concerned about roominess and safety. In general, it holds true that "You can't be all things to all people," and experience has demonstrated that firms that specialize in meeting the needs of one group of consumers over another tend to be more profitable.

Generically, there are three approaches to marketing. In the *undifferentiated* strategy, all consumers are treated as the same, with firms not making any specific efforts to satisfy particular groups.

This may work when the product is a standard one where one competitor really can't offer much that another one can't. Usually, this is the case only for commodities. In the *concentrated* strategy, one firm chooses to focus on one of several segments that exist while leaving other segments to competitors.

For example, Southwest Airlines focuses on price sensitive consumers who will forego meals and assigned seating for low prices. In contrast, most airlines follow the *differentiated* strategy: They offer high priced tickets to those who are inflexible in that they cannot tell in advance when they need to fly and find it impractical to stay over a Saturday.

These travellers—usually business travellers—pay high fares but can only fill the planes up partially. The same airlines then sell some of the remaining seats to more price sensitive customers who can buy two weeks in advance and stay over. Note that segmentation calls for some tough choices. There may be a large number of variables that can be used to differentiate consumers of a given product category; yet, in practice, it becomes impossibly cumbersome to work with more than a few at a time. Thus, we need to determine which variables will be *most* useful in distinguishing different groups of consumers. We might thus decide, for example, that the variables that are most relevant in separating different kinds of soft drink consumers are preference for taste vs. low calories, preference for Cola vs. non-cola taste, price sensitivity—willingness to pay for brand names; and heavy vs. light consumers. We now put these variables together to arrive at various combinations.

Several different kinds of variables can be used for segmentation:

- Demographic variables essentially refer to personal statistics such as income, gender, education, location, ethnicity, and family size. Campbell's soup, for instance, has found that Western U.S. consumers on the average prefer spicier soups—thus, you get a different product in the same cans at the East and West coasts. Facing flat sales of guns in the traditional male dominated market, a manufacturer came out with the Lady Remmington, a more compact, handier gun more attractive to women. Taking this a step farther, it is also possible to segment on *lifestyle and values*."
- Some consumers want to be seen as similar to others, while a different segment wants to stand apart from the crowd.
- Another basis for segmentation is *behaviour*. Some consumers are "brand loyal"—i.e., they tend to stick with their preferred brands even when a competing one is on sale. Some consumers are "heavy" users while others are "light" users. For example, research conducted by the wine industry shows that some 80% of the product is consumed by 20% of the consumers—presumably a rather intoxicated group.
- One can also segment on *benefits sought*, essentially bypassing demographic explanatory variables. Some consumers, for example, like scented soap while others prefer the "clean" feeling of unscented soap. Some consumers use toothpaste primarily to promote oral health, while another segment is more interested in breath freshening.

In the next step, we decide to target one or more segments. Our choice should generally depend on several factors. First, how well are existing segments served by *other* manufacturers? It will be more difficult to appeal to a segment that is already well served than to one whose needs are not currently being served well. Secondly, how large is the segment, and how can we expect it to grow?.

Thirdly, do we have strengths as a company that will help us appeal particularly to one group of consumers? Firms may already have an established reputation. While McDonald's has a great reputation for fast, consistent quality, family friendly food, it would be difficult to convince consumers that McDonald's now offers gourmet food.

Thus, McD's would probably be better off targeting families in search of consistent quality food in nice, clean restaurants. Positioning involves *implementing* our targeting.

For example, Apple Computer has chosen to position itself as a maker of user-friendly computers. Thus, Apple has done a lot through its advertising to promote itself, through its unintimidating icons, as a computer for "non-geeks." The Visual C software programming language, in contrast, is aimed a "techies."

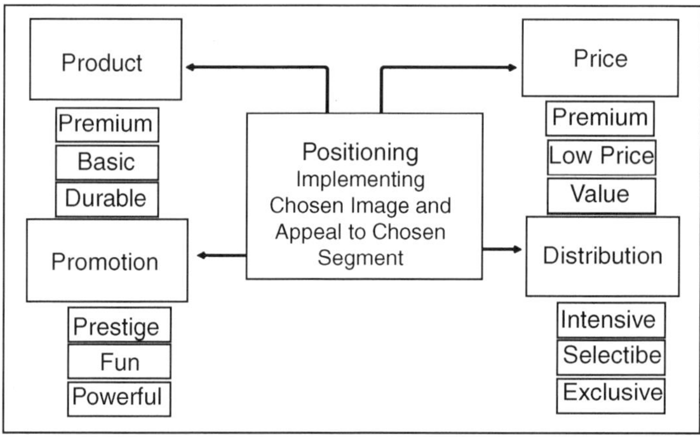

Michael Treacy and Fred Wiersema suggested in their 1993 book The Discipline of Market Leaders that most successful firms fall into one of three categories:

1. Operationally excellent firms, which maintain a strong competitive advantage by maintaining exceptional efficiency, thus enabling the firm to provide reliable service to the customer at a significantly lower cost than those of less well organized and well run competitors. The emphasis here is mostly on low cost, subject to reliable performance, and less value is put on customizing the offering for the specific customer. Wal-Mart is an example of this discipline. Elaborate logistical designs allow goods to be moved at the lowest cost, with extensive systems predicting when specific quantities of supplies will be needed.
2. Customer intimate firms, which excel in serving the specific needs of the individual customer well. There is less emphasis on efficiency, which is sacrificed for providing more precisely what is wanted by the customer. Reliability is also stressed. Nordstrom's and IBM are examples of this discipline.

3. Technologically excellent firms, which produce the most advanced products currently available with the latest technology, constantly maintaining leadership in innovation. These firms, because they work with costly technology that need constant refinement, cannot be as efficient as the operationally excellent firms and often cannot adapt their products as well to the needs of the individual customer. Intel is an example of this discipline.

Treacy and Wiersema suggest that in addition to excelling on one of the three value dimensions, firms must meet acceptable levels on the other two. Wal-Mart, for example, does maintain some level of customer service. Nordstrom's and Intel both must meet some standards of cost effectiveness. The emphasis, beyond meeting the minimum required level in the two other dimensions, is on the dimension of strength. *Repositioning* involves an attempt to change consumer perceptions of a brand, usually because the existing position that the brand holds has become less attractive.

Sears, for example, attempted to reposition itself from a place that offered great sales but unattractive prices the rest of the time to a store that consistently offered "everyday low prices." Repositioning in practice is very difficult to accomplish. A great deal of money is often needed for advertising and other promotional efforts, and in many cases, the repositioning fails. To effectively attempt repositioning, it is important to understand how one's brand and those of competitors are perceived.

One approach to identifying consumer product perceptions is *multidimensional scaling*. Here, we identify how products are perceived on two or more "dimensions," allowing us to plot brands against each other. It may then be possible to attempt to "move" one's brand in a more desirable direction by selectively promoting certain points. There are two main approaches to multi-dimensional scaling.

In the *a priori* approach, market researchers identify dimensions of interest and then ask consumers about their perceptions on each dimension for each brand. This is useful when the market researcher knows which dimensions are of interest and the customer's perception on each dimension is relatively clear.

In the *similarity rating* approach, respondents are not asked about their perceptions of brands on any specific dimensions. Instead, subjects are asked to rate the extent of *similarity* of different pairs of products. Using a computer algorithms, the computer then identifies positions of each brand on a map of a given number of dimensions.

The computer does not reveal what each dimension means—that must be left to human interpretation based on what the variations in each dimension appears to reveal. This second method is more useful when no specific product dimensions have been identified as being of particular interest or when it is not clear what the variables of difference are for the product category.

CONCEPT OF MARKETING MANAGEMENT

Marketing Management is a business discipline which is focused on the practical application of marketing techniques and the management of a firm's marketing resources and activities. Rapidly emerging forces of globalization have compelled firms to market beyond the borders of their home country making International marketing highly significant and an integral part of a firm's marketing strategy. Marketing managers are often responsible for influencing the level, timing, and composition of customer demand accepted definition of the term. In part, this is because the role of a marketing manager can vary significantly based on a business' size, corporate culture, and industry context.

For example, in a large consumer products company, the marketing manager may act as the overall general manager of his or her assigned product To create an effective, cost-efficient Marketing management strategy, firms must possess a detailed, objective understanding of their own business and the market in which they operate. In analyzing these issues, the discipline of marketing management often overlaps with the related discipline of strategic planning.

STRUCTURE

Traditionally, marketing analysis was structured into three areas: Customer analysis, Company analysis, and Competitor analysis. More recently, it has become fashionable in some marketing circles to divide these further into certain five "Cs": Customer analysis, Company analysis, Collaborator analysis, Competitor analysis, and analysis of the industry Context. Customer analysis is to develop a schematic diagram for market segmentation, breaking down the market into various constituent groups of customers, which are called customer segments or market segmentation's.

Marketing managers work to develop detailed profiles of each segment, focusing on any number of variables that may differ among the segments: demographic, psycho graphic, geographic, behavioural, needs-benefit, and other factors may all be examined. Marketers also attempt to track these segments' perceptions of the various products in the market using tools such as perceptual mapping. In company analysis, marketers focus on understanding the company's cost structure and cost position relative to competitors, as well as working to identify a firm's core competencies and other competitively distinct company resources. Marketing managers may also work with the accounting department to analyse the profits the firm is generating from various product lines and customer accounts.

The company may also conduct periodic brand audits to assess the strength of its brands and sources of brand equity. The firm's collaborators may also be profiled, which may include various suppliers, distributors and other channel partners, joint venture partners, and others. An analysis of complementary products may also be performed if such products exist. Marketing management employs various tools from economics and competitive strategy to analyse the industry context in which the firm operates. These include Porter's five forces, analysis of strategic groups of competitors, value chain analysis and others.

Depending on the industry, the regulatory context may also be important to examine in detail. In Competitor analysis, marketers build detailed profiles of each competitor in the market, focusing especially on their relative competitive strengths and weaknesses using SWOT analysis. Marketing managers will examine each competitor's cost structure, sources of profits, resources and competencies, competitive positioning and product differentiation, degree of vertical integration, historical responses to industry developments, and other factors. Marketing management often finds it necessary to invest in research to collect the data required to perform accurate marketing analysis. As such, they often conduct market research to obtain this information.

Marketers employ a variety of techniques to conduct market research, but some of the more common include:

- Qualitative marketing research, such as focus groups
- Quantitative marketing research, such as statistical surveys
- Experimental techniques such as test markets
- Observational techniques such as ethnographic observation

Marketing managers may also design and oversee various environmental scanning and competitive intelligence processes to help identify trends and inform the company's marketing analysis.

Marketing Strategy

If the company has obtained an adequate understanding of the customer base and its own competitive position in the industry, marketing managers are able to make their own key strategic decisions and develop a marketing strategy designed to maximize the revenues and profits of the firm. The selected strategy may aim for any of a variety of specific objectives, including optimizing short-term unit margins, revenue growth, market share, long-term profitability, or other goals. To achieve the desired objectives, marketers typically identify one or more target customer segments which they intend to pursue.

Customer segments are often selected as targets because they score highly on two dimensions: The segment is attractive to serve because it is large, growing, makes frequent purchases, is not price sensitive or other factors; and The company has the resources and capabilities to compete for the segment's business, can meet their needs better than the competition, and can do so profitably. In fact, a commonly cited definition of marketing is simply "meeting needs profitably." The implication of selecting target segments is that the business will subsequently allocate more resources to acquire and retain customers in the target segment(s) than it will for other, non-targeted customers.

In some cases, the firm may go so far as to turn away customers who are not in its target segment.The doorman at a swanky nightclub, for example, may deny entry to unfashionably dressed individuals because the business has made a strategic decision to target the "high fashion" segment of nightclub patrons. In conjunction with targeting decisions, marketing managers will identify the desired positioning they want the company, product, or brand to occupy in the target customer's mind.

This positioning is often an encapsulation of a key benefit the company's product or service offers that is differentiated and superior to the benefits offered by competitive products. For example, Volvo has traditionally positioned its products in the automobile market in North America in order to be perceived as the leader in "safety", whereas BMW has traditionally positioned its brand to be perceived as the leader in "performance." Ideally, a firm's positioning can be maintained over a long period of time because the company possesses, or can develop, some form of sustainable competitive advantage. The positioning should also be sufficiently relevant to the target segment such that it will drive the purchasing behaviour of target customers.

Implementation Planning

After the firm's strategic objectives have been identified, the target market selected, and the desired positioning for the company, product or brand has been determined, marketing managers focus on how to best implement the chosen strategy. Traditionally, this has involved implementation planning across the "4Ps" of marketing: Product management, Pricing, Place, and People. Now a new P has been added making it a total of 5P's. The 5th P is Politics which affects marketing in a significant way.

Taken together, the company's implementation choices across the 4(5)Ps are often described as the marketing mix, meaning the mix of elements the business will employ to "go to market" and execute the marketing strategy. The overall goal for the marketing mix is to consistently deliver a compelling value proposition that reinforces the firm's chosen positioning, builds customer loyalty and brand equity among target customers, and achieves the firm's marketing and financial objectives. In many cases, marketing management will develop a marketing plan to specify how the company will execute the chosen strategy and achieve the business' objectives.

The content of marketing plans varies from firm to firm, but commonly includes:

- An executive summary
- Situation analysis to summarize facts and insights gained from market research and marketing analysis
- The company's mission statement or long-term strategic vision

- A statement of the company's key objectives, often subdivided into marketing objectives and financial objectives
- The marketing strategy the business has chosen, specifying the target segments to be pursued and the competitive positioning to be achieved
- Implementation choices for each element of the marketing mix (the 4(5)Ps)

Project, Process, and Vendor Management

Once the key implementation initiatives have been identified, marketing managers work to oversee the execution of the marketing plan. Marketing executives may therefore manage any number of specific projects, such as sales force management initiatives, product development efforts, channel marketing programmes and the execution of public relations and advertising campaigns. Marketers use a variety of project management techniques to ensure projects achieve their objectives while keeping to established schedules and budgets.

More broadly, marketing managers work to design and improve the effectiveness of core marketing processes, such as new product development, brand management, marketing communications, and pricing. Marketers may employ the tools of business process reengineering to ensure these processes are properly designed, and use a variety of process management techniques to keep them operating smoothly. Effective execution may require management of both internal resources and a variety of external vendors and service providers, such as the firm's advertising agency. Marketers may therefore coordinate with the company's Purchasing department on the procurement of these services.

Organizational Management and Leadership

Marketing management may spend a fair amount of time building or maintaining a marketing orientation for the business. Achieving a market orientation, also known as "customer focus" or the "marketing concept", requires building consensus at the senior management level and then driving customer focus down into the organization. Cultural barriers may exist in a given business unit or functional area that the marketing manager must address in order to achieve this goal. Additionally, marketing executives often act as a "brand champion" and work to enforce corporate identity standards across the enterprise.

In larger organizations, especially those with multiple business units, top marketing managers may need to coordinate across several marketing departments and also resources from finance, research and development, engineering, operations, manufacturing, or other functional areas to implement the marketing plan. In order to effectively manage these resources, marketing executives may need to spend much of their time focused on political issues and inte-departmental negotiations. The effectiveness of a marketing manager may therefore depend on his or her ability to make the internal "sale" of various marketing programmes equally as much as the external customer's reaction to such programmes.

Reporting, Measurement, Feedback and Control Systems

Marketing management employs a variety of metrics to measure progress against objectives. It is the responsibility of marketing managers – in the marketing department or elsewhere – to ensure that the execution of marketing programmes achieves the desired objectives and does so in a cost-efficient manner.

Marketing management therefore often makes use of various organizational control systems, such as sales forecasts, sales force and reseller incentive programmes, sales force management systems, and customer relationship management tools. Recently, some software vendors have begun using the term "marketing operations management" or "marketing resource management" to describe systems that facilitate an integrated approach for controlling marketing resources. In some cases, these efforts may be linked to various supply chain management systems, such as enterprise resource planning, material requirements planning, efficient consumer response, and inventory management systems. Measuring the return on investment of and marketing effectiveness various marketing initiatives is a significant problem for marketing management.

Various market research, accounting and financial tools are used to help estimate the ROI of marketing investments. Brand valuation, for example, attempts to identify the percentage of a company's market value that is generated by the company's brands, and thereby estimate the financial value of specific investments in brand equity. Another technique, integrated marketing communications is a CRM database-driven approach that attempts to estimate the value of marketing mix executions based on the changes in customer behaviour these executions generate.

EVOLUTION OF MARKETING

Marketing as we know it today began in the 1970's with the birth of the "marketing orientation". During the first stage of capitalism business had a production orientation. Business was concerned with production, manufacturing, and efficiency issues. By the mid 1950's a second stage emerged, the sales orientation stage. Business's prime concern was to sell what it produced. By the early 1970's a third stage, the marketing orientation stage emerged as businesses came to realise that consumer needs and wants drove the whole process. Marketing research became important. Businesses realised it was futile putting a lot of production and sales effort into products that people did not want. Some commentators claim that we are now on the verge of a fourth stage, one of a personal marketing orientation. They believe that the technology is available today to market to people on an individual basis. They feel it is no longer necessary to think in broad aggregated terms like market segments or target markets. Marketing has become an academic discipline in itself, with tertiary degrees in the field now routinely awarded. Masters and Doctrinal degrees can be obtained in numerous subcategories of marketing including: Marketing Research, Consumer Behaviour, International Marketing, Industrial Marketing, Consumer Marketing, Product Management, and e-Marketing.

TYPES OF MARKETING

If you want your company to succeed, at some point you will need to begin marketing your products or services. The old adage that the worst type of advertising is no advertising is still true. No matter what your marketing budget may be, there are many different types of marketing that you can take advantage of. Let's take a look at a few of the more proven techniques that combine low cost with major results.

ONLINE MARKETING

Online marketing has opened up incredible avenues for small businesses. Thanks to companies like Google and Overture, you can place ads for your company right along side the big guns at competitive prices. Never before has it been easier to market your business than it is right now. New forms of online marketing are also making headway. Online video ads are easy and cheap to shoot and give you the kind of exposure that was previously limited to expensive national television campaigns. With low production costs and reasonable pricing, you can run an online video campaign at a fraction of the cost of traditional advertising.

OFFLINE MARKETING

The benefits of traditional marketing cannot be overlooked in our digital age. Many companies are reaping the benefits of combining online and offline marketing techniques. For example, you can use direct mail or local advertising to drive potential customers to your site. This is a great and proven combination that results in increased traffic and better conversions.

You can actually save money on print campaigns by relying on your website to do the actual selling while the print ad can function as a pointer. You'll save money using less words while building brand awareness. Radio ads are still a proven way to increase awareness of your company. If you are new to radio marketing, try placing a sample ad with a local station. They'll be able to assist you in producing your first ad until you get the hang of the process.

WORD OF MOUTH MARKETING

Word of mouth is still one of the most powerful forms of advertising on the planet. The best word of mouth comes from satisfied customers. Go the extra mile for them, and really work towards building relationships with your customers. This will result not only in more leads but they'll keep coming back to you in the future. Try running special promotions or coupons for these regular customers to help them feel that they are special and you'll really be able to continue to build on these relationships in the future.

The best marketing strategies take advantage of all the different types of advertising. By spreading your ad dollars around you can be assured of greater success and better interaction with the public. Start small by combining a special promotion that will run both in print and online avenues at the same time. You can keep track of the success of each method by using coupon codes to see which form suits your company the best.

TELEMARKETING

Telemarketing is a method of direct marketing in which a salesperson solicits prospective customers to buy products or services, either over the phone or through a subsequent face to face or Web conferencing appointment scheduled during the call. Telemarketing can also include recorded sales pitches programmed to be played over the phone via automatic dialing. Telemarketing has come under fire in recent years, being viewed as an annoyance by many.

History

Many believe that in the 1950s, DialAmerica Marketing, Inc became the first company completely dedicated to inbound and outbound telephone sales and services. The company, spun off and sold by Time, Inc. magazine in 1976, became the largest provider of telephone sales and services to magazine publishing companies. The term telemarketing was first used extensively in the late 1970s to describe Bell System communications which related to new uses for the outbound WATS and inbound Toll-free services.

Categories

The two major categories of telemarketing are Business-to-business and Business-to-consumer.

Subcategories:

- Lead Generation, the gathering of information
- Sales, using persuasion to sell a product or service
- Outbound, proactive marketing in which prospective and preexisting customers are contacted directly
- Inbound, reactive reception of incoming orders and requests for information. Demand is generally created by advertising, publicity, or the efforts of outside salespeople.

Procedure

Telemarketing may be done from a company office, from a call centre, or from home. It may involve either a live operator or a recorded message, in which case it is known as "automated telemarketing" using voice broadcasting. "Robocalling" is a form of voice broadcasting which is most frequently associated with political messages. An effective telemarketing process often involves two or more calls.

The first call determines the customer's needs. The final call motivates the customer to make a purchase. Prospective customers are identified by various means, including past purchase history, previous requests for information, credit limit, competition entry forms, and application forms. Names may also be purchased from another company's consumer database or obtained from a telephone directory or another public list. The qualification process is intended to determine which customers are most likely to purchase the product or service.

Charitable organizations, alumni associations, and political parties often use telemarketing to solicit donations. Marketing research companies use telemarketing techniques to survey the prospective or past customers of a client's business in order to assess market acceptance of or satisfaction with a particular product, service, brand, or company. Public opinion polls are conducted in a similar manner. Telemarketing techniques are also applied to other forms of electronic marketing using e-mail or fax messages, in which case they are frequently considered spam by other people.

Negative Perceptions and Criticism

Telemarketing has been negatively associated with various scams and frauds, such as pyramid schemes, and with deceptively overpriced products and services. Fraudulent telemarketing companies are frequently referred to as "telemarketing boiler rooms" or simply "boiler rooms". Telemarketing is often criticized as an unethical business practice due to the perception of high-pressure sales techniques during unsolicited calls.

Telemarketers marketing telephone companies may participate in telephone slamming, the practice of switching a customer's telephone service without their knowledge or authorization. Telemarketing calls are often considered an annoyance, especially when they occur during the dinner hour, early in the morning, or late in the evening.

A recent trend in telemarketing is to use robocalls: Automated telephone calls that use both computerized autodialers and computer-delivered pre-recorded messages in a sales pitch. These often include intentionally deceptive tactics, with computer recorded messages saying things like "Don't panic but this is your final notice" or "We have already attempted to contact you through the mail." These messages are often outright lies, intended to incite concern or fear in the potential customer. Robocalls are known for failing to add numbers to their do-not-call list and repeatedly interrupting individuals at all hours of the day.

Regulations

In some countries telemarketing is subject to regulatory and legislative controls related to consumer privacy and protection.

United States of America

It is not known exactly when telemarketing officially became legal in the United States of America. Telemarketing in the United States of America is restricted at the federal level by the Telephone Consumer Protection Act of 1991 and the FTC's Telemarketing Sales Rule. The FCC derives regulatory authority from the TCPA, adopted as CFR 64.1200. Many professional associations of telemarketers have codes of ethics and standards that member businesses follow to encourage public confidence.

Some jurisdictions have implemented "Do Not Call" lists through industry organizations or legislation; telemarketers are restricted from initiating contact with participating consumers.

Legislative versions often provide for heavy penalties on companies which call individuals on these listings. The U.S. Federal Trade Commission has implemented a National Do Not Call Registry in an attempt to reduce intrusive telemarketing nationwide.

Telemarketing corporations and trade groups challenged this as a violation of commercial speech rights. However, the U.S. 10th Circuit Court of Appeals upheld the National Do Not Call Registry on February 17, 2004. Companies that use telemarketing as a sales tool are governed by the United States Federal regulations outlined in the TSR and the TCPA. In addition to these Federal regulations, telemarketers calling nationally must also adhere to separate state regulations. Most states have adapted "do not call" files of their own, of which only some states share with the U.S. Federal Do Not Call registry.

Each U.S. state also has its own regulations concerning: permission to record, permission to continue, no rebuttaling statutes, Sunday and Holiday calls; as well as the fines and punishments exacted for violations. September 1, 2009, FTC regulations banning most robocall went into effect. Telemarketing techniques are increasingly used in political campaigns. Because of free-speech issues, the laws governing political phone calls are much less stringent than those applying to commercial messages. Even so, a number of states have barred or restricted political robocalls.

Canada

In Canada, telemarketing is regulated by Federal Government, specifically handled by Canadian Radio-television and Telecommun-ications Commission.

Australia

Telemarketing in Australia is restricted by the Australian Federal Government and policed by the Australian Communications and Media Authority. Australian Federal legislation provides for a restriction in calling hours for both Research and Marketing calls. In 2007 a Do Not Call Register was established for Australian inbound telephone numbers. The register allows a user to register private use telephone numbers. Australian Federal Legislation limits the types of marketing calls that can be made to these registered telephone numbers; however, research calls are allowed.

Other exemptions include calls made by charities and political members, parties and candidates Inbound telemarketing is another major industry. It involves both live operators and IVR—Interactive Voice Response. IVR is also known as audiotext or automated call processing. Usually, major television campaigns and advertisers use toll-free telephone number that are answered by IVR service bureaus. Such service bureaus have the technology and call capacity to process the large amounts of simultaneous calls that occur when an toll-free telephone number is advertised on television.

Technology

- Autodialer
- Automatic call distributor
- Customer relationship management
- Predictive dialer
- Private Branch eXchange
- Teleblock

E-MARKETING

E-Marketing is essentially part of marketing. But what is the difference between eMarketing and Internet or web marketing? What are the eMarketing tools? And how do marketers plan for eMarketing? This session aims to answer these questions. So the place to begin defining *eMarketing* is to consider where it fits within the subject of marketing. So let's start with a definition of marketing.

The American Marketing Association definition is as follows:

- Marketing is an organizational function and a set of processes for creating, communicating and delivering value to customers and for managing customer relationships in ways that benefit the organization and its stakeholders.

Therefore eMarketing by its very nature is one aspect of an organizational function and a set of processes for creating, communicating and delivering value to customers and for managing customer relationships in ways that benefit the organization and its stakeholders. As such an aspect, eMarketing has its own approaches and tools that contribute to the achievement of marketing goals and objectives. This also helps us to differentiate between eMarketing and E-commerce, since E-Commerce is simply buying and selling online.

Difference between e-Marketing and Internet or Web Marketing

There is no real difference between eMarketing and internet or web marketing. However, with the arrival of mobile technologies such as PDA's and 3G mobile phones, as well as Interactive Television, both terms tend to be stretched to include these new media technologies.

- Internet [or web] marketing is achieving marketing objectives through applying digital technologies.
- e-Marketing is achieving marketing objectives through use of electronic communications technology.

Whilst this distinction is wholly acceptable, it is difficult to see where the distinction lies between digital technologies and electronic communications technologies, especially with the convergence of technologies such as mobile devices.

The e-Marketing Tools

The Internet has a number of tools to offer to the marketer:

- A company can distribute via the Internet.
- A company can use the Internet as a way of building and maintaining a customer relationship.
- The money collection part of a transaction could be done online e.g. electricity and telephone bills.
- Leads can be generated by attracting potential customers to sign-up for short periods of time, before signing up for the long-term e.g. which.co.uk.
- The Internet could be used for advertising e.g. Google Adwords.
- Finally, the web can be used as a way of collecting direct responses e.g. as part of a voting system for a game show.

How do Marketers Plan for e-Marketing

There are two ways of looking at this:

1. An existing organization may embark upon some eMarketing as part of their marketing plan.
2. An organization trades solely on the Internet and so their marketing plan focuses purely on eMarketing.

The marketing plan in either case is the next step, whether focused upon eMarketing or all marketing.

The next sessions focus upon a tailor-made eMarketing plan which conforms to the acronym AOSTC.

- A – Audit—An audit of internal strengths and weaknesses, an external opportunities and threats.

- O – Objectives—SMART eMarketing objectives.
- S – Strategy—e-Marketing strategies.
- T – Tactics—an e-Marketing mix.
- C – Controls—measuring the performance of our eMarketing plan.

SERVICES MARKETING

Services marketing is a form of marketing which focuses on selling services. Services can be tricky to sell and the marketing approach for them is much different than the approach for products. Some companies offer both products and services and must use a mixture of styles; for example, a store whi ch sells computers also tends to offer services such as helping people select computers and providing computer repair.

Such a store must market both its products and the supporting services it offers to appeal to customers. When people market services, the goal is not to get customers to buy a product, but to get people to do business with a particular company, often in a specific location. For example, a restaurant offers a service: It provides food to customers, both on-site and in to-go form in many cases. When the restaurant markets itself, it must convince people that it is preferable to other restaurants and that its facility is worth the trip. As with the marketing of products, the marketing of services covers issues like what is being offered, what the price point is, how it compares to similar things, and why people should choose that particular iteration over other options.

With services, which are often intangible in nature, consumers must also be convinced through services marketing that the service is something they need which will have some sort of benefit. There are different approaches which can be taken in services marketing, depending on how people want the position the company and what kind of messages they want people to take away from the marketing. A company might want to project itself as reliable and trustworthy if it offers a service like security, or fun loving and adventurous for services like travel planning.

In all cases, people must be shown why it is that they would want to pay for services the company offers. Marketing schools usually discuss various techniques which can be used in services marketing. People may also develop their own techniques as they practice marketing in the real world and learn more about what people look for, how they shop for services, and what makes a service appealing.

Often, the goal is to establish a personal relationship with customers so that they will return for the company's services in the future, rather than taking their business elsewhere. The loyalty is often to the quality of the service, rather than to a specific brand or image, and this makes services marketing somewhat different than product marketing, in which it is the value of the product which is important.

MARKETING PLAN

A marketing plan is a written document that details the necessary actions to achieve one or more marketing objectives. It can be for a product or service, a brand, or a product line. Marketing plans cover between one and five years. A marketing plan may be part of an overall business plan. Solid marketing strategy is the foundation of a well-written marketing plan. While a marketing plan contains a list of actions, a marketing plan without a sound strategic foundation is of little use.

THE MARKETING PLANNING PROCESS

Marketing process can be realised by the marketing mix in step 4. The last step in the process is the marketing controlling. In most organizations, "strategic planning" is an annual process, typically covering just the year ahead. Occasionally, a few organizations may look at a practical plan which stretches three or more years ahead. To be most effective, the plan has to be formalized, usually in written form, as a formal "marketing plan."

The essence of the process is that it moves from the general to the specific, from the vision to the mission to the goals to the corporate objectives of the organization, then down to the individual action plans for each part of the marketing programme. It is also an interactive process, so that the draft output of each stage is checked to see what impact it has on the earlier stages, and is amended.

MARKETING PLANNING AIMS AND OBJECTIVES

Behind the corporate objectives, which in themselves offer the main context for the marketing plan, will lie the "corporate mission," which in turn provides the context for these corporate objectives. In a sales-oriented organization, the marketing planning function designs incentive pay plans to not only motivate and reward frontline staff fairly but also to align marketing activities with corporate mission. This "corporate mission" can be thought of as a definition of what the organization is, of what it does: "Our business is ...". This definition should not be too narrow, or it will constrict the development of the organization; a too rigorous concentration on the view that "We are in the business of making meat-scales," as IBM was during the early 1900s, might have limited its subsequent development into other areas.

On the other hand, it should not be too wide or it will become meaningless; "We want to make a profit" is not too helpful in developing specific plans. Abell suggested that the definition should cover three dimensions: "customer groups" to be served, "customer needs" to be served, and "technologies" to be utilized. Thus, the definition of IBM's "corporate mission" in the 1940s might well have been: "We are in the business of handling accounting information [customer need] for the larger US organizations-[customer group] by means of punched cards [technology]."

Perhaps the most important factor in successful marketing is the "corporate vision." Surprisingly, although not by the popular exponents of corporate strategy - indeed, it was perhaps the main theme of the book by Peters and Waterman, in the form of their "Superordinate Goals." "In Search of Excellence" said: "Nothing drives progress like the imagination.

The idea precedes the deed." If the organization in general, and its chief executive in particular, has a strong vision of where its future lies, then there is a good chance that the organization will achieve a strong position in its markets. This will be not least because its strategies will be consistent and will be supported by its staff at all levels. In this context, all of IBM's marketing activities were underpinned by its philosophy of "customer service," a vision originally promoted by the charismatic Watson dynasty. The emphasis at this stage is on obtaining a complete and accurate picture.

A "traditional" - albeit product-based - format for a "brand reference book" was suggested by Godley more than three decades ago:

- *Financial data*: Facts for this part will come from management accounting, costing and finance parts.
- *Product data*: From production, research and development.
- *Sales and distribution data*: Sales, packaging, distribution parts.
- *Advertising, sales promotion, merchandising data*: Information from these departments.
- *Market data and miscellany*: From market research, who would in most cases act as a source for this information. His sources of data, however, assume the resources of a very large organization. In most organizations they would be obtained from a much smaller set of people.

It is apparent that a marketing audit can be a complex process, but the aim is simple: "it is only to identify those existing factors which will have a significant impact on the future plans of the company." It is clear that the basic material to be input to the marketing audit should be comprehensive.

Accordingly, the best approach is to accumulate this material continuously, as and when it becomes available; since this avoids the otherwise heavy workload involved in collecting it as part of the regular, typically annual, planning process itself - when time is usually at a premium.

Even so, the first task of this annual process should be to check that the material held in the current facts book or facts files actually is comprehensive and accurate, and can form a sound basis for the marketing audit itself.

The structure of the facts book will be designed to match the specific needs of the organization, but one simple format - suggested by Malcolm McDonald - may be applicable in many cases.

This splits the material into three groups:

1. *Review of the marketing environment*: A study of the organization's markets, customers, competitors and the overall economic, political,

cultural and technical environment; covering developing trends, as well as the current situation.

2. *Review of the detailed marketing activity*: A study of the company's marketing mix; in terms of the 7 Ps -
3. *Review of the marketing system*: A study of the marketing organization, marketing research systems and the current marketing objectives and strategies. The last of these is too frequently ignored. The marketing system itself needs to be regularly questioned, because the validity of the whole marketing plan is reliant upon the accuracy of the input from this system, and `garbage in, garbage out' applies with a vengeance.
   - *Portfolio planning*: In addition, the coordinated planning of the individual products and services can contribute towards the balanced portfolio.
   - 80:20 *rule*: To achieve the maximum impact, the marketing plan must be clear, concise and simple. It needs to concentrate on the 20 per cent of products or services, and on the 20 per cent of customers, which will account for 80 per cent of the volume and 80 per cent of the profit.
   - 7 *P's*: Product, Place, Price and Promotion, Physical Environment, People, Process. The 7 P's can sometimes divert attention from the customer, but the framework they offer can be very useful in building the action plans.

It is only at this stage that the active part of the marketing planning process begins. This next stage in marketing planning is indeed the key to the whole marketing process.

The"marketing objectives" state just where the company intends to be at some specific time in the future. James Quinn succinctly defined objectives in general as: Goals state what is to be achieved and when results are to be accomplished, but they do not state"how" the results are to be achieved. They typically relate to what products will be where in what markets. They are essentially about the match between those"products" and"markets." Objectives for pricing, distribution, advertising and so on are at a lower level, and should not be confused with marketing objectives.

They are part of the marketing strategy needed to achieve marketing objectives. To be most effective, objectives should be capable of measurement and therefore"quantifiable." This measurement may be in terms of sales volume, money value, market share, percentage penetration of distribution outlets and so on. An example of such a measurable marketing objective might be"to enter the market with product Y and capture 10 per cent of the market by value within one year." As it is quantified it can, within limits, be unequivocally monitored, and corrective action taken as necessary. The marketing objectives must usually be based on the organization's financial objectives; converting these financial measurements into the related marketing measurements. He went on to explain his view of the role of"policies," with which strategy is most often confused:"Policies are rules or guidelines that express the'limits' within which action should occur."Simplifying somewhat, marketing strategies can be seen as the means, or"game plan," by which marketing objectives will be achieved and, in the framework that we have chosen to use, are generally concerned with the 8 P's.

Examples are:

1. *Price*: The amount of money needed to buy products
2. *Product*: The actual product
3. *Promotion*: Getting the product known
4. *Placement*:Where the product is located
5. *People*: Represent the business
6. *Physical environment*: The ambiance, mood, or tone of the environment
7. *Process*: How do people obtain your product
8. *Packaging*: How the product will be protected

In principle, these strategies describe how the objectives will be achieved. The 7 P's are a useful framework for deciding how the company's resources will be manipulated to achieve the objectives. However, they are not the only framework, and may divert attention from the real issues. The focus of the strategies must be the objectives to be achieved - not the process of planning itself. Only if it fits the needs of these objectives should you choose, as we have done, to use the framework of the 7 P's. The strategy statement can take the form of a purely verbal description of the strategic options which have been chosen.

Alternatively, and perhaps more positively, it might include a structured list of the major options chosen. One aspect of strategy which is often overlooked is that of "timing." Exactly when it is the best time for each element of the strategy to be implemented is often critical. Taking the right action at the wrong time can sometimes be almost as bad as taking the wrong action at the right time.

Timing is, therefore, an essential part of any plan; and should normally appear as a schedule of planned activities.Having completed this crucial stage of the planning process, you will need to re-check the feasibility of your objectives and strategies in terms of the market share, sales, costs, profits and so on which these demand in practice. As in the rest of the marketing discipline, you will need to employ judgment, experience, market research or anything else which helps you to look at your conclusions from all possible angles.

Detailed Plans and Programmes

At this stage,you will need to develop your overall marketing strategies into detailed plans and programme. Although these detailed plans may cover each of the 7 P's, the focus will vary, depending upon your organization's specific strategies. A product-oriented company will focus its plans for the 7 P's around each of its products. A market or geographically oriented company will concentrate on each market or geographical area. Each will base its plans upon the detailed needs of its customers, and on the strategies chosen to satisfy these needs. Brochures and Websites are used effectively. Again, the most important element is, indeed, that of the detailed plans, which spell out exactly what programmes and individual activities will take place over the period of the plan. Without these specified - and preferably quantified - activities the plan cannot be monitored, even in terms of success in meeting its objectives.It is these programmes and activities which will then constitute the "marketing" of the organization over the period. As a result, these detailed marketing programmes are the most important, practical outcome of the whole planning process.

These plans must therefore be:

- *Clear*: They should be an unambiguous statement of 'exactly' what is to be done.
- *Quantified*: The predicted outcome of each activity should be, as far as possible, quantified, so that its performance can be monitored.
- *Focused*: The temptation to proliferate activities beyond the numbers which can be realistically controlled should be avoided. The 80:20 Rule applies in this context too.
- *Realistic*: They should be achievable.
- *Agreed*: Those who are to implement them should be committed to them, and agree that they are achievable. The resulting plans should become a working document which will guide the campaigns taking place throughout the organization over the period of the plan. If the marketing plan is to work, every exception to it must be questioned; and the sessions learnt, to be incorporated in the next year's planning.

CONTENT OF THE MARKETING PLAN

A marketing plan for a small business typically includes Small Business Administration Description of competitors, including the level of demand for the product or service and the strengths and weaknesses of competitors.

- Description of the product or service, including special features
- Marketing budget, including the advertising and promotional plan
- Description of the business location, including advantages and disadvantages for marketing
- Pricing strategy
- Market Segmentation

MEASUREMENT OF PROGRESS

The final stage of any marketing planning process is to establish targets so that progress can be monitored. Accordingly, it is important to put both quantities and timescales into the marketing objectives and into the corresponding strategies.

Changes in the environment mean that the forecasts often have to be changed. Along with these, the related plans may well also need to be changed. Continuous monitoring of performance, against predetermined targets, represents a most important aspect of this.

However, perhaps even more important is the enforced discipline of a regular formal review. Again, as with forecasts, in many cases the best planning cycle will revolve around a quarterly review. Best of all, at least in terms of the quantifiable aspects of the plans, if not the wealth of backing detail, is probably a quarterly rolling review - planning one full year ahead each new quarter. Of course, this does absorb more planning resource; but it also ensures that the plans embody the latest information, and - with attention focused on them so regularly - forces both the plans and their implementation to be realistic. Plans only have validity if they are actually used to control the progress of a company: their success lies in their implementation, not in the writing'.

PERFORMANCE ANALYSIS

The most important elements of marketing performance, which are normally tracked, are:

Market Share Analysis

Few organizations track market share though it is often an important metric. Though absolute sales might grow in an expanding market, a firm's share of the market can decrease which bodes ill for future sales when the market starts to drop.

Where such market share is tracked, there may be a number of aspects which will be followed:

- Overall market share
- Segment share - that in the specific, targeted segment
- Relative share -in relation to the market leaders
- Annual fluctuation rate of market share
- Also the specific market sharing of customers.

Expense Analysis

The key ratio to watch in this area is usually the 'marketing expense to sales ratio'; although this may be broken down into other elements.

Financial Analysis

The "bottom line" of marketing activities should at least in theory, be the net profit.

There are a number of separate performance figures and key ratios which need to be tracked:

- Gross contribution<>net profit
- Gross profit<>return on investment
- Net contribution<>profit on sales

There can be considerable benefit in comparing these figures with those achieved by other organizations; using, for instance, the figures which can be obtained from 'The Centre for Interfirm Comparison'. The most sophisticated use of this approach, however, is typically by those making use of PIMS, initiated by the General Electric Company and then developed by Harvard Business School, but now run by the Strategic Planning Institute. The performance analyses concentrate on the quantitative measures which are directly related to short-term performance. But there are a number of indirect measures, essentially tracking customer attitudes, which can also indicate the organization's performance in terms of its longer-term marketing strengths and may accordingly be even more important indicators.

Some useful measures are:

- *Market research*: Including customer panels
- *Lost business*: The orders which were lost because, for example, the stock was not available or the product did not meet the customer's exact requirements
- *Customer complaints*: How many customers complain about the products or services, or the organization itself, and about what

Use of Marketing Plans

A formal, written marketing plan is essential; in that it provides an unambiguous reference point for activities throughout the planning period. However, perhaps the most important benefit of these plans is the planning process itself. This typically offers a unique opportunity, a forum, for information-rich and productively focused discussions between the various managers involved. The plan, together with the associated discussions, then provides an agreed context for their subsequent management activities, even for those not described in the plan itself. Additionally, marketing plans are included in business plans, offering data showing investors how the company will grow and most importantly, how they will get a return on investment.

BUDGETS AS MANAGERIAL TOOLS

The classic quantification of a marketing plan appears in the form of budgets. Because these are so rigorously quantified, they are particularly important. They should, thus, represent an unequivocal projection of actions and expected results.

What is more, they should be capable of being monitored accurately; and, indeed, performance against budget is the main management review process.

The purpose of a marketing budget is, thus, to pull together all the revenues and costs involved in marketing into one comprehensive document. It is a managerial tool that balances what is needed to be spent against what can be afforded, and helps make choices about priorities.

It is then used in monitoring performance in practice. The marketing budget is usually the most powerful tool by which you think through the relationship between desired results and available means. Its starting point should be the marketing strategies and plans, which have already been formulated in the marketing plan itself; although, in practice, the two will run in parallel and will interact. At the very least, the rigorous, highly quantified, budgets may cause a rethink of some of the more optimistic elements of the plans.

MARKETING RESEARCH

Managers need information in order to introduce products and services that create value in the mind of the customer. But the perception of value is a subjective one, and what customers value this year may be quite different from what they value next year. As such, the attributes that create value cannot simply be deduced from common knowledge.

Rather, data must be collected and analysed. The goal of marketing research is to provide the facts and direction that managers need to make their more important marketing decisions. To maximize the benefit of marketing research, those who use it need to understand the research process and its limitations.

MARKETING RESEARCH VS. MARKET RESEARCH

These terms often are used interchangeably, but technically there is a difference. Market research deals specifically with the gathering of information about a market's size and trends. Marketing research covers a wider range of activities.

While it may involve market research, marketing research is a more general systematic process that can be applied to a variety of marketing problems.

THE VALUE OF INFORMATION

Information can be useful, but what determines its real value to the organization?

In general, the value of information is determined by:

- The ability and willingness to act on the information.
- The accuracy of the information.
- The level of indecisiveness that would exist without the information.
- The amount of variation in the possible results.
- The level of risk aversion.

- The reaction of competitors to any decision improved by the information.
- The cost of the information in terms of time and money.

THE MARKETING RESEARCH PROCESS

Once the need for marketing research has been established, most marketing research projects involve these steps:

- Define the problem
- Determine research design
- Identify data types and sources
- Design data collection forms and questionnaires
- Determine sample plan and size
- Collect the data
- Analyse and interpret the data
- Prepare the research report

PROBLEM DEFINITION

The decision problem faced by management must be translated into a market research problem in the form of questions that define the information that is required to make the decision and how this information can be obtained. Thus, the decision problem is translated into a research problem. For example, a decision problem may be whether to launch a new product. The corresponding research problem might be to assess whether the market would accept the new product. The objective of the research should be defined clearly. To ensure that the true decision problem is addressed, it is useful for the researcher to outline possible scenarios of the research results and then for the decision maker to formulate plans of action under each scenario. The use of such scenarios can ensure that the purpose of the research is agreed upon before it commences.

RESEARCH DESIGN

Marketing research can classified in one of three categories:

1. Exploratory research
2. Descriptive research
3. Causal research

These classifications are made according to the objective of the research. In some cases the research will fall into one of these categories, but in other cases different phases of the same research project will fall into different categories.

- Exploratory research has the goal of formulating problems more precisely, clarifying concepts, gathering explanations, gaining insight, eliminating impractical ideas, and forming hypotheses. Exploratory research can be performed using a literature search, surveying certain people about their experiences, focus groups, and case studies. When surveying people, exploratory research studies would not try to acquire a representative sample, but rather, seek to interview those who are knowledgeable and who might be able to provide insight concerning the relationship among variables. Case studies can include contrasting situations or benchmarking against an organization known for its excellence. Exploratory research may develop hypotheses, but it does not seek to test them. Exploratory research is characterized by its flexibility.

- Descriptive research is more rigid than exploratory research and seeks to describe users of a product, determine the proportion of the population that uses a product, or predict future demand for a product. As opposed to exploratory research, descriptive research should define questions, people surveyed, and the method of analysis prior to beginning data collection. In other words, the who, what, where, when, why, and how aspects of the research should be defined. Such preparation allows one the opportunity to make any required changes before the costly process of data collection has begun.

  There are two basic types of descriptive research: longitudinal studies and cross-sectional studies. Longitudinal studies are time series analyses that make repeated measurements of the same individuals, thus allowing one to monitor behaviour such as brand-switching. However, longitudinal studies are not necessarily representative since many people may refuse to participate because of the commitment required. Cross-sectional studies sample the population to make measurements at a specific point in time. A special type of cross-sectional analysis is a cohort analysis, which tracks an aggregate of individuals who experience the same event within the same time interval over time. Cohort analyses are useful for long-term forecasting of product demand.
- Causal research seeks to find cause and effect relationships between variables. It accomplishes this goal through laboratory and field experiments.

DATA TYPES AND SOURCES

Secondary Data

Before going through the time and expense of collecting primary data, one should check for secondary data that previously may have been collected for other purposes but that can be used in the immediate study. Secondary data may be internal to the firm, such as sales invoices and warranty cards, or may be external to the firm such as published data or commercially available data.The government census is a valuable source of secondary data. Secondary data has the advantage of saving time and reducing data gathering costs. The disadvantages are that the data may not fit the problem perfectly and that the accuracy may be more difficult to verify for secondary data than for primary data. Some secondary data is republished by organizations other than the original source. Because errors can occur and important explanations may be missing in republished data, one should obtain secondary data directly from its source. One also should consider who the source is and whether the results may be biased.

There are several criteria that one should use to evaluate secondary data:

- Whether the data is useful in the research study.
- How current the data is and whether it applies to time period of interest.
- Errors and accuracy - whether the data is dependable and can be verified.
- Presence of bias in the data.
- Specifications and methodologies used, including data collection method, response rate, quality and analysis of the data, sample size and sampling technique, and questionnaire design.
- Objective of the original data collection.
- Nature of the data, including definition of variables, units of measure, categories used, and relationships examined.

Primary Data

Often, secondary data must be supplemented by primary data originated specifically for the study at hand.

Some common types of primary data are:

- Demographic and socioeconomic characteristics
- Psychological and lifestyle characteristics
- Attitudes and opinions
- *Awareness and knowledge*: For example, brand awareness
- *Intentions*: For example, purchase intentions. While useful, Intentions are not a reliable indication of actual future behaviour.
- *Motivation*: A person's motives are more stable than his/her behaviour, so motive is a better predictor of future behaviour than is past behaviour.
- Behaviour

Primary data can be obtained by communication or by observation. Communication involves questioning respondents either verbally or in writing. This method is versatile, since one needs only to ask for the information; however, the response may not be accurate. Communication usually is quicker and cheaper than observation. Observation involves the recording of actions and is performed by either a person or some mechanical or electronic device.

Observation is less versatile than communication since some attributes of a person may not be readily observable, such as attitudes, awareness, knowledge, intentions, and motivation. Observation also might take longer since observers may have to wait for appropriate events to occur, though observation using scanner data might be quicker and more cost effective. Observation typically is more accurate than communication. Personal interviews have an interviewer bias that mail-in questionnaires do not have. For example, in a personal interview the respondent's perception of the interviewer may affect the responses.

QUESTIONNAIRE DESIGN

The questionnaire is an important tool for gathering primary data. Poorly constructed questions can result in large errors and invalidate the research data, so significant effort should be put into the questionnaire design. The questionnaire should be tested thoroughly prior to conducting the survey.

MEASUREMENT SCALES

Attributes can be measured on nominal, ordinal, interval, and ratio scales:

- Nominal numbers are simply identifiers, with the only permissible mathematical use being for counting.
  Example: Social security numbers.
- Ordinal scales are used for ranking. The interval between the numbers conveys no meaning. Median and mode calculations can be performed on ordinal numbers.
  Example: Class ranking
- Interval scales maintain an equal interval between numbers. These scales can be used for ranking and for measuring the interval between two numbers. Since the zero point is arbitrary, ratios cannot be taken between numbers on an interval scale; however, mean, median, and mode are all valid.
  Example: Temperature scale
- Ratio scales are referenced to an absolute zero values, so ratios between numbers on the scale are meaningful. In addition to mean, median, and mode, geometric averages also are valid.
  Example: Weight

VALIDITY AND RELIABILITY

The validity of a test is the extent to which differences in scores reflect differences in the measured characteristic. Predictive validity is a measure of the usefulness of a measuring instrument as a predictor. Proof of predictive validity is determined by the correlation between results and actual behaviour.

Construct validity is the extent to which a measuring instrument measures what it intends to measure. Reliability is the extent to which a measurement is repeatable with the same results. A measurement may be reliable and not valid. However, if a measurement is valid, then it also is reliable and if it is not reliable, then it cannot be valid. One way to show reliability is to show stability by repeating the test with the same results.

ATTITUDE MEASUREMENT

Many of the questions in a marketing research survey are designed to measure attitudes. Attitudes are a person's general evaluation of something.

Customer attitude is an important factor for the following reasons:

- Attitude helps to explain how ready one is to do something.
- Attitudes do not change much over time.
- Attitudes produce consistency in behaviour.
- Attitudes can be related to preferences.

Attitudes can be measured using the following procedures:

- *Self-reporting*: Subjects are asked directly about their attitudes. Self-reporting is the most common technique used to measure attitude.
- *Observation of behaviour*: Assuming that one's behaviour is a result of one's attitudes, attitudes can be inferred by observing behaviour. For example, one's attitude about an issue can be inferred by whether he/she signs a petition related to it.
- *Indirect techniques*: Use unstructured stimuli such as word association tests.
- *Performance of objective tasks*: Assumes that one's performance depends on attitude. For example, the subject can be asked to memorize the arguments of both sides of an issue. He/she is more likely to do a better job on the arguments that favour his/her stance.
- *Physiological reactions*: Subject's response to a stimuli is measured using electronic or mechanical means. While the intensity can be measured, it is difficult to know if the attitude is positive or negative.
- *Multiple measures*: A mixture of techniques can be used to validate the findings, especially worthwhile when self-reporting is used.

There are several types of attitude rating scales:

- *Equal-appearing interval scaling*: A set of statements are assembled. These statements are selected according to their position on an interval scale of favourableness. Statements are chosen that has a small degree of dispersion. Respondents then are asked to indicate with which statements they agree.
- *Likert method of summated ratings*: A statement is made and the respondents indicate their degree of agreement or disagreement on a five point scale.
- Semantic differential scale - a scale is constructed using phrases describing attributes of the product to anchor each end. For example, the left end may state, "Hours are inconvenient" and the right end

may state, "Hours are convenient". The respondent then marks one of the seven blanks between the statements to indicate his/her opinion about the attribute.

- *Stapel Scale*: Similar to the semantic differential scale except that
  - Points on the scale are identified by numbers,
  - Only one statement is used and if the respondent disagrees a negative number should marked, and
  - There are 10 positions instead of seven. This scale does not require that bipolar adjectives be developed and it can be administered by telephone.
- *Q-sort technique*: The respondent if forced to construct a normal distribution by placing a specified number of cards in one of 11 stacks according to how desirable he/she finds the characteristics written on the cards.

SAMPLING PLAN

The sampling frame is the pool from which the interviewees are chosen. The telephone book often is used as a sampling frame, but have some shortcomings. Telephone books exclude those households that do not have telephones and those households with unlisted numbers. Since a certain percentage of the numbers listed in a phone book are out of service, there are many people who have just moved who are not sampled. Such sampling biases can be overcome by using random digit dialing. Mall intercepts represent another sampling frame, though there are many people who do not shop at malls and those who shop more often will be over-represented unless their answers are weighted in inverse proportion to their frequency of mall shopping.

In designing the research study, one should consider the potential errors. Two sources of errors are random sampling error and non-sampling error. Sampling errors are those due to the fact that there is a non-zero confidence interval of the results because of the sample size being less than the population being studied.

Non-sampling errors are those caused by faulty coding, untruthful responses, respondent fatigue, etc. There is a tradeoff between sample size and cost.

The larger the sample size, the smaller the sampling error but the higher the cost. After a certain point the smaller sampling error cannot be justified by the additional cost. While a larger sample size may reduce sampling error, it actually may increase the total error. There are two reasons for this effect. First, a larger sample size may reduce the ability to follow up on non-responses. Second, even if there is a sufficient number of interviewers for follow-ups, a larger number of interviewers may result in a less uniform interview process.

DATA COLLECTION

In addition to the intrinsic sampling error, the actual data collection process will introduce additional errors. These errors are called non-sampling errors. Some non-sampling errors may be intentional on the part of the interviewer, who may introduce a bias by leading the respondent to provide a certain response. The interviewer also may introduce unintentional errors, for example, due to not having a clear understanding of the interview process or due to fatigue. Respondents also may introduce errors.

A respondent may introduce intentional errors by lying or simply by not responding to a question. A respondent may introduce unintentional errors by not understanding the question, guessing, not paying close attention, and being fatigued or distracted. Such non-sampling errors can be reduced through quality control techniques.

DATA ANALYSIS - PRELIMINARY STEPS

Before analysis can be performed, raw data must be transformed into the right format. First, it must be edited so that errors can be corrected or omitted. The data must then be coded; this procedure converts the edited raw data into numbers or symbols. A codebook is created to document how the data was coded. Finally, the data is tabulated to count the number of samples falling into various categories. Simple tabulations count the occurrences of each variable independently of the other variables.

Cross tabulations, also known as contingency tables or cross tabs, treats two or more variables simultaneously. However, since the variables are in a two-dimensional table, cross tabbing more than two variables is difficult to visualize since more than two dimensions would be required. Cross tabulation can be performed for nominal and ordinal variables. Cross tabulation is the most commonly utilized data analysis method in marketing research. Many studies take the analysis no further than cross tabulation. This technique divides the sample into sub-groups to show how the dependent variable varies from one subgroup to another. A third variable can be introduced to uncover a relationship that initially was not evident.

CONJOINT ANALYSIS

The conjoint analysis is a powerful technique for determining consumer preferences for product attributes.

HYPOTHESIS TESTING

A basic fact about testing hypotheses is that a hypothesis may be rejected but that the hypothesis never can be unconditionally accepted until all possible evidence is evaluated. In the case of sampled data, the information set cannot be complete. So if a test using such data does not reject a hypothesis, the conclusion is not necessarily that the hypothesis should be accepted.

The null hypothesis in an experiment is the hypothesis that the independent variable has no effect on the dependent variable. The null hypothesis is expressed as H0. This hypothesis is assumed to be true unless proven otherwise. The alternative to the null hypothesis is the hypothesis that the independent variable does have an effect on the dependent variable. This hypothesis is known as the alternative, research, or experimental hypothesis and is expressed as H1. This alternative hypothesis states that the relationship observed between the variables cannot be explained by chance alone.

There are two types of errors in evaluating a hypotheses:

1. *Type I error*: Occurs when one rejects the null hypothesis and accepts the alternative, when in fact the null hypothesis is true.
2. *Type II error*: Occurs when one accepts the null hypothesis when in fact the null hypothesis is false.

Because their names are not very descriptive, these types of errors sometimes are confused. Some people jokingly define a Type III error to occur when one confuses Type I and Type II. To show the difference, it is useful to consider a trial by jury in which the null hypothesis is that the defendant is innocent. If the jury convicts a truly innocent defendant, a Type I error has occurred. If, on the other hand, the jury declares a truly guilty defendant to be innocent, a Type II error has occurred.

Hypothesis testing involves the following steps:

- Formulate the null and alternative hypotheses.
- Choose the appropriate test.
- Choose a level of significance —determine the rejection region.
- Gather the data and calculate the test statistic.
- Determine the probability of the observed value of the test statistic under the null hypothesis given the sampling distribution that applies to the chosen test.
- Compare the value of the test statistic to the rejection threshold.
- Based on the comparison, reject or do not reject the null hypothesis.
- Make the marketing research conclusion.

In order to analyse whether research results are statistically significant or simply by chance, a test of statistical significance can be run.

TESTS OF STATISTICAL SIGNIFICANCE

The chi-square (C^2) goodness-of-fit test is used to determine whether a set of proportions have specified numerical values. It often is used to analyse bivariate cross-tabulated data.

Some examples of situations that are well-suited for this test are:

- A manufacturer of packaged products test markets a new product and wants to know if sales of the new product will be in the same relative proportion of package sizes as sales of existing products.
- A company's sales revenue comes from Product A (50%), Product B

(30%), and Product C (20%). The firm wants to know whether recent fluctuations in these proportions are random or whether they represent a real shift in sales.

The chi-square test is performed by defining k categories and observing the number of cases falling into each category. Knowing the expected number of cases falling in each category, one can define chi-squared as:

$$c^2 = \mathring{a}(O_i - E_i)^2 / E_i$$

where:

O_i = The number of observed cases in category i,

E_i = The number of expected cases in category i,

k = The number of categories,

the summation runs from i = 1 to i = k. Before calculating the chi-square value, one needs to determine the expected frequency for each cell. This is done by dividing the number of samples by the number of cells in the table. To use the output of the chi-square function, one uses a chi-square table. To do so, one needs to know the number of degrees of freedom. For chi-square applied to cross-tabulated data, the number of degrees of freedom is equal to,

(number of columns – 1) (number of rows – 1)

This is equal to the number of categories minus one. The conventional critical level of 0.05 normally is used. If the calculated output value from the function is greater than the chi-square look-up table value, the null hypothesis is rejected.

ANOVA

Another test of significance is the Analysis of Variance test. The primary purpose of ANOVA is to test for differences between multiple means. Whereas the t-test can be used to compare two means, ANOVA is needed to compare three or more means. If multiple t-tests were applied, the probability of a TYPE I error increases as the number of comparisons increases. One-way ANOVA examines whether multiple means differ. The test is called an F-test. ANOVA calculates the ratio of the variation between groups to the variation within groups. While ANOVA was designed for comparing several means, it also can be used to compare two means. Two-way ANOVA allows for a second independent variable and addresses interaction.

To run a one-way ANOVA, use the following steps:

- Identify the independent and dependent variables.
- Describe the variation by breaking it into three parts - the total variation, the portion that is within groups, and the portion that is between groups. The total variation is the sum of the squares of the differences between each value and the grand mean of all the values in all the groups. The in-group variation is the sum of the squares of the differences in each element's value and the group mean. The

variation between group means is the total variation minus the in-group variation.

- Measure the difference between each group's mean and the grand mean.
- Perform a significance test on the differences.
- Interpret the results.

This F-test assumes that the group variances are approximately equal and that the observations are independent. It also assumes normally distributed data; however, since this is a test on means the Central Limit Theorem holds as long as the sample size is not too small. ANOVA is efficient for analyzing data using relatively few observations and can be used with categorical variables. Note that regression can perform a similar analysis to that of ANOVA.

DISCRIMINANT ANALYSIS

Analysis of the difference in means between groups provides information about individual variables, it is not useful for determine their individual impacts when the variables are used in combination. Since some variables will not be independent from one another, one needs a test that can consider them simultaneously in order to take into account their interrelationship.

One such test is to construct a linear combination, essentially a weighted sum of the variables. To determine which variables discriminate between two or more naturally occurring groups, discriminant analysis is used. Discriminant analysis can determine which variables are the best predictors of group membership. It determines which groups differ with respect to the mean of a variable, and then uses that variable to predict new cases of group membership. Essentially, the discriminant function problem is a one-way ANOVA problem in that one can determine whether multiple groups are significantly different from one another with respect to the mean of a particular variable.

A discriminant analysis consists of the following steps:

- Formulate the problem.
- Determine the discriminant function coefficients that result in the highest ratio of between-group variation to within-group variation.
- Test the significance of the discriminant function.
- Interpret the results.
- Determine the validity of the analysis.

Discriminant analysis analyses the dependency relationship, whereas factor analysis and cluster analysis address the interdependency among variables.

FACTOR ANALYSIS

Factor analysis is a very popular technique to analyse interdependence.

Factor analysis studies the entire set of interrelationships without defining variables to be dependent or independent. Factor analysis combines variables to create a smaller set of factors. Mathematically, a factor is a linear combination of variables. A factor is not directly observable; it is inferred from the variables.

The technique identifies underlying structure among the variables, reducing the number of variables to a more manageable set. Factor analysis groups variables according to their correlation. The factor loading can be defined as the correlations between the factors and their underlying variables. A factor loading matrix is a key output of the factor analysis. An example matrix is shown below.

	Factor 1	Factor 2	Factor 3
Variable 1			
Variable 2			
Variable 3			
Column's Sum of Squares:			

Each cell in the matrix represents correlation between the variable and the factor associated with that cell. The square of this correlation represents the proportion of the variation in the variable explained by the factor. The sum of the squares of the factor loadings in each column is called an eigenvalue. An eigenvalue represents the amount of variance in the original variables that is associated with that factor.

The communality is the amount of the variable variance explained by common factors. A rule of thumb for deciding on the number of factors is that each included factor must explain at least as much variance as does an average variable.

In other words, only factors for which the eigenvalue is greater than one are used. Other criteria for determining the number of factors include the Scree plot criteria and the percentage of variance criteria. To facilitate interpretation, the axis can be rotated. Rotation of the axis is equivalent to forming linear combinations of the factors. A commonly used rotation strategy is the varimax rotation. Varimax attempts to force the column entries to be either close to zero or one.

CLUSTER ANALYSIS

Market segmentation usually is based not on one factor but on multiple factors. Initially, each variable represents its own cluster. The challenge is to find a way to combine variables so that relatively homogenous clusters can be formed. Such clusters should be internally homogenous and externally heterogeneous. Cluster analysis is one way to accomplish this goal. Rather than being a statistical test, it is more of a collection of algorithms for grouping objects, or in the case of marketing research, grouping people. Cluster analysis is useful in the exploratory phase of research when there are no a-priori hypotheses.

Cluster analysis steps:

- Formulate the problem, collecting data and choosing the variables to analyse.
- *Choose a distance measure*: The most common is the Euclidean distance. Other possibilities include the squared Euclidean distance, city-block distance, Chebychev distance, power distance, and per cent disagreement.
- Choose a clustering procedure.
- Determine the number of clusters. They should be well separated and ideally they should be distinct enough to give them descriptive names such as professionals, buffs, etc.
- Profile the clusters.
- Assess the validity of the clustering.

MARKETING RESEARCH REPORT

The format of the marketing research report varies with the needs of the organization.

The report often contains the following parts:

- Authorization letter for the research
- Table of Contents
- List of illustrations
- Executive summary
- Research objectives
- Methodology
- Results
- Limitations
- Conclusions and recommendations
- Appendices containing copies of the questionnaires, etc.

CONCLUDING THOUGHTS

Marketing research by itself does not arrive at marketing decisions, nor does it guarantee that the organization will be successful in marketing its products. However, when conducted in a systematic, analytical, and objective manner, marketing research can reduce the uncertainty in the decision-making process and increase the probability and magnitude of success.

MARKETING INFORMATION SYSTEMS

The Internet is rapidly changing the way business views marketing information systems. New business models present challenges and opportunities as organizations seek to adopt "ebusiness" methodologies in the search for competitive advantage. Organizations of all sizes are feeling the "ripple effect" of Internet-enabled customers, supply chains and competitors. This pressure is particularly acute in the marketing function where information technology touches the customer and is increasingly becoming the key to creating superior customer value. The importance of marketing information is particularly apparent as the economy continues to emphasize services as a primary source of value. Services are heavily information dependent. Information is rapidly becoming a service in its own right. Even in industries that are primarily manufacturing in nature, the information content of the final product is rapidly increasing. Mass customization, often described as "one-to-one" marketing or the customizing of products and services for individual customers, is heavily dependent on comprehensive and timely customer information. Modern marketing organizations, with their focus on the Internet, exhibit different characteristics than their "old economy" brethren.

They create and manage the customer interface where interactions are more virtual than face-to-face. They leverage IT technology to integrate and coordinate with customers and business partners to rapidly achieve measurable business results. The emphasis in on the rapid conversion of knowledge into customer value which depends on the ability to develop, deploy, and manage powerful new marketing information systems. The key to competitive advantage depends on the firm's ability to convert knowledge into customer relationships, reduced time to market and lower costs.

To survive in highly competitive markets, companies need to be able to develop the marketing function and scale it up on "Internet time" with best-of-class decision support solutions for customer relationship management, sales force automation, market research, marketing communications, logistics, and product development. The purpose of this document is to provide an overview of the MkIS as it is evolving into an Internet-based system.

DEFINITION—MARKETING INFORMATION SYSTEM

Simply put, a MkIS is a computerized system that is designed to provide an organized flow of information to enable and support the marketing activities of an organization. The MkIS serves collaborative, analytical and operational needs. In the collaborative mode, the MkIS enables managers to share information and work together virtually. In addition, the MkIS can enable marketers to collaborate with customers on product designs and customer requirements. The analytical function is addressed by decision support applications that enable marketers to analyse market data on customers, competitors, technology and general market conditions.

These insights are becoming the foundation for the development of marketing strategies and plans. The MkIS addresses operational needs through customer management systems that focus on the day-to-day processing of customer transactions from the initial sale through customer service. MkIS systems are designed to be comprehensive and flexible in nature and to integrate with each other functionally. They are formal, forward looking and essential to the organization's ability to create competitive advantage. The MkIS is the firm's "window on the world" and, increasingly, it is the primary customer interface.

THE STRATEGIC ROLE OF THE MARKETING INFORMATION SYSTEMS

Historically, the role of the marketing function has been to support "make and sell" business strategies that emphasized increases in market share over the creation of long-term customer value. This view started to change after World War II with the recognition that satisfying the customer's needs and wants should be the focus of a firm's business activities.

The emphasis on the customer elevated the importance of marketing as a core business function on a par with research and development and production. The marketing function has become the firm's window to the world in the sense that it must monitor the marketing environment for changes in buyer behaviour, competition, technology, economic conditions, and government policies. Marketing is a "strategic" function in that marketing activities enable organizations to identify and adapt to changes in the market environment. The strategic function of marketing is further emphasized as Internet-based technologies have enabled radically new approaches to selling where information technology for the first time touches customers and provides new means for collecting marketing information. In a knowledge-intensive economy, the ability to collect, analyse and act upon marketing information more rapidly than the competition is the core competency from which competitive advantage flows. Marketing information systems provide the information technology backbone for the marketing organization's strategic operations.

In a broader sense, the MkIS creates an organized and timely flow of information required by marketing decision makers. It involves the equipment, software, databases, and also the procedures, methodologies and people necessary for the system to meet its organizational objectives. MkIS encompasses a broad spectrum of activities from simple transaction processing complex marketing strategy decision making.

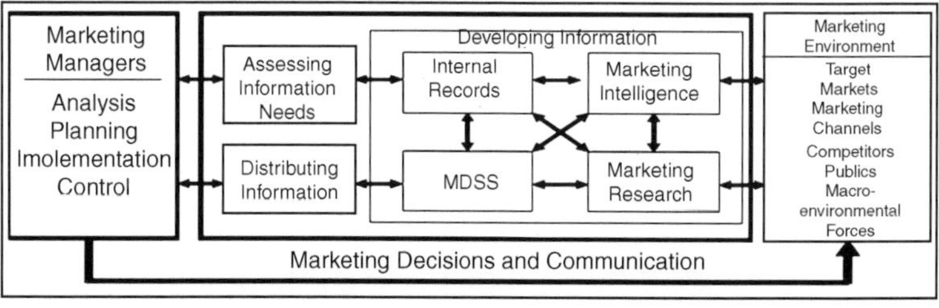

Fig. The Marketing Information System.

THE ROLE OF THE INTERNET

Information technology has transformed how firms conduct business. For example, financial service providers such as banks, stockbrokers and insurance companies could not do business today without their client-server-based information technology. This technology has long supported marketing activities. However, it is the recent advent of the Internet, and especially the browserbased World Wide Web, which has ignited a revolution in MkISs.

The term "cybermarketing" is often used to describe the Internet's convergence of computers, information systems, telecommunications and the customer with the marketing process. Internet marketing is characterized by interactivity, graphical user interfaces, multimedia content, and one-to-one connectivity. Internet technologies are not only providing new ways to reach the customer, but also to enable the reengineering of the entire marketing process and, indeed, the entire enterprise. It is no longer acceptable to view marketing as a standalone activity with lengthy time lapses between product concept, marketing strategy and commercialization.

Marketing has become interactive and real time. The rapidly growing field of marketing automation encompasses customer management functions to support e-commerce. As depicted in Figure, customer management applications include marketing decision support systems, customer relationship management, sales force automation, customer service and e-commerce activities.

These activities are often described as "front office" customer-oriented activities. "Back office" enterprise resource planning activities include manufacturing, finance and human resources. "Supply chain management" activities encompass electronic procurement, inventory management, quality management and logistics systems to link an organization with its suppliers. These three elements comprise the enterprise information system.

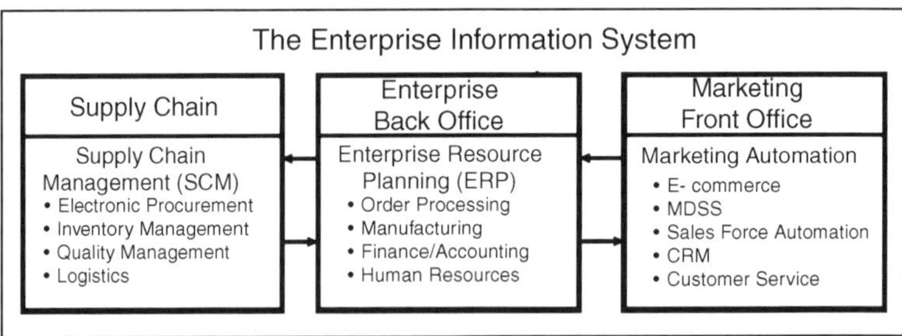

Fig. The Interfaces of MKIS

Large integrated enterprise software companies such as Oracle, SAP, PeopleSoft, and IBM address all three major applications and they are beginning to use Web-based technologies to redesign business processes throughout the organization. The result is leaner organizations, faster response times, and lower costs.

Decisionmakers are able to integrate information from customers, suppliers, and the internal organization to obtain an enterprise-wide view of their ability to develop and execute marketing strategy.

Until truly integrated browser-based systems are widely in use, the principal challenge for marketers is to tie e-commerce generated data with legacy information systems in order to create a unified view of each customer. Marketers will need to understand all the various ways that customers are touching the business through existing interfaces and e-commerce.

Many of the older interfaces, such as telemarketing centres, point of sale systems, and the sales force are likely to be supported by legacy client-server technology. Marketers need to consolidate data from those systems with that from the Web-based ecommerce sources into a holistic view of the customer and make it available to decisionmakers.

BENEFITS OF THE MARKETING INFORMATION SYSTEM

The MkIS increases the number of options available to decision-makers and supports every element of marketing strategy. MkIS affects marketing's interfaces with customers, suppliers and other partners.

The primary benefits of the MkIS impact in the areas of functional integration, market monitoring, strategy development, and strategy implementation:

- *Market Monitoring*: Through the use of market research and marketing intelligence activities the MkIS can enable the identification of emerging market segments, and the monitoring of the market environment for changes in consumer behaviour, competitor activities, new technologies, economic conditions and governmental policies. Market research is situational in nature and focuses on specific strategic or tactical marketing initiatives. Marketing intelligence is continuous in nature and involves monitoring and analyzing a broad range of market-based activities and information sources. There are three major sources of market information. The first is syndicated data published by market research companies and industry associations. Company-sponsored primary research is another option. It is much more focused since you ask specific questions of respondents within your markets. But, it is considerably more expensive and time consuming. Perhaps the best data available are your own customer's behaviour captured from web site viewing, point of sale transactions, and systematic feed back from the sales force.
- *Strategy Development*: The MkIS provides the information necessary to develop marketing strategy. It supports strategy development for new products, product positioning, marketing communications, pricing, personal selling, distribution, customer service and

partnerships and alliances. The MkIS provides the foundation for the development information system-dependent e-commerce strategies.

- *Strategy Implementation*: The MkIS provides support for product launches, enables the coordination of marketing strategies, and is an integral part of sales force automation, customer relationship management, and customer service systems implementations. The MkIS enables decisionmakers to more effectively manage the sales force as well as customer relationships. Some customer management software companies are extending their CRM applications to include partner relationship management capabilities. This has become increasingly important as many marketers are choosing to outsource important marketing functions and form strategic alliances to address new markets.
- *Functional integration*: The MkIS enables the coordination of activities within the marketing department and between marketing and other organizational functions such as engineering, production, product management, finance, manufacturing, logistics, and customer service.

MARKETING INFORMATION SYSTEM FUNCTIONAL COMPONENTS

As shown in Figure, a MkIS consists of four major components:

1. User interfaces,
2. Applications software,
3. Databases, and
4. Systems support.

1. *User Interfaces*: The essential element of the MkIS is the managers who will use the system and the interfaces they need to effectively analyse and use marketing information. The design of the system will depend on what type of decisions managers need to make. The interface includes the type of hardware that will be used, the way information is analysed, formatted and displayed, and how reports are to be compiled and distributed. Issues to resolve are ease of use, security, cost, and access.

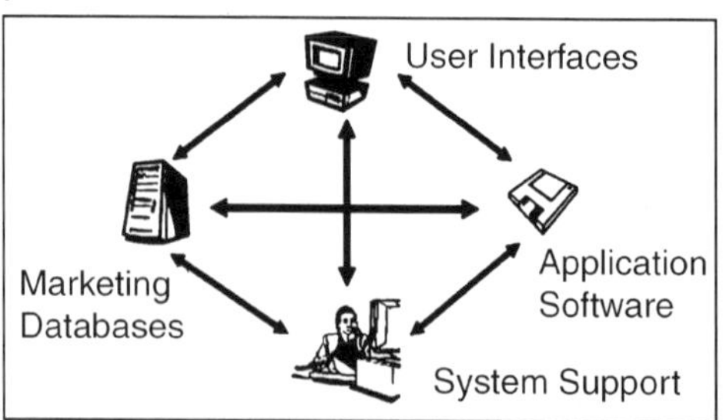

Fig. MKIS Functional Components.

2. *Applications Software*: These are the programmes that marketing decision makers use to collect, analyse, and manage data for the purpose of developing the information necessary for marketing decisions. Examples include the marketing decisions support software and customer management software for on-line sales and customer service.
3. *Marketing Databases*: A marketing database is a system in which marketing data files are organized d stored. Data may be collected from internal and external sources. Internal sources largely result from transactions. They provide data from e-commerce sites, sales results, shipping data, inventories, and product profitability. External sources include market research, competitor intelligence, credit bureaus, and financial institutions. Data can be organized in a flat file or a relational database. For instance, each row could represent a customer with the columns providing name, identification number, and purchase information.
4. *System Support*: This component consists of system managers who manage and maintain the systems assets including software and hardware network, monitor its activities and ensure compliance with organizational policies. This function may also include a help desk for system users.

MARKETING DECISION SUPPORT SYSTEM

Marketing decision support systems constitute a set of core applications of the MkIS. The MDSS provides computer-based tools, models, and techniques to support the marketing manager's decision process. In the general case, MDSS is optimized for queries of historical data. MDSS data typically are derived from both internal and external market sources. The MDSS features inquiry and report generation functions where the manager can access marketing data, analyse it statistically, and use the results to determine an optimal course of action.

Marketing Decisions Support System Functions

The MDSS can provide analytical models for forecasting, simulation, and optimization. MDSS tools include simple spreadsheets such as Excel, statistical analysis packages such as SPSS and SAS, on-line analytical processing tools, data mining applications, and neural networks. The MDSS provides the user with the ability to explore multiple options.

Typical MDSS functions include models and tools for:

- *Sensitivity analysis*: Decision-makers can explore changes in a strategic variable such as price and model its impact on demand or competitive behaviour.
- *What-if analysis*: Can be easily accomplished with a spreadsheet.

Revenues and costs can be manipulated to show the impact of each variable on profits and cash flows.

- *Goal setting*: Analysis focuses on the desired result and builds the resource base necessary to accomplish the goal.
- *Exception reporting*: Analysis looks for results that exceed or fall short of stated goals or benchmarks. Which products or segments exceeded sales forecasts? Sometimes called gap analysis.
- *Pareto analysis*: Analysis looks for activities that generate disproportionate results. For instance, the top 20 per cent of customers may account for 80 per cent of sales revenues.
- *Forecasting models*: Econometric models are used to analyse time series data for the purpose of predicting future sales and market share levels.
- *Simulation models*: Monte Carlo simulations address marketing decision making under conditions of uncertainty. Variables such as the market price, unit variable cost, and quantity sold are not known ahead of the product investment decision. Simulation models allow the marketer to analyse risk and assess the probabilities of likely outcomes of their decisions.
- *Scorecards and dashboards*: Scorecard systems can present a consistent framework for tracking the effectiveness of marketing activities. They often have different modules for senior executives, marketing managers, product managers, and customer service managers. Scorecard systems allow the user to "drill down" on an analytic and workflow basis to determine the status of any strategic initiative. Dashboards allow frontline managers to monitor their critical performance indicators. These systems are often used in conjunction with "best practice" standards for call-centre-based customer support.

MDSS Analyses

Marketers typically use MDSS models and tools to analyse markets, customers, competitors, and internal operations.

The following list presents some of the most common types of issues targeted by MDSS analyses:

- *Market segment analysis*: Use of modeling techniques to identify segments and analyse economic trends, demographics and behaviour.
- *Market share analysis*: Analyse trends and determinants of market share.
- *Competitor analysis*: Analysis of competitors' market positions, economics customer base, and marketing strategies.
- *Pricing analysis*: Identifies and analyses the factors that influence a firm's ability to set prices including price elasticity and demand analysis. Includes internal economics and market related factors.

- *Cost analysis*: Studies a firm's overall cost structure and its impact on product cost. Margin analysis combines cost analysis with pricing analysis. Variance analysis looks for explanations of costs overages and underages.
- *Sales analysis*: Studies the distribution of a firm's sales by region, product, brand, sales territory, etc.
- *Sales forecasting*: Develops estimates of sales potential by product, region, sales territory, brand, etc.
- *Sales force productivity*: Studies sales force effectiveness and efficiency and contributing factors.
- *Advertising analysis*: Analyses advertising effectiveness, media choices and brand awareness.
- *Distribution*: Analyses channel decisions from economic and strategic perspectives.
- *Simulation*: Simulates decision making under various strategic scenarios.
- *Customer satisfaction*: Analyses issues concerning the customer's expectations and outcomes with the product.

Data Warehousing

IBM defines a data warehouse as a place that stores enterprise data designed to facilitate management decisions. In essence, a data warehouse provides the basis for an analytical system where periodic data points are collected and stored at specified times for future analysis. Data warehousing enables marketers to capture, organize, and store potentially useful data about customers and markets for decision-making purposes.

Every record of a transaction or interaction with a customer, supplier, channel member, or sales person is an opportunity to create knowledge. Firms collect data from these day-today business operations. In order for this data to be useful, it is often organized and stored in a data warehouse. Simply put, a marketing data warehouse is a repository for data that has been collected from internal and external data sources. Each customer generates a stream of transaction records over time.

Data sources may include scanner data, billing records, applications, registration forms, warranty forms, call reports, customer service inquiries, and web site data. Data warehousing enables the firm to organize and store this data for analysis purposes.

By careful analysis of this and other data, firms can design more effective and efficient ways to serve their customers. Data warehouses exist to support the decision-making process by providing ready access to market and customer data. The Internet has shifted power away from marketers to customers by lowering search costs and providing greater choice. Competitors are only a "click" away.

Consequently, marketers need to work smarter to create and manage the one-to-one relationships that customers desire. This goal requires increased knowledge about customer preferences, behaviours, and value expectations in order to create better products and services. Conversely, marketers need to understand which customers are the most valuable to them over time. They need to regularly monitor and evaluate the "lifetime value" of each customer in order to determine which customers to continue investing in and which ones to drop.

Data Warehouse Processes

Data warehouses can provide narrow or broad strategic views of key marketing activities for the purpose of generating higher customer value and business returns. Data warehousing activities commonly support customer relationship management, product development, and customer service delivery.

Data warehouse architectures are based on the following three processes:

1. *Data collection*: Processes need to be developed for capturing data from the appropriate internal and external sources and then organizing, verifying, integrating and otherwise preparing it for loading into the database.
2. *Data management*: This step involves formatting and storing that data for easy access by data warehouse users.
3. *Data access*: This process involves specialized tools to query the data, analyse it and create and distribute useful business reports.

Data warehouses are an integral part of the MDSS. They provide the ability to access data for creating marketing operations reports, analyse sales results over time, identifying and mapping patterns, trends, that may be emerging in the market, and enabling the development of new products, pricing, market segmentation strategies, marketing communications campaigns, and distribution channels.

Data Marts

A data mart is a scaled-down version of a data warehouse. It is more focused, less complex, and holds a subset of the entire data, often in summary form. It is usually designed for a smaller number of users. They provide fast, specialized access and applications. They are sometimes call departmental data warehouses. Data marts are useful when it is not feasible for a data warehouse to meets the needs of all potential users. Data marts enable a more limited number of users to exert greater control over the data they need.

Data marts enable increased data access speed and minimize preemption of user queries. They also minimize performance sacrifices inherent in large data warehouses by enabling small groups to get the data they most need when they need it. They may also include specialized data sets that can be analysed with statistical or data mining tools. Not all the data in the data mart need come from the data warehouse. A marketing researcher may overlay customer purchase histories from the data warehouse with Geographic information system data from a commercial service and store it in the data mart.

Data Mining

Internet-based marketing strategies generate extremely large data sets from customer interactions. Purchase histories, financial records, customer service records, and web site usage are just some of the data that reside in customer databases. In order to transform this mountain of diverse data into operationally useful information, marketers are increasingly using data mining procedures. Data mining is the computer-based exploration and analysis of large quantities of data in order to discover meaningful patterns and rules for the purpose of improving marketing, sales, and customer support operations.

The combination of data mining procedures with data warehousing enables the MDSS to move beyond just support for the operational processes in the marketing organization and to focus on actual customer behaviour. Data mining and data warehousing provide the means and the infrastructure for extracting strategic opportunity from knowledge of the customer.

The Data Mining Process

Large multinational organizations produce much more marketing data per day than its managers can assimilate. The Internet facilitates the rapid growth of data on a worldwide basis. But, exponential growth of data can, paradoxically, lead to a situation where more data leads to less information as managers become swamped by the flood of data that defies ready interpretation.

Marketers need to develop procedures for processing, filtering and interpreting this data for strategic marketing purposes. Data mining is essentially the engine for a knowledge-based marketing strategy. It provides the ability to collect, process, disseminate, and act upon information more rapidly than the competition that is essential to for the creation of first-mover advantage. The first step in the process is to collect data on what the customer does. On-line transaction processing systems do precisely that. Virtually everything a customer does when purchasing a product or service generates a string of transaction records.

If the customer calls an "800" number to order a product, the phone company will capture data on the time of the call, the number dialed and the duration of the call. The marketing company will generate similar data in addition to that on products and services purchased, catalogue referenced, special offers, credit card number, order size, and time since last purchase.

Further transactions are generated by the order entry, billing, and shipping systems. The bank and the shipping company will log further transactions. The customer may need to call customer service to solve post-purchase problems. Internet transactions can generate even more data as the customer's purchase behaviour can be linked to web-browsing behaviour within a site and throughout the web. This data can then be linked to purchase histories, financial history and other personal-identity information.

Data Mining Tasks

After the data have been collected and reside in the data warehouse, approaches to analyzing the data are considered. Data mining methodologies may encompass a range of approaches from rigorous scientific methodologies and hypothesis testing to qualitative sifting through massive amounts of data in search of relationships. The type of analysis typically is a function of the task the researcher wants the data mining exercise to accomplish.

Typical data mining tasks include:

- *Classification*: A predetermined classification code is assigned to a database record. Decision tree analysis techniques are commonly associated with this task.
- *Estimation*: Input data are used to estimate continuous variables such as age, income, and likely behaviours. Neural networks are often used for estimation.
- *Affinity Grouping*: Rules of association are developed from the data and used to group variables that seem to go together. Market basket analysis is a preferred technique that analyses the linkages between items consumers buy in a basket of items.
- *Description*: Summary observations are made about the data that serve to increase the understanding of the phenomena that generated the data. Description often motivates further research and data analysis. Market basket analysis, query tools, and visualization techniques are commonly used.
- *Clustering*: Used to segment a large heterogeneous population into homogeneous clusters based on measures of similarity. The researcher must determine the meaning of each cluster. Clustering algorithms are used to analyse the data.
- *Prediction*: Records are classified based on predicted future values or behaviours. Neural networks, market basket analysis, and decision trees are common techniques.

Data Mining Techniques

Researchers looking for behavioural insights in large customer databases commonly use the following data mining techniques.

- *Market Basket Analysis*: Searches for associations in the data such as professional women who drive 5-Series BMWs also use web-enabled mobile phones. The weakness of the technique is there are an infinite number of possible rules in any given database and only a few have marketing importance. The problem is to find them. Techniques works best when the researcher has an idea of what to look for.

- *Cluster Analysis*: Based on the hypothesis that customers of the same type will exhibit similar behaviours. K-means cluster analysis is the most common method. The purpose is to assign objects to groups that are relatively homogeneous within and heterogeneous between.
- *Decision Trees*: Decision trees enable classification for directed data mining. Simple rules are often used to divide the data into subsets in which key attributes can be more readily evaluated. Decision trees can facilitate prediction by linking customer characteristics with purchase behaviours.
- *Query Tools*: Structured Query Language is often used for conducting a preliminary analysis of a data set. Data summaries such as simple averages, frequencies, and cross-tabulations are useful for looking for patterns and rules that may form the basis for more structured analyses.
- *Neural Networks*: Neural networks are a class of tools that are used for classification, clustering and prediction. These networks are computer models that simulate the neural connections in the human brain. There are two critical stages for using neural networks—the encoding stage where the network is trained to perform a task and the decoding stage where network executes the assigned task. In practice, these machine learning tools are used to identify loyal customer clusters, find fraudulent credit card transactions, diagnose medical conditions, and predict the failure rate of aircraft engines.

On-line Analytical Processing (OLAP)

OLAP is a family of analysis and reportgenerating tools that are used to access large databases. It enables partially aggregated data or full reports to be stored in a multidimensional format for fast, convenient access and analysis. OLAP methods are based on databases that allow multidimensional views of business data. OLAP is useful for visualization of relationships between pre-designated variables. OLAP applications are used achieve a higher view of the data such as total sales or profitability by product line, sales territory, or market segment.

The OLAP database is usually updated in batch mode from multiple sources. OLAP is optimized for analysis and reporting. In contrast, users of on-line transaction processing (OLTP) applications are involved with creating, updating, or retrieving individual customer records. OLTP databases are optimized for updating transactions. An OLAP system essentially stores answers to predefined business questions for report generation needs. The user can choose from a predetermined set of options for types of data and display formats. Output is typically in the form of charts, graphs, tables or maps. OLAP solves the problem of distributing information to large numbers of users with diverse reporting needs. OLAP relieves the long response times that can be encountered when many users need to repeatedly query large databases for extended periods of time.

Time series data are probably the most common dimensionality in an OLAP database. Marketers want to look at trends in all aspects of the business—sales trends, market trends, pricing trends, profitability trends, etc. OLAP can compare current results with prior periods, calculate year-to-date results, and present other comparative historical data. OLAP can also present multiple hierarchies and classes within given dimensions.

For instance, data may be "drilled down" by "state-county-city-customer" or "sales region-sales district-sales personcustomer." OLAP may be used in conjunction with data mining, but it is not a substitute. OLAP tools are powerful and fast tools for generating reports on data, whereas data mining tools find patterns in the data. OLAP users are constrained in the questions they can ask since OLAP and only answer the questions that the data formats were designed to address. They cannot go back to the original data and search for new solutions. Therefore, data mining is more powerful than OLAP.

Geographical Information Systems

GIS systems enable marketers to geographically map their customers, competitors, suppliers, sales concentrations, prospects, suppliers and partners. Site selection, trade-area analysis, environmental analysis, territory design, network planning, risk analysis are common applications. Newer systems have integrated global positioning system (GPS) capability for location reports from resources in motion such as mapping transportation fleet movements, sales representative reporting, and locating and managing key assets in real time. GIS data provide powerful new visualization opportunities for customer data that can link consumer behaviour to a fixed location at a specified time.

Geographical Information System Marketing Applications

- *Customer location*: Links behavioural data from customer master files, subscription lists, support and warranty claims, transaction history and identity with time and location information. This is very powerful information for mapping and predicting consumer behaviour. The advent of mobile ecommerce will enable marketers to identify and map consumers at the actual point of purchase. The wireless carriers will be able to provide this data.
- *Geographic market information*: Links marketing data to physical maps.

Data may be classified by county, city, ZIP code, Census tract, etc.

- *Marketing activity location*: Links POS transactions, distribution patterns, direct response results, sales forecasts, advertising expense, etc. to geographic location.
- *Business location*: Labels business facilities on a map that can display retail density, population density, buying power, media coverage, etc.
- *Marketing resource location*: Links assets in motion to physical location through GPS from trucks, autos, aircraft and wireless devices.

CUSTOMER MANAGEMENT SYSTEMS

Companies need a method for viewing all customer and marketing-related information in an integrated way. Often marketing organizations maintain multiple databases for each business and marketing activity with data that is not easily integrated for strategic or operational purposes. A new generation of software that is Internet based gathers information from customer service, Web sites, direct mail operations, telemarketing, field sales, customer service, distributors, retailers and suppliers for the purpose of managing marketing, sales and customer service activities.

The major applications families are commonly referred to as sales force automation (SFA) and customer relationship management (CRM) systems.

Some CRM systems are fully integrated with SFA applications and some are standalone. The worldwide market for such systems is projected to grow five times faster than the overall software market, from $5 billion in 1999 to more than $22 billion in 2003.

Sales Force Automation

SFA is a customer management tool that is one of the fastest growing elements of the MkIS. SFA applications are often integrated with the CRM system. SFA involves the application of information technology to the sales function or, more appropriately, to the activities leading to a sale. These activities include acquiring sales leads, managing the sales opportunity, closing the sale and managing the customer relationship. The historic role of personal selling has been to move the product—to generate transactions.

As selling has become increasingly more professional, sales people emphasize building relationships with customers that will generate loyalty-based repeat transactions over time. Relationship building often necessitates that the sales person has consultative and advisory skills in addition to product knowledge and sales abilities. Team-based selling places emphasis on role specialization, collaboration and coordination. Customers have become more sophisticated as well.

Requirements for customised solutions, rapid response times and the need for concurrent and post-sale service have greatly increased the need for information technology in the sales process. The goals of SFA are to increase the effectiveness of the sales organization, improve its efficiency and to create superior value for the customer. Sales effectiveness focuses on getting the sale by improving lead generation, qualifying prospects, coordinating sales efforts, and tracking commitments.

Effectiveness is a function of improving the sales process. Sales efficiency is evaluated by measuring the return on sales efforts. SFA can improve sales efficiency by reducing sales cycle time, by managing workflow, and tracking the current status of critical activities related to the sale.

Proposal generation, opportunity management, fulfillment, and follow up are facilitated by SFA. Superior customer value is achieved when the customer expectations are exceeded. It is a primary determinant of customer satisfaction. SFA enables better understanding of customer expectations and management of the customer account.

The Sales Process

The typical field sales process consists of a series of steps that are designed to lead to a sale. The typical role of the MkIS is to support the sales process steps of lead generation, sales process management, and account management.

- *Lead generation*: Leads represent potential customers. The identification of a lead is the beginning of the sales cycle. After leads are identified, they must be qualified. This process involves gathering information about the lead and comparing the result against qualifying criteria. The lead generation process is becoming more automated with regard to obtaining more pre-qualifying information directly from the lead and augmenting it from commercial and other databases such as credit bureaus. The advent of Web-based technologies is driving this trend. Qualified leads are then distributed to the sales force.
- *Sales Process Management*: This process starts when the sales person receives the lead information. The primary information system need is for a convenient method to track the process and store data the data generated at each stage. There are a number of sub-steps to this stage of the process.
  - *Verification of the opportunity*: The sales person usually contacts the lead and attempts to verify the existence and nature of an opportunity including its size, timing, and appropriateness of the products and services of the selling company. Sales people will also desire to verify the lead's ability to purchase, identify the names of key decision-makers and influencers, and the level of budget authority. This information is entered into the sales database.
  - *The Sales Call*: If the lead is amenable and the opportunity

justifies it, a sales call is scheduled. Information may be sent to the prospect and a custom presentation may be created. The SFA system is used to provide a single point of interface for the sales person to coordinate the activities leading up to the sales call. After the call, the SFA system is updated with customer requirements, new information and commitments made by the sales person.

- *Opportunity Management*: If the sales person is successful, the next step is typically the receipt of a request for proposal (RFP) from the prospective customer. The RFP will generally state the customer's requirements and the date for the final submission. Follow-on visits may be necessary to clear up or identify new requirements. The prospect may want to visit the seller's manufacturing site. The final product of this stage is the creation of a proposal and price quote to be presented to the prospect. This document should build a sound economic case for the purchase. All these interactions, requirements, commitments, and competitor information are tracked by the SFA system that provides the database, tools and templates to generate the proposal.
- *Closing the Sale*: The presentation of the proposal and the price quote is the start of the closing process. Even if the sales person has done a good job of presenting the business case, further negotiations may be necessary to close the sale. If all objections are met and the proposal is accepted the close is successful. If not, the sales team will need to debrief the sessions learned to determine why the proposal was not accepted. The outcomes are recorded in the SFA system.

• *Account Management*: The automation of the sales process may result in a standalone system that is not integrated with other management systems. However, SFA is increasingly being integrated with the overall CRM system. This is especially true of the account management function. Since the primary goal of the CRM system is to manage the customer relationship in order to generate repeat sales, a good sales person will want to keep track of the status of a new account and how well the customer is being served. This is especially true if the account is to become "referenceable" to other prospects. The account management function of the CRM system enables the sales person to track order entry, order processing, shipment, and installation. The sales person may need to ensure that post-sales service is delivered or monitor the results of and installation and track the customer's satisfaction. The ability to track outcomes and interact with the customer in order to reassess needs and create new opportunities is a major benefit that flows from effective account management.

Sales Force Automation Tools

SFA tools consist of software applications that enable the salesperson to better target sales opportunities and manage the sales cycle. The tools are increasingly available bundled as integrated suites that are Internet enabled, accessible through a browser and linked to the CRM system.

The software applications may be categorized as:

- *Document management tools*: These tools support all stages of the sales process. They include word processors, graphics programmes, spreadsheets, e-mail, expense reports, proposal generators, and "product configurators." A Web-accessible sales library or encyclopedia of previously developed product information, brochures, product demonstrations, presentations, financial information, price lists, white documents, and public relations materials is a key resource for sales force productivity.
- *Personal management tools*: These tools focus on increasing the efficiency and effectiveness of the sales teams efforts. They typically include calendar and scheduling programmes, contact management systems, and call reporting capabilities.
- *Process management tools:* These tools are used to keep track of customer requirements and sales commitments. They include opportunity management systems, project management systems, account management systems, order-entry systems, telemarketing systems, team-selling systems.

Increasingly, with the rise of Web-based hosting and the application service provider (ASP) industry, SFA applications and databases are being hosted by third-party specialists and accessed remotely on the Internet. With the ASP model, client companies are essentially outsourcing all or part of there IS function. Remote hosting raises issues of security and scalability. The advantages of an ASP approach are its browser-based simplicity, rapid implementation, and lower cost of deployment. Most ASP applications use a subscription-based pricing model. Some vendors are proposing that renting the application or paying by the transaction may become the pricing model of the future.

Customer Relationship Management

The Internet has facilitated a fundamental shift in market power from sellers to buyers. Customers, newly endowed with the power of market information, have much different expectations than before. Customers can easily move their business to another vendor with the click of a mouse. They have access to the same cost data as their suppliers and they demand 24x7 customer service. Customers now have almost unlimited ability for interactions with organizations through the Web in addition to the traditional phone and mail methods. Company web sites facilitate information search, shopping and customer support. E-mail communication can target specific offers on a one-to-one basis. Understanding and meeting demanding expectations has placed a renewed emphasis on managing customer relationships. The primary goal of CRM systems is to increase the return on marketing expenditures by enabling the understanding of the complete history of a firm's interactions with its customers.

CRM applications can deliver targeted solutions that promote customer loyalty as measured by increased response to promotions, purchase frequencies and volume, and minimizes the time between orders. CRM systems are able to target marketing communications to likely buyers, facilitate sales efforts and deliver customer service. CRM systems increase revenue, lower costs and optimize customer lifetime value.

Customer Relationship Management Design Principles

The CRM field is rapidly evolving into an integrated discipline that manages all of a company's touches with the customer.

Accordingly, several design principles have evolved as the foundation for CRM development:

- The CRM system should offer the customer multiple channels for communication such as the telephone, e-mail, fax, on-line or some combination. Each channel should lead to an interaction that satisfies customer expectations. Customers must be able to choose the method that best meets their needs on each occasion.
- Each CRM interaction should deliver value to the customer. The CRM system must be able to determine what value is required and deliver it quickly whether it is a product or service transaction or a customer service request.
- The CRM system integrates the customer throughout the firm's value chain. Customers should be able to reach into all necessary functions of the organization not just to the sales organization, or customer service, but to manufacturing and even the CEO. Better integration of the customer into the process can lead to higher levels of trust, loyalty and repeat purchases. The cost of acquiring a new customer often far exceeds that of retaining existing ones.
- Knowledge is captured during each CRM interaction. The CRM system should capture knowledge about the customer and the customer's relationship with the company over time. Sales and customer support histories should be analysed for indications of how well the vendor is doing in meeting customers' needs and how valuable the customer is to the marketer.

Customer Relationship Management Functions

CRM applications provide the customer-related information that is necessary to drive a firm's ebusiness activities. Better customer information enables more effective demand forecasting, product launches and marketing campaigns. CRM functions are sometimes referred to as the company's "front office."

CRM functionality includes:

- E-commerce support
- Sales force automation
- Telesales and call centre automation
- Direct mail and catalog sales
- E-mail and e-newsletter response
- Web sales and personalization
- Analysis of Web generated data
- Traditional customer support and service
- On-line support and customer service
- Mobile support through laptops, handheld devices.
- Training

Modern CRM systems are fully integrated with the "back office" elements of the enterprise resource planning (ERP) system such as accounting, manufacturing, project management, and human resources. This integration enables the sharing of customer information that can impact the operations of the enterprise and vice versa. Common customer definitions, price lists, employee definitions, service requests, call histories, order histories, contracts, service level agreements are accessible by all who need them. Correspondingly, marketing can access information on items such as new product development, product costs, order status, delivery dates and backorders.

PRIVACY AND THE MARKETING INFORMATION SYSTEM

Privacy in the Internet Age has become a major concern for customers and marketers alike. Webenabled marketing information systems have the potential to collect highly sensitive and voluminous information on customers, competitors, suppliers and channel members. The speed in which this information can be collected, analysed and acted upon can provide real competitive advantage to the user.

This information can be used to better serve customers, streamline a company's operations, and develop better strategy. Some marketers use the data to better target advertising and marketing plans. Others sell or trade the data with other Web sites. Unfortunately, guidelines for how this information is collected, how it may be used, and how it is to be protected are not widely accepted. Since most non-IS people use privacy, confidentiality and security interchangeable, it is important to clarify some definitions before moving on.

Privacy, as marketers define it, is the right not to be contacted or marketed to unless the customer has granted specific permission or "opted in."

Security means keeping unauthorized persons from gaining access by breaking into the information system. Confidentiality is defined as maintaining appropriate controls on information so that only those authorized can access or use it. A marketer may respect a customer's privacy and only contact her after gaining permission, but they may have an insecure system that allows hackers to access credit card transaction data. Alternatively, a marketer may respect privacy rights and have a very secure system, but inadvertently releases a patient's health care record to the news media. In order to avoid these and other pitfalls, marketers must act to increase system security, establish confidentiality procedures and training, and implement privacy policies. The remainder of this part will focus on privacy issues as a representative case.

Tracking Internet Users

It is axiomatic that no one is anonymous on the Web. At the current state of technology, marketers are able to develop customer profiles and track their behaviour over the Web. Soon marketers will be able to track the locations and behaviours of Web-enabled cell phone and other wireless device users. The public uproar over such capabilities has caused several Web advertising networks to abandon efforts to link Web-use profiles to personal information. In order to track consumers on the Web, enabling IS infrastructure has been developed that links a surfer's Web-behaviour to his Internet Protocol (IP) address. Once that occurs the information gathering begins.

The following infrastructure elements are essential to the information model of the Internet:

- *Advertising networks*: Web-based advertising agencies such as DoubleClick, Engage, and 24/7 create profiles of Web surfers by tracking their on-line behaviours. Ads are customised and presented on-line to those most likely to buy when they visit supported Web sites.
- *Cookies*: A tiny text file that is placed on a consumer's hard drive when they first visit a site. It allows the site to track the user's behaviour on the site. Most Web users are not knowledgeable about cookies. If a consumer removes the cookies from the browser most membership-based sites will prompt for user names and passwords and install another cookie.
- *IP Address*: A number used to identify a consumer's personal computer so that Web data can be sent. These addresses enable profiling and ad targeting. IP addresses can be associated with behavioural and personal information.
- *On-line Profiling*: Web sites build consumer profiles of page viewing,

time spent and shopping behaviour by combining cookies with other information. This sounds ominous, but the ostensible reason is to provide better automated service.

- *Personal Information*: This includes the consumer's name, address, credit card number, driver's license number, social security number, and consumer behaviour that is linked to customers personal identity. Most consumers are still reticent about e-commerce because they fear for the safety of their personal information. Identity theft is a rising problem.
- *Referers*: This is information that a Web browser passes along as a surfer moves from site to site. Referers are commonly collected and used to target advertising.
- *Registrations*: This is personal information that is collected when a consumers fills out a sign-up form on a web site. Data can be sold or shared. Many firms do not closely follow their stated privacy policies with regard to selling customer data.

Developing a Privacy Policy

Forward-looking Web marketers are at the forefront of the consumer privacy movement. Advertising network firms were caught on the wrong side of this issue and have suffered greatly in terms of company image and market capitalization. There is a growing realization that Web marketers should post disclosure notices on what information a company collects and how it is used or shared. At present privacy policies vary widely from marketer to marketer and there is no monitoring of their effectiveness. Concerned marketers are reacting to privacy concerns in an attempt to ameliorate consumer fears and to head off potential government regulation.

The major actions marketers are taking include:

- *Disclosure of privacy practices*: Smart marketers should clearly and prominently explain what information is collected, how it is tracked, how it is used, and under what conditions it is disclosed to partners. New technology may help solve the privacy problem. Soon the P3P software standard will allow consumers to set privacy preferences in their browsers that will alert them when a site's privacy policy differs from their desires.
- *Ask permission*: Web users should be able to opt in, especially if the data to be collected is sensitive. Sensitive data include medical information, financial information, insurance claims, and consumer behaviour that can be traced to the individual by name. Opt-In means the site cannot collect personal information unless the user gives permission. Opt-Out is a default situation where the site collects personal data and is free to use or sell it unless the consumer specifically denies permission

- *Allow access*: Consumers should be allowed access to the personal data each site has collected on them in a manner similar to the access they have to their credit report. Perhaps this can be accomplished by enabling consumers to obtain the aggregated profiles the advertising network firms have constructed. Consumers should be allowed to correct or delete inaccurate data.
- *Establish industry-wide privacy rules*: The On-line Privacy Alliance is an association of leading global companies and trade associations dedicated to the protection of privacy on-line. They are working to educate on-line businesses on the need for a standardized privacy policy to inform customers about what information is being collected, how it is used, how it is protected, and how people can access the information to prevent errors and how to opt-out.

2

Nature of International Marketing

PROCESS OF INTERNATIONAL MARKETING

A study of international marketing should begin with an understanding of what marketing is and how it operates in an international context. A definition adopted by the AMA is used as a basis for the definition of international marketing given here: international marketing is the multinational process of planning and executing the conception, pricing, promotion, and distribution of ideas, goods, and services to create exchanges that satisfy individual and organizational objectives. Only the word *multinational* has been added. That word implies that marketing activities are undertaken in several countries and that such activities should somehow be coordinated across nations. This definition is not completely free of limitations. By placing individual objectives at one end of the definition and organizational objectives at the other, the definition stresses a relationship between a consumer and an organization.

In effect, it fails to do justice to the significance of business-to-business marketing, which involves a transaction between two organizations. In the world of international marketing, governments, quasigovernment agencies, and profit-seeking and nonprofit entities are frequently buyers. Companies such as Boeing and Bechtel, for example, have nothing to do with consumer products. Likewise, Russia's export agency, Rosoboronexport, has adopted a Western-style marketing approach to sell arms for the country's 1700 defence plants. Its cheery sales representatives and giant TV screens show Russian jets and helicopters in action. In addition, Rosoboronexport offers competitive prices and will modify the products to suit its customers. Nonetheless, the definition does offer several advantages by carefully describing the essential characteristics of international marketing. First, what is to be exchanged is not restricted to tangible products but may include concepts and services as well.When the United Nations promotes such concepts as birth control and breast-feeding, this should be viewed as international marketing. Second, the definition removes the implication that international marketing applies only to market or business transactions.

International nonprofit marketing, which has received only scant attention, should not be overlooked. Governments are very active in marketing in order to attract foreign investment. Religion is also a big business and has been marketed internationally for centuries, though most people prefer not to view it that way. Even the Vatican is now using modern marketing.

The Holy See has launched a mass-licensing programme that put images from the Vatican Library's art collection, architecture, and manuscripts on Tshirts, glassware, and candles. The Vatican Radio, wanting to market the Pope's voice in the USA and Europe, has hired a music distributor to market compact disks and cassettes of Pope John II reciting the rosary. Third, the definition recognizes that it is improper for a firm to create a product first and then look for a place to sell it. Rather than seeking consumers for a firm's existing product, it is often more logical to determine consumer needs before creating a product. For overseas markets, the process may call for a modified product.

In some cases, following this approach may result in foreign needs being satisfied in a new way. Fourth, the definition acknowledges that "place" is only part of the marketing mix and that the distance between markets makes it neither more nor less important than the other parts of the mix. It is thus improper for any firms to regard their international function as simply to export available products from one country to another. Finally, the "multinational process" implies that the international marketing process is not a mere repetition of using identical strategies abroad. The four Ps of marketing must be integrated and coordinated across countries in order to bring about the most effective marketing mix.

In some cases, the mix may have to be adjusted for a particular market for better impact. Coca-Cola's German and Turkish divisions, for example, have experimented with berry-flavored Fanta and a pear-flavored drink respectively.

In other cases, a multinational marketer may find it more desirable to use a certain degree of standardization if the existing market differences are somewhat artificial and can be overcome. As in the case of General Electric Co.'s GE Medical Systems, it went too far in localizing its medical imaging products to compete with local competitors.

Its managers designed and marketed similar products for different markets. Overcustomizing such big-ticket products is an expensive and wasteful duplication of effort.

INTERNATIONAL DIMENSIONS OF MARKETING

One way to understand the concept of international marketing is to examine how international marketing differs from similar concepts. Domestic marketing is concerned with the marketing practices within a researcher's or marketer's home country. From the perspective of domestic marketing, marketing methods used outside the home market are foreign marketing.

A study becomes comparative marketing when its purpose is to contrast two or more marketing systems rather than examine a particular country's marketing system for its own sake. Similarities and differences between systems are identified.

Some marketing textbooks differentiate international marketing from global marketing because international marketing in its literal sense signifies marketing between nations. The word *international* may thus imply that a firm is not a corporate citizen of the world but rather operates from a home base. For those authors, global or world marketing is the preferred term, since nothing is foreign or domestic about the world market and global opportunities.

One might question whether the subtle difference between international marketing and multinational marketing is significant. For practical purposes, it is merely a distinction without a difference. As a matter of fact, multinational firms themselves do not make any distinction between the two terms. It is difficult to believe that International Business Machines will become more global if it changes its corporate name to Multinational Business Machines.

Likewise, there is no compelling reason for American Express and British Petroleum to change their names to, say, Global Express and World Petroleum. For purposes of the discussion in this text, international, multinational, and global marketing are used interchangeably.

DOMESTIC MARKETING VS. INTERNATIONAL MARKETING

It would beg the question to say that life and death are similar in nature, except in degree. As pointed out by Lufthansa, it would be just as *incorrect to say that domestic and international marketing are similar in nature but not in scope,* meaning that international marketing is nothing but domestic marketing on a larger scale. Domestic marketing involves one set of uncontrollables derived from the domestic market. International marketing is much more complex because a marketer faces two or more sets of uncontrollable variables originating from various countries. The marketer must cope with different cultural, legal, political, and monetary systems.

Digital Microwave Corporation's annual report makes this point very clear when it states:

- The Company is subject to the risks of doing business internationally, including unexpected changes in regulatory requirements, fluctuations in foreign currency exchange rates, imposition of tariffs and other barriers and restrictions, the burdens of complying with a variety of foreign laws, and general economic and geopolitical conditions, including inflation and trade relationships.

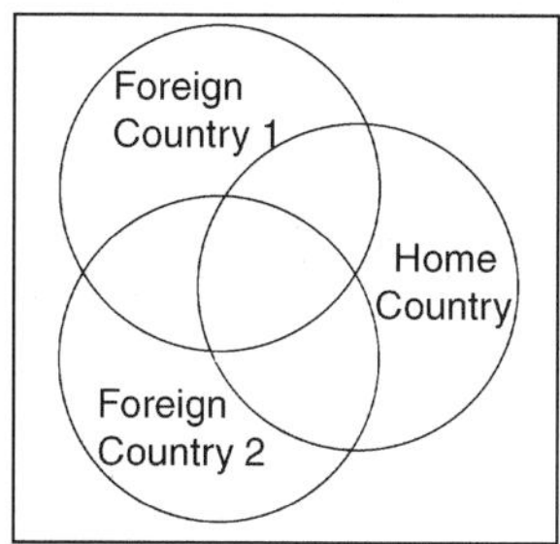

Fig. Environmental Divergence and Convergence

As shown in Figure, the two or more sets of environmental factors overlap, indicating that some similarities are shared by the countries involved. A firm's marketing mix is determined by the uncontrollable factors within each country's environment as well as by the interaction between the sets.

For optimum results, a firm's marketing mix may have to be modified to conform to a different environment, though wholesale modification is not often necessary.The degree of overlap of the sets of uncontrollable variables will dictate the extent to which the four Ps of marketing must change–the more the overlap, the less the modification. The varying environments within which the marketing plan is implemented may often rule out uniform marketing strategies across countries. McDonald's, although world renowned for its American symbols and standardization, has actually been flexible overseas. Recognizing the importance of foreign markets and local customs, the company customises its menu by region. In fact, it has even excluded beef from its menu in India in deference to the country's Hindu tradition.

THE APPLICABILITY OF MARKETING

Marketing is a *universal* activity that is widely applicable, regardless of the political, social, and economic systems of a country. However, it does not mean that consumers in all parts of the world must or should be satisfied in exactly the same way. Consumers from various countries are significantly different due to varying culture, income, level of economic development, and so on.

Therefore, consumers may use the same product without having the same need or motive, and in turn may use different products to satisfy the same need. For example, different kinds of foods are used in different countries to satisfy the same hunger need. Further, Americans and Europeans may use gas or electric heat to keep warm, whereas people in India may meet the same need by burning cow dung.

Too often, marketing mix is confused with marketing principles. Sound marketing principles are universal. One basic principle states that marketers should adopt the marketing concept. Regardless of their nationalities, marketers everywhere should be customer-oriented. However, this universal principle in no way implies a uniform marketing mix for all markets.To be customer-oriented does not mean that the same marketing strategy should be repeated in a different environment.

MULTINATIONAL CORPORATIONS (MNCS)

PROS AND CONS

Multinational corporations (MNCs) are major actors in the world of international business. The mention of MNCs usually elicits mixed reactions. On the one hand, MNCs are associated with exploitation and ruthlessness. They are often criticized for moving resources in and out of a country, as they strive for profit without much regard for the country's social welfare. In addition, they erode a nation's sovereignty. One study found that globalization undermined domestic airline competition policy. Is globalization detrimental to environment? This question is based on a premise that globalization encourages location of polluting industries in countries with low environmental regulations. Based on survey data from companies in China, globalization has positive environmental effects because of selfregulation pressures on firms in low-regulation countries. "Multinational ownership, multinational customers, and exports to developed countries increase self-regulation of environmental performance."

The size of a domestic market and other factors are much more important than pollution costs. The attractiveness of China is due more to its market size than its relatively lax pollution-control laws. From the 1970s through the early 1990s, the average amount spent by US manufacturers to comply with pollutioncontrol laws accounted for about 1 per cent of their total costs, and this cost of pollution control is not high enough to justify international relocation.

On a positive note, MNCs have power and prestige. Also in defence of MNCs, more and more of them have been trying to be responsible members of society. In addition, MNCs create social benefit by facilitating economic balance. Given the fact that natural resources and factors of production are unevenly distributed around the globe, MNCs can act as an effective and efficient mechanism to use these precious resources.

MULTINATIONALITY AND MARKET PERFORMANCE

At one time, it was thought that the relationship between a firm's degree of multinationality and its market performance was a linear and positive one. While studies have found a relationship, the linkage is not straightforward. One recent study found a curvilinear relationship instead. Increasing levels of multinationality provide significant performance benefits up to a certain optimum level. Once that optimum level is achieved, any further increase of multinationality results in decelerating benefits and accelerating costs. In other words,multinationality has both positive and negative impacts on performance. The positive impacts originate in MNCs' ability to leverage scale economies, access new technologies, and arbitrage factor cost differentials across multiple locations.The negative effects later emerge because of higher costs associated with coordination and control, administrative systems to manage culturally distinct markets, and diverse human resources.

Other factors further complicate the relationship. One cross-sectional analysis of twelve industries over a seven-year period found that the "impact of multinationality on both financial and operational performance is moderated by a firm's R&D and marketing capabilities."

CHARACTERISTICS OF MNCS

MNC is not a one-dimensional concept.There is no single criterion that proves satisfactory at all times in identifying an MNC. Varying definitions are not necessarily convergent. As a result, whether or not a company is classified as an MNC depends in part on what set of criteria is used.

Definition by Structure

An MNC has at least three significant dimensions: structural, performance, and behavioral. Structural requirements for definition as an MNC include the number of countries in which the firm does business and the citizenship of corporate owners and top managers. Pfizer, stating that it is a truly global company, does business in more than 150 countries.

Citicorp satisfies the requirement for multinationalism through the citizenship of members of its top management.The company has done as much as other major American MNCs to diversify its management. In Asia, a native of Pakistan is in charge of the firm's $800 million finance business for all of Asia apart from Japan. His colleague, an Indian national, heads the consumer business.They are two of the eight non-Americans in the elite group of fifteen executive vice-presidents.

Definition by Performance

Definition by performance depends on such characteristics as foreign earnings, sales, and assets.These performance characteristics indicate the extent of the commitment of corporate resources to foreign operations and the amount of rewards from that commitment.

The greater the commitment and reward, the greater the degree of internationalization. Japanese and British firms have routinely shown willingness to commit their corporate resources to overseas assets.

Kraft, North America's largest food company, has long dominated US grocery-store shelves with such powerful brands as Philadelphia Cream Cheese, Oreo cookies,Tang, Jell-O, Kool-Aid, Life Savers, Planters peanuts, and Lunchables prepackaged meals for kids. Remarkably, it has sixty-one brands with more than $100 million in sales. Virtually all US grocery stores need some of Kraft's products. Internationally, it is a different matter. In Australia, Kraft Macaroni and Cheese and Oscar Mayer hot dogs are not readily available.While Kraft derives 27 per cent of its total revenues from overseas, the figure pales when compared with H.J. Heinz's 44 per cent, McDonald's 50+ per cent, and Coca-Cola Co.'s 80+ per cent. Furthermore, Kraft trails Nestlé and Unilever in foreign markets, with only 9 per cent of its sales coming from developing countries.

Human resources or overseas employees are customarily considered as part of the performance requirements rather than as part of the structural requirements, though the desirability of separating lower level employees from top management is questionable.A preferable analysis would be to treat the total extent of the employment of personnel in other countries as another indicator of the structure of the company. In any case, the willingness of a company to use overseas personnel satisfies a significant criterion for multinationalism.Avon, for example, employs 370,000 Japanese women to sell its products house to house across Japan. Siemens, well known worldwide for its consumer and industrial products, has some 300,000 employees in 124 countries.

Definition by Behaviour

Behaviour is somewhat more abstract as a measure of multinationalism than either structure or performance, though it is no less important. This requirement concerns the behavioral characteristics of top management. Thus, a company becomes more multinational as its management thinks more internationally. Such thinking, known as geocentricity, must be distinguished from two other attitudes or orientations, known as ethnocentricity and polycentricity.

Ethnocentricity

Ethnocentricity is a strong orientation towards the home country. Markets and consumers abroad are viewed as unfamiliar and even inferior in taste, sophistication, and opportunity.

The usual practice is to use the home base for the production of standardized products for export in order to gain some marginal business. Centralization of decision making is thus a necessity. Caterpillar Inc.'s chairman recalled that, while making sales calls in Africa in his younger days, pricing decisions were often forced upon him from headquarters even though those decisions did not fit the local market.

Polycentricity

Polycentricity, the opposite of ethnocentricity, is a strong orientation to the host country. The attitude places emphasis on differences between markets that are caused by variations within, such as in income, culture, laws, and politics. The assumption is that each market is unique and consequently difficult for outsiders to understand.

Thus, managers from the host country should be employed and allowed to have a great deal of discretion in market decisions. A significant degree of decentralization is thus common across the overseas divisions. A drawback of polycentricity is that it often results in duplication of effort among overseas subsidiaries. Similarities among countries might well permit the development of efficient and uniform strategies.

Geocentricity

Geocentricity is a compromise between the two extremes of ethnocentricity and polycentricity. It could be argued that this attitude is the most important of the three. Geocentricity is an orientation that considers the whole world rather than any particular country as the target market. A geocentric company might be thought of as *denationalized* or *supranational*. As such, "international" or "foreign" departments or markets do not exist because the company does not designate anything international or foreign about a market.

Corporate resources are allocated without regard to national frontiers, and there is no hesitation in making direct investment abroad when warranted. There is a high likelihood that a geocentric company does not identify itself with a particular country. Therefore, it is often difficult to determine the firm's home country except through the location of its headquarters and its corporate registration. Business is "nationalityless," and companies should attempt to lose their national identity. As such, a corporation should not mind moving its headquarters to a more hospitable environment.

The chairman of Japanese retail giant Yaohan International Group, for example, moved the firm's headquarters as well as his family and personal assets to Hong Kong to take advantage of Hong Kong's low taxes and hub location in Asia. To reward his faith in China, the Chinese government permitted Yaohan to build shopping malls in China. Geocentric firms take the view that, even though countries may differ, differences can be understood and managed. In coordinating and controlling the global marketing effort, the company adapts its marketing programme to meet local needs within the broader framework of its total strategy.

It is important to coordinate the activities of local subsidiaries and those of the headquarters. One study found important divergence between home and away in various aspects of the marketing process.This divergence may result in poor relationships, dysfunctional conflict, and ineffectiveness. The geocentric approach combines aspects of centralization and decentralization in a synthesis that allows some degree of flexibility.The firm may designate one country subsidiary as its research and development center while appointing another subsidiary in another country to specialize in manufacturing certain products. Although the corporation provides overall guidance so as to achieve maximum efficiency of its global system, the various aspects of the local operations may or may not be centralized as long as they meet local market needs. Geocentric firms compete with each other on a worldwide basis rather than at a local level. There is evidence that geocentricity and companies' international practices are related. One study found that managers' worldmindedness was a significant determinant of international trade propensity. Another study employed the GEOCENTRIC scale to measure international human resources managers' mind-set concerning the impact of nationality on the selection and careers of managers.

The index of a geocentric mind-set was found to be significantly related to the percentage of sales and employees abroad as well as the number of countries with manufacturing operations. A study of the EPRG framework found that firms exhibiting an ethnocentric orientation emphasize the home market and export to psychologically close markets. In addition, these firms believe that marketing adaptation is not necessary. In contrast, polycentric, regiocentric, and geocentric firms export to psychologically distant markets. Adaptation increases as psychological distance between home and host markets increases.

THE PROCESS OF INTERNATIONALIZATION

The literature describes a number of stages of internationalization. Many companies may have begun as domestic firms concentrating on their own domestic markets before shifting or expanding the focus to also cover international markets. As they become more international, they are supposed to move from being sporadic exporters to being frequent exporters before finally doing manufacturing abroad. It is thus useful to investigate the stages of internationalization.

One study found evidence to support the hypothesis that there are four identifiable stages in a firm's internationalization. The four stages are: nonexporters, export intenders, sporadic exporters, and regular exporters.

The process shows how firms were constrained initially by resource limitations and a lack of export commitment, and how they are able to become more and more internationalized as more resources are allocated to international activity. Based on his review of a number of the internationalization models which specify the various stages of internationalization, Andersen has proposed his own U-model which has received mixed empirical support.

There are four stages:

1. No regular export activities,
2. Export via independent representatives,
3. Establishment of an overseas sales subsidiary, and
4. Overseas production/manufacturing.

The development is supposed to take place initially within a specific country before being repeated across countries. More recently, an increasingly global economy has given birth to a new theory which states that some companies are destined to go global from the outset, thus bypassing the stages of internationalization. Several Silicon Valley companies do not see the need to have a business model first for the US market before going overseas.

Instead, their mission is global almost from birth.As such, from the beginning, they may employ engineers in India, manufacture in Taiwan, and sell in Europe. At present, there is no conclusive evidence to show that domestic firms have generally indeed progressed from one stage to another as prescribed on their way to becoming more internationally oriented. Likewise, no empirical evidence has been provided so far to support the competing hypothesis that some firms are "born global" in the sense that their mission is to become MNCs which engage in international business activities from the outset.

BENEFITS OF INTERNATIONAL MARKETING

International marketing daily affects consumers in many ways, though its importance is neither well understood nor appreciated. Government officials and other observers seem always to point to the negative aspects of international business. Many of their charges are more imaginary than real.

SURVIVAL AND GROWTH

For companies to survive, they need to grow. Because most countries are not as fortunate as the USA in terms of market size, resources, and opportunities, they must trade with others to survive. Since most European nations are relatively small in size, they need foreign markets to achieve economies of scale so as to be competitive with American firms. International competition may not be a matter of choice when survival is at stake. A study of five medical sector industries found that international expansion was necessary when foreign firms entered a domestic market.

However, only firms with previously substantial market share and international experience could expand successfully. Moreover, firms that retrenched after an international expansion disappeared. Even American marketers cannot ignore the vast potential of international markets. The world market is more than four times larger than the US market. In the case of Amway Corp., a privately held US manufacturer of cosmetics, soaps, and vitamins, Japan represents a larger market than the USA.

SALES AND PROFITS

Foreign markets constitute a large share of the total business of many firms that have wisely cultivated markets abroad. The case of Coca-Cola clearly emphasizes the importance of overseas markets. International sales account for more than 80 per cent of the firm's operating profits. In terms of operating profit margins, they are less than 15 per cent at home but twice that amount overseas.

For every gallon of soda that Coca-Cola sells, it earns 37 cents in Japan–a marked difference from the mere 7 cents per gallon earned in the USA.The Japanese market contributes about $350 million in operating income to Coca-Cola, making Japan the company's most profitable market. With consumption of Coca-Cola's soft drinks averaging 296 eight-ounce servings per person per year in the USA, the US market is clearly saturated. Non-US consumption, on the other hand, averages only about forty servings and offers great potential for future growth.

DIVERSIFICATION

Demand for most products is affected by such cyclical factors as recession and such seasonal factors as climate.The unfortunate consequence of these variables is sales fluctuations, which can frequently be substantial enough to cause layoffs of personnel. One way to diversify a company's risk is to consider foreign markets as a solution to variable demand. Such markets even out fluctuations by providing outlets for excess production capacity.

Cold weather, for instance, may depress soft drink consumption. Yet not all countries enter the winter season at the same time, and some countries are relatively warm all year round. Bird, USA Inc., a Nebraska manufacturer of go-carts and minicars for promotional purposes, has found that global selling has enabled the company to have year-round production. A similar situation pertains to the business cycle: Europe's business cycle often lags behind that of the USA. That domestic and foreign sales operate in differing economic cycles works in the favour of General Motors and Ford because overseas operations help smooth out the business cycles of the North American market.

INFLATION AND PRICE MODERATION

The benefits of export are readily self-evident. Imports can also be highly beneficial to a country because they constitute reserve capacity for the local economy.Without imports, there is no incentive for domestic firms to moderate their prices. The lack of imported product alternatives forces consumers to pay more, resulting in inflation and excessive profits for local firms. This development usually acts as a prelude to workers' demand for higher wages, further exacerbating the problem of inflation.

EMPLOYMENT

Trade restrictions, such as the high tariffs caused by the 1930 Smoot-Hawley Bill, which forced the average tariff rates across the board to climb above 60 per cent, contributed significantly to the Great Depression and have the potential to cause widespread unemployment again. Unrestricted trade, on the other hand, improves the world's GDP and enhances employment generally for all nations. Unfortunately, there is no question that globalization is bound to hurt some workers whose employers are not cost competitive. Some employers may also have to move certain jobs overseas so as to reduce costs. As a consequence, some workers will inevitably be unemployed. It is extremely difficult to explain to those who must bear the brunt of unemployment due to trade that there is a net benefit for the country.

STANDARDS OF LIVING

Trade affords countries and their citizens higher standards of living than otherwise possible.Without trade, product shortages force people to pay more for less. Products taken for granted, such as coffee and bananas, may become unavailable overnight. Life in most countries would be much more difficult were it not for the many strategic metals that must be imported.

Trade also makes it easier for industries to specialize and gain access to raw materials, while at the same time fostering competition and efficiency. A diffusion of innovations across national boundaries is a useful by-product of international trade. A lack of such trade would inhibit the flow of innovative ideas.

The World Bank's studies have shown that increased openness to trade is associated with the reduction of poverty in most developing countries. Those developing countries which chose growth through trade grew twice as fast as those nations which chose more restrictive trade regimes. "Open trade has offered developing nations widespread gains in material well being, as well as gains in literacy, education and life expectancy."

UNDERSTANDING OF MARKETING PROCESS

International marketing should not be considered a subset or special case of domestic marketing.When an executive is required to observe marketing in other cultures, the benefit derived is not so much the understanding of a foreign culture. Instead, the real benefit is that the executive actually develops a better understanding of marketing in one's own culture. For example, Coca-Cola Co. has applied the lessons learned in Japan to the US and European markets. The study of international marketing can thus prove to be valuable in providing insights for the understanding of behavioral patterns often taken for granted at home. Ultimately, marketing as a discipline of study is more effectively studied.

CONCLUSION

This stage has provided an overview of the process and of the basic issues of international marketing. Similar to domestic marketing, international marketing is concerned with the process of creating and executing an effective marketing mix in order to satisfy the objectives of all parties seeking an exchange. International marketing is relevant regardless of whether or not the activities are for profit. It is also of little consequence whether countries have the same level of economic development or political ideology, since marketing is a universal activity that has application in a variety of circumstances. The benefits of international marketing are considerable. Trade moderates inflation and improves both employment and the standard of living, while providing a better understanding of the marketing process at home and abroad.

For many companies, survival or the ability to diversify depends on the growth, sales, and profits from abroad. The more commitment a company makes to overseas markets in terms of personnel, sales, and resources, the more likely it is that it will become a multinational corporation. This is especially true when the management is geocentric rather than ethnocentric or polycentric. Since many view MNCs with envy and suspicion, the role of MNCs in society, their benefits as well as their abuses will continue to be debated. The marketing principles may be fixed, but a company's marketing mix in the international context is not. Certain marketing practices may or may not be appropriate elsewhere, and the degree of appropriateness cannot be determined without careful investigation of the market in question.

CASE STUDY

SONY: THE SOUND OF ENTERTAINMENT

The name Sony, derived from the Latin word sonus for sound and combined with the English word sonny, was adapted for Japanese tongues. It is the most recognized brand in the USA, outranking McDonald's and Coke. Sony Corp. has $60 billion in worldwide sales, with 80 per cent from overseas and 30 per cent alone from the USA. Sony's stock is traded on twenty-three exchanges around the world, and foreigners own 23 per cent of the stock. Transnational Corporations and Export Competitiveness, in terms of value-added sales, Sony is ranked No. 80. In other words, Sony is larger than such economies as Uruguay, the Dominican Republic,Tunisia, Slovakia, Croatia, Guatemala, and Luxembourg.

In addition, in terms of foreign assets, Sony is No. 22. Out of its total assets of $68,129 million, it has $30,214 million in foreign assets. It also derives $42,768 million from foreign sales out of its total sales of $63,664 million. Some years ago, the company made an early move into local manufacturing, and 35 per cent of the firm's manufacturing is done overseas. For instance, Sony makes TV sets in Wales and the USA, thus enabling the company to earn revenues and pay its bills in the same currency. Sony has recently ceased its production of video products in Taiwan and has moved the operation to Malaysia and China in order to employ cheaper labour. But Sony will establish a technology center in Taiwan for product design, engineering, and procurement.

Sony has some 181,800 employees worldwide, 109,080 of whom are non-Japanese. In the USA, 150 out of its 7100 employees are Japanese.Virtually alone among Japanese companies, Sony has a policy of giving the top position in its foreign operations to a local national. For example, a European runs Sony's European operations.

Sony was also the first major Japanese firm to have a foreigner as a director. Sony's late co-founder, Akio Morita, even talked about moving the company's headquarters to the USA but concluded that the effort would be too complicated. Sony Corp. of America, located in New York, was Sony's US umbrella company in charge of the US operations that included Sony Pictures Entertainment and Sony Music Entertainment. Because the president, an American, failed to stop rampant overspending of Sony Pictures Entertainment, Sony ousted him and took a $2.5 billion write-off. Sony's CEO Nobuyuki Idei has stripped the New York headquarters of all operational responsibility for the US market and turned it into a second headquarters and strategic planning center for the USA.

The overall management of Sony's US operations will be left to Tokyo. Many of New York's functions will be delegated to Sony Pictures and Sony Music, both of which will report to Tokyo. Idei said: "I want to make a more direct extension of Sony headquarters in Japan.We don't need to manage Sony Pictures and Sony Music from New York." Incidentally, Idei has been described by friends as "un-Japanese" because he speaks his mind and demands candor from others. Sources: "Sony's New World," Business Week, May 27, 1996, 100ff. Business Week/21st Century Capitalism, 90. "Sony's Idei Tightens Reins Again on Freewheeling US Operations," Wall Street Journal, January 24, 1997; "Sony Video Products Shift to Malaysia, China," San José Mercury News, September 23, 2000; World Investment Report 2002: Transnational Corporations and Export Competitiveness, Division on Investment,Technology and Enterprise Development, UNCTAD, 2002, 90; and "The Top Foreign Companies," Forbes, July 23, 2002, 124ff.

Points to Consider

Do you consider Sony to be an MNC? What are the criteria that you use to make this determination? You need to provide factual evidence to show how these criteria are or are not met.

3

Customer Relationship Management (CRM)

CONCEPT

Customer relationship management is a broadly recognized, widely-implemented strategy for managing a company's interactions with customers, clients and sales prospects. It involves using technology to organize, automate, and synchronize business processes—principally sales activities, but also those for marketing, customer service, and technical support. The overall goals are to find, attract, and win new clients, nurture and retain those the company already has, entice former clients back into the fold, and reduce the costs of marketing and client service. Customer relationship management denotes a company-wide business strategy embracing all client-facing departments and even beyond. When an implementation is effective, people, processes, and technology work together to increase profitability, and reduce operational costs.

RELATED TRENDS

Many CRM vendors offer Web-based tools and software as a service which are accessed via a secure Internet connection and displayed in a Web browser. These applications are sold as subscriptions, with customers not needing to invest in the acquisition and maintenance of IT hardware, and subscription fees are a fraction of the cost of purchasing software outright.

PHASES OF CRM

The three phases in which CRM help to support the relationship between a business and its customers are, to:

1. *Acquire*: A CRM can help a business in acquiring new customers through excellent contact management, direct marketing, selling and fulfillment.
2. *Enhance*: A web-enabled CRM combined with customer service tools offers customers excellent service from a team of trained and skilled sales and service specialists, which offers customers the convenience of one-stop shopping.

3. *Retain*: CRM software and databases enable a business to identify and reward its loyal customers and further develop its targeted marketing and relationship marketing initiatives.

CHALLENGES

Tools and workflows can be complex to implement, especially for large enterprises. Previously these tools were generally limited to contact management: monitoring and recording interactions and communications. Software solutions then expanded to embrace deal tracking, territories, opportunities, and at the sales pipeline itself.

Next came the advent of tools for other client-facing business functions. These technologies have been, and still are, offered as on-premises software that companies purchase and run on their own IT infrastructure. Often, implementations are fragmented; isolated initiatives by individual departments to address their own needs. Systems that start disunited usually stay that way: siloed thinking and decision processes frequently lead to separate and incompatible systems, and dysfunctional processes.

TYPES/VARIATIONS

Sales Force Automation

Sales force automation involves using software to streamline all phases of the sales process, minimizing the time that sales representatives need to spend on each phase. This allows sales representatives to pursue more clients in a shorter amount of time than would otherwise be possible. At the heart of SFA is a Contact management system for tracking and recording every stage in the sales process for each prospective client, from initial contact to final disposition. Many SFA applications also include insights into opportunities, territories, sales forecasts and workflow automation, quote generation, and product knowledge. Newly-emerged priorities are modules for Web 2.0 e-commerce and pricing.

Marketing

CRM systems for marketing help the enterprise identify and target potential clients and generate qualified leads for the sales team. A key marketing capability is tracking and measuring multichannel campaigns, including e-mail, search, social media, telephone and direct mail. Metrics monitored include clicks, responses, leads, deals, and revenue. This has been superseded by marketing automation and Prospect Relationship Management solutions which track customer behaviour and nurture them from first contact to sale, often cutting out the active sales process altogether.

Customer Service and Support

Recognizing that service is an important differentiator, organizations are increasingly turning to technology platforms to help them improve their clients' experience while aiming to increase efficiency and minimize costs. Even so, a 2009 study revealed that only 39% of corporate executives believe their employees have the right tools and authority to solve client problems.". The core for these applications has been and still is comprehensive call centre solutions, including such features as intelligent call routing, computer telephone integration and escalation capabilities.

Analytics

Relevant analytics capabilities are often interwoven into applications for sales, marketing, and service. These features can be complemented and augmented with links to separate, purpose-built applications for analytics and business intelligence. Sales analytics let companies monitor and understand client actions and preferences, through sales forecasting, data quality, and dashboards that graphically display. Marketing applications generally come with predictive analytics to improve segmentation and targeting, and features for measuring the effectiveness of online, offline, and search marketing campaign.

Web analytics have evolved significantly from their starting point of merely tracking mouse clicks on Web sites. By evaluating "buy signals," marketers can see which prospects are most likely to transact and also identify those who are bogged down in a sales process and need assistance. Marketing and finance personnel also use analytics to assess the value of multi-faceted programmes as a whole.

These types of analytics are increasing in popularity as companies demand greater visibility into the performance of call centres and other service and support channels, in order to correct problems before they affect satisfaction levels. Support-focused applications typically include dashboards similar to those for sales, plus capabilities to measure and analyse response times, service quality, agent performance, and the frequency of various issues.

Integrated/Collaborative

Departments within enterprises — especially large enterprises — tend to function with little collaboration. More recently, the development and adoption of these tools and services have fostered greater fluidity and cooperation among sales, service, and marketing. This finds expression in the concept of collaborative systems which uses technology to build bridges between departments.

For example, feedback from a technical support centre can enlighten marketers about specific services and product features clients are asking for. Reps, in their turn, want to be able to pursue these opportunities without the burden of re-entering records and contact data into a separate SFA system. Owing to these factors, many of the top-rated and most popular products come as integrated suites.

Small Business

Basic client service can be accomplished by a contact manager system, an integrated solution that lets organizations and individuals efficiently track and record interactions, including e-mails, documents, jobs, faxes, scheduling, and more. These tools usually focus on accounts rather than individual contacts. They also generally include opportunity insight for tracking sales pipelines plus added functionality for marketing and service. As with larger enterprises, small businesses are finding value in online solutions, especially for mobile and telecommuting workers.

Social Media

Social media sites like Twitter, LinkedIn and Facebook are amplifying the voice of people in the marketplace and are having profound and far-reaching effects on the ways in which people buy. Customers can now research companies online and then ask for recommendations through social media channels, making their buying decision without contacting the company.

Details on companies are now also shared online. People are using social media to share opinions and experiences on companies, products and services. As social media is not as widely moderated or censored as mainstream media, individuals can say anything they want about a company or brand, whether pro or con.

Increasingly, companies are looking to gain access to these conversations and take part in the dialogue. More than a few systems are now integrating to social networking sites. Social media promoters cite a number of business advantages, such as using online communities as a source of high-quality leads and a vehicle for crowd sourcing solutions to client-support problems. Companies can also leverage client stated habits and preferences to personalize and even "hyper-target" their sales and marketing communications.

Some analysts take the view that business-to-business marketers should proceed cautiously when weaving social media into their business processes. These observers recommend careful market research to determine if and where the phenomenon can provide measurable benefits for client interactions, sales and support..

It is often found that people feel that interaction is peer to peer between them and their contacts and resent the company involvement, responding with negatives about that company.

Non-profit and Membership-based

Systems for non-profit and membership-based organizations help track constituents and their involvement in the organization. Capabilities typically include tracking the following: fund-raising, demographics, membership levels, membership directories, volunteering and communications with individuals. Many include tools for identifying potential donors based on previous donations and participation. In light of the growth of social networking tools, there may be some overlap between social/community driven tools and non-profit/membership tools.

STRATEGY

For larger-scale enterprises, a complete and detailed plan is required to obtain the funding, resources, and company-wide support that can make the initiative of choosing and implementing a system successful.

Benefits must be defined, risks assessed, and cost quantified in three general areas:

- *Processes*: Though these systems have many technological components, business processes lie at its core. It can be seen as a more client-centric way of doing business, enabled by technology that consolidates and intelligently distributes pertinent information about clients, sales, marketing effectiveness, responsiveness, and market trends. Therefore, a company must analyse its business workflows and processes before choosing a technology platform; some will likely need re-engineering to better serve the overall goal of winning and satisfying clients. Moreover, planners need to determine the types of client information that are most relevant, and how best to employ them.
- *People*: For an initiative to be effective, an organization must convince its staff that the new technology and workflows will benefit employees as well as clients. Senior executives need to be strong and visible advocates who can clearly state and support the case for change. Collaboration, teamwork, and two-way communication should be encouraged across hierarchical boundaries, especially with respect to process improvement.
- *Technology*: In evaluating technology, key factors include alignment with the company's business process strategy and goals, including the ability to deliver the right data to the right employees and sufficient ease of adoption and use. Platform selection is best undertaken by a carefully chosen group of executives who understand the business processes to be automated as well as the software issues. Depending upon the size of the company and the breadth of data, choosing an application can take anywhere from a few weeks to a year or more.

IMPLEMENTATION

Implementation Issues

Increases in revenue, higher rates of client satisfaction, and significant savings in operating costs are some of the benefits to an enterprise. Proponents emphasize that technology should be implemented only in the context of careful strategic and operational planning.

Implementations almost invariably fall short when one or more facets of this prescription are ignored:

- *Poor planning*: Initiatives can easily fail when efforts are limited to choosing and deploying software, without an accompanying rationale, context, and support for the workforce. In other instances, enterprises simply automate flawed client-facing processes rather than redesign them according to best practices.
- *Poor integration*: For many companies, integrations are piecemeal initiatives that address a glaring need: improving a particular client-facing process or two or automating a favoured sales or client support channel. Such "point solutions" offer little or no integration or alignment with a company's overall strategy. They offer a less than complete client view and often lead to unsatisfactory user experiences.
- *Towards a solution*: Overcoming siloed thinking. Experts advise organizations to recognize the immense value of integrating their client-facing operations. In this view, internally-focused, department-centric views should be discarded in favour of reorienting processes towards information-sharing across marketing, sales, and service. For example, sales representatives need to know about current issues and relevant marketing promotions before attempting to cross-sell to a specific client. Marketing staff should be able to leverage client information from sales and service to better target campaigns and offers. And support agents require quick and complete access to a client's sales and service history.

Adoption Issues

Historically, the landscape is littered with instances of low adoption rates. In 2003, a Gartner report estimated that more than $1 billion had been spent on software that was not being used. More recent research indicates that the problem, while perhaps less severe, is a long way from being solved. According to CSO Insights, less than 40 per cent of 1,275 participating companies had end-user adoption rates above 90 per cent.

In a 2007 survey from the U.K., four-fifths of senior executives reported that their biggest challenge is getting their staff to use the systems they had installed. Further, 43 per cent of respondents said they use less than half the functionality of their existing system; 72 per cent indicated they would trade functionality for ease of use; 51 per cent cited data synchronization as a major issue; and 67 per cent said that finding time to evaluate systems was a major problem. With expenditures expected to exceed $11 billion in 2010, enterprises need to address and overcome persistent adoption challenges.

Specialists offer these recommendations for boosting adoptions rates and coaxing users to blend these tools into their daily workflow:

- *Choose a system that is easy to use*: All solutions are not created equal.

Some vendors offer more user-friendly applications than others, and simplicity should be as important a decision factor as functionality.

- *Choose the right capabilities*: Employees need to know that time invested in learning and usage will yield personal advantages. If not, they will work around or ignore the system.
- *Provide training*: Changing the way people work is no small task, and help is usually a requirement. Even with today's more usable systems, many staffers still need assistance with learning and adoption
- *Lead by example*: Showing employees that upper management fully supports the use of a new application by using the application themselves may increase the likelihood that employees will adopt the application.

PRIVACY AND DATA SECURITY SYSTEM

One of the primary functions of these tools is to collect information about clients, thus a company must consider the desire for privacy and data security, as well as the legislative and cultural norms. Some clients prefer assurances that their data will not be shared with third parties without their prior consent and that safeguards are in place to prevent illegal access by third parties.

MARKET STRUCTURES

This market grew by 12.5 per cent in 2008, from revenue of $8.13 billion in 2007 to $9.15 billion in 2008. The following table lists the top vendors in 2006-2008.

Vendor	2008 Revenue	2008 Share (%)	2007 Revenue	2007 Share (%)	2006 Revenue	2006 Share (%)
SAP	2,055	22.5 (–2.8)	2,050.8	25.3	1,681.7	26.6
Oracle	1,475	16.1	1,319.8	16.3	1,016.8	15.5
Salesforce.com	965	10.6	676.5	8.3	451.7	6.9
Microsoft	581	6.4	332.1	4.1	176.1	2.7
Amdocs	451	4.9	421.0	5.2	365.9	5.6
Others	3,620	39.6	3,289.1	40.6	2,881.6	43.7
Total	9,147	100	8,089.3	100	6,573.8	100

THE IMPORTANCE OF CRM CUSTOMER RELATIONSHIP MANAGEMENT

CRM Customer Relationship Management is one of the newest innovations in customer service today. CRM stands for customer relationship management and helps the management and customer service staffs cope with customer concerns and issues. CRM involves gathering a lot of data about the customer. The data is then used to facilitate customer service transactions by making the information needed to resolve the issue or concern readily available to those dealing with the customers. This results in more satisfied customers, a more profitable business and more resources available to the support staff. Furthermore, CRM Customer Relationship Management systems are a great help to the management in deciding on the future course of the company.

There is much data needed for the CRM system to work. These fields include the customer name, address, date of transactions, pending and finished transactions, issues and complaints, status of order, shipping and fulfillment dates, account information, demographic data and many more. This information is important in providing the customer the answer that he or she needs to resolve the issue without having to wait for a long time and without going to several departments.

With just a few mouse clicks, a customer support representative for example can track the location of the customer's package or order. This is infinitely better than the cumbersome process of tracking shipments previously. Furthermore, the customer service representative will also be able to see the previous concerns of the customer.

This is a great help especially if the customer is calling about the same issue since he or she will not have to repeat the story all over again. This results in less time in resolving the issue, thus, higher productivity of the support staff.

CRM Customer Relationship Management systems are also important to the top management because it provides crucial data like customer satisfaction and efficiency of service by the frontline crews. A piece of customer relationship management software will also be able to generate the needed reports for product development or new concepts. Furthermore, this system will also be a great help for the top management in deciding the company's future course of action, whether it involves phasing out one of the products on the shelves or making adjustments to one of the products sold.

The reports generated by CRM systems are also invaluable to your advertising and marketing planners, as they will be able to pinpoint which ideas works and which do not. Because of CRM systems, you will be able to release advertisements or plan marketing campaigns more in tune with your target market. This will also lead to more responses to your advertisement and a more effective marketing campaign.

Successful integration of a CRM Customer Relationship Management system in your company, however, might not be as easy as it seems. The following might give you an insight why CRM systems fail in some companies... Most companies fail to prepare for CRM systems. By this, I mean that most companies fail to integrate all the departments that need to share the information for it to be effective. Furthermore, CRM units scattered all over the company's departments is often more effective than just making one big CRM department. This will ensure that each department will get the information and data that they need.

A CRM system will also help you a lot in expanding your business. As CRM systems are capable of handling enormous amounts of data, CRM systems will help you a lot in coping with the increased numbers of customers and data. With a CRM Customer Relationship Management system installed and properly utilized, you can be sure that all data is maximized and used to ensure that your business will be successful and your customers a lot more satisfied than before.

PROBLEMS IN CUSTOMER RELATIONSHIP MANAGEMENT

From the business and international catastrophes of the past two years, a new information technology initiative has arisen. It is called customer relationship management and it is dedicated to improving through automated, especially Internet-driven, means the entire arena of customer service and interaction. If the amount of print space, conference literature and position advertisements devoted to a topic is a criterion for importance, CRM is a hot button for the IT industry as well as the entire business world. In reality, customer-driven applications have been in existence for years. Successful sales and marketing organizations have always used the principles which CRM now formalizes.

So it is important that the CRM starts with an organization vision and mission, which should become part of the mind-set of employees. The objective of CRM is to give customers satisfactory and pleasant experiences in doing business with an organization. Such experiences will result in more profitable business. CRM technology enables the organization to apply sound relationship development and maintenance principles on a larger scale within the organization. In the application of CRM technology, techniques used by successful sales and marketing people become available to all employees. However, the employees must be trained and incentivised to take advantage of this powerful tool.

The advent of the Internet, personal computers, sophisticated database management systems capable of handling very large volumes of data efficiently, hand-held technologies, GUI-based workstations, data distribution and access facilities have made the CRM concept workable and have significantly raised management's expectations.

Enabling technologies and the thrust towards a customer-centric business focus have brought CRM applications to the forefront as a viable approach for increased competitiveness and profitability. Unfortunately, the success rate in realizing potential benefits from CRM projects is still lower than expected and, in fact, many projects fail even before a first phase is completed.

In the rush to implement a CRM application, many potential problems and pitfalls are being overlooked. Some involve the same considerations and principles that have been important for years, but many of these have a new twist. This object walks through a number of major potential problem areas and their impact on the success of a CRM project. For each problem, solutions are suggested.

Several broad categories of problems exist: conceptual, managerial and technical. However, the most important underlying theme of these problems is that they involve everyone, from senior business executives, sales and marketing management, customer representatives to IT technical personnel. The best way to solve problems is, of course, to anticipate them pro-actively and not let them become problems.

PROBLEM NO. 1 – MANY MISUNDERSTANDINGS ABOUT CRM EXIST

The most significant problem is the perception that CRM is a magic bullet, a panacea for all customer support problems. This is simply not true. This perception and the expectations that follow from it are potentially catastrophic. Overselling something as "new and hot" as CRM is likely to occur and have serious consequences for the next new and hot project. Any future CRM effort could be seriously compromised, not to mention the reputation of the IS department. This, in turn, will continue to deprive the organization of the benefits that should accrue from CRM

Another conceptual pitfall is management does not understand the consequences of not having access to integrated, cleansed and consistent data, which is the technical goal. The issue of stewardship vs. ownership will surface very quickly, opening up potential political issues that have long been dormant or which have been avoided by costly manual compilation of data.

Because CRM provides answers to queries of internal as well as external customers, the entire process of creating CRM is subject to misunderstanding. The CRM application is an enabler, not a substitute for human relationship. Failure to distinguish between the availability of value- added data and the users' ability to use the data for better customer service cause an expectation gap.

In addition, the amount of time required to be spent with management and users who understand real customer relationship needs is almost always underestimated. Some tasks, such as vision development, analysis and requirements definition for CRM, should be carried out differently than with traditional IT system development.

Solution

The best solution to heading off problems is systematic education and communication with all levels of the organization, especially the executive sponsor, the project team, key users and data stewards. The education must clearly communicate that in CRM, technology contributes only 20 per cent of the total effort. Having the quality data is another 20 per cent. The rest is requirement analysis, system design, training the users and assuring that this application does, in fact, improve customer relationships. The CRM project team must consist of successful salespeople, customer reps, knowledgeable users, data analysts and the CRM package expert. The team must be aware of what can and can't be done with CRM, and what its problems are. Management must be appropriately educated on what to expect and not to expect. They must be made aware of their commitment. Time spent in education is never wasted.

PROBLEM NO. 2 – THE SCOPE OF THE CRM PROJECT IS INAPPROPRIATE

While the proper choice of scope is critical to all projects, doubtless dating from the very earliest systems, the correct CRM focus should be based on customer expectations, which could vary with the customer segments in your industry. For example, the needs of a retail customer are significantly different than a wholesale or institutional customer. If you combine both segments in one project phase and try to fit in one straightjacket, you could have serious problems. In the case of one state government, the scope of a major CRM project included all member departments. The definition of information delivery and data architecture to enable CRM simply proved to be too much for the group. This, coupled with the lack of strong executive management, caused the project to fail. In addition, if the definition of scope is too large, the analysis and implementation becomes complex, takes too long and people lose interest.

Solution

A sound solution to the scope issue is based on the understanding that the organization is on a learning curve in applying CRM. Try starting small, following the KISS rule. This is an old but successful approach technique to dealing with new things. The scope for CRM implementation could be one customer segment where users are receptive, knowledgeable and are available to work with you, and quality data is easily available. Any area you select must in any case have a committed executive sponsor. The use of time-boxing techniques can also help control the project scope. For instance, limit the analysis to no more than four weeks and design and implementation to four weeks. Allow adequate time for piloting and field testing which should be another four weeks. This will leave adequate time for attending to infrastructure requirements and can still provide a usable facility as soon as practicable. It will also reinforce the value of the starting-small approach.

PROBLEM NO. 3 – THE CRM PROJECT HAS NO COMMITTED EXECUTIVE SPONSOR

The most serious – and usually fatal – problem is lack of an executive sponsor with an absolutely burning desire to see the project through. Without the blessing of strong sponsorship, any project can fail. A conflict in scope may develop, the right resources may not be available and user participation may be inadequate.

However, some of the subtle pitfalls in dealing with data that must be consistent across enterprise components can also cause unanticipated difficulties. It is quite common, for instance, for groups, even small ones, to be unable to agree on common definitions of data and delivery mechanisms.

Moreover, when the attempt is made to define requirements for several disparate customer segments together, this phenomenon can become more pronounced. As companies move to a greater degree of customer focus, these types of problems will surface with increasing frequency and severity.

Last, but not the least, is the need for data quality. At times the effort and commitment required to assure adequate data quality for CRM is much more than anticipated. The effect of not having the right executive sponsor to make the appropriate commitment can cause a project to bog down beyond help.

Solution

The solution to this problem is clear and obvious; the sponsor of the project must be an executive with sufficient clout as well as having a need for CRM. This person should have a track record sufficient to devote the adequate resources to the project. In addition, he or she should have the authority to make final decisions on the myriad issues of data definition, delivery mechanism and quality metrics that will inevitably arise in a CRM project.

In one chemical company, for instance, the inability of groups to agree on a common definition of terms such as "head count" and "net sales" caused an impasse. The issue was resolved promptly and decisively by the controller, keeping the project on schedule. Sponsorship by an executive with a burning desire and with budgets, stature and the ability to make prompt and final decisions will see a project through to success in most cases.

PROBLEM NO. 4 – THE CRM PROJECT TEAM MAY LACK SKILLS AND EXPERIENCE

Foremost among technical problems is lack of skills and experience in all stages of the CRM project. The application of traditional techniques in definition of requirements, for instance, will not work. Using a structured approach with its reliance on data and process models will lead only up a blind alley, since modern CRM techniques are concerned with answering customer questions, solving customer problems and giving customers pleasant experiences in doing business with your organization. Analysis to define these needs, aside from standard reports and customer communications, may be a highly iterative process, continuing even after the CRM system is populated with data. Not knowing this in advance may cause serious underestimation of project costs and time to complete. Traditional modeling techniques will not be able to determine how many different ways data may be summarized or sorted. Not understanding the level of detail required by queries can also cause having either too much detailed data, or too little. Another shortcoming of traditional modeling techniques is that they do not address well data that may be highly summarized or derived. Not understanding this may result in data structures that are inadequate.

Many technical people with data modeling or database experience may think they know how to design for CRM. But without firsthand experience some of the problems unique to CRM analysis and design, the project timeline will run longer than planned. At worst it could end up as a major failure. Either way it could easily disappoint executive sponsors and other clientele, running the risk of jeopardizing future CRM efforts.

Solution

The most effective solution is to have an experienced high-level individual who can lead, staff, educate and who is available throughout the initial project from start to finish. This will not only insure project success but will also instill in the organization the necessary level of confidence to continue with expansion of CRM. Having experience in using a particular set of tools is necessary but not sufficient. More critical is having experience in implementing a successful CRM environment with satisfied customers.

In addition, specialized training in the form of in-house workshops for the project team will pay off both in the short and long run. Initially the team's learning curve will be reduced and many wrong turns prevented. And for the long term, the entire organization will benefit sooner from the increased credibility that a first success will bring. The following steps are recommended for planning and analysis in order to plan the system implementation.

Planning

The team must consist of users as well as business area experts. A steering committee comprised of senior executives including the Sponsor is necessary to communicate the vision, set a direction and make crucial decisions on desired quality metrics. The time line, as a general rule, should not be more than for four months for first phase.

Requirement Analysis:

- Define market/customer segmentation. The analysis should treat each segment separately if necessary.
- Set short-term and long-term goals along with the metrics to be used.
- Identify key stakeholders internal as well as external.
- Define the interaction points with the customer for the whole life cycle of the customer interaction.

- For each segment, define customer expectations for the quality service.
- For each segment, define the expectations of the internal user.
- For each segment, define decisions to be made, problems to be solved, questions to be answered and reports to be made.
- Define the trend and promotional analysis needs.
- Define data needs with timeliness, summarization, historical period and naming and formatting for the users.
- Identify the sources of data.
- Define data quality and the cleansing required.
- Define privacy/security constraints.

Prototyping

If you are making drastic changes in the current environment, you should prototype deliverables for the user's understanding and proof of concept. Once the system developed or tailored you should pilot it with a small subset of the users. At this time you would develop manuals and training material for users.

PROBLEM NO. 5 – RISKS INHERENT IN USING NEW TECHNOLOGY MAY INCREASE

The risk of using new technology is always a critical factor in IS projects. However, in the case of CRM, which is conceptually different and may have a large user base, the usual risks of pioneering are increased.

Most of the salespeople have their own way of managing their relationships and oftentimes resist the discipline as well as constraints of an automated system. The technology can be new both to the parent organization and to its users as well. Coupled with a lack of organizational experience, the results can be devastating and expensive. Mixing vendors, especially in the emerging Internet market, could also be catastrophic.

Some CRM technology is, and probably will be for some time, in a state of flux. Since most of the CRM users are less proficient in computer skills, the bells and whistles so attractive to IT professionals in new technology could be at best underutilized and at worst wasted. In addition, the presence of bugs, which are known to crop up in new technology, could turn users off very easily following on the heels of a lengthy gestation period for CRM. Remember, as with all new things, idiosyncrasies in new technology may surface at inopportune moments, since Murphy's Law has not yet been repealed for CRM.

Another aspect of the risk in employing new technology is not knowing what additional requirements or restrictions it may impose. If it is necessary to acquire and learn new technology, the time and effort required can detract from the most important part of the CRM effort, analysis and requirements definition. A result of this may be a misallocation of project resources and the attendant loss of time as well as a depletion of customer and management resources.

Solution

Wherever possible use existing, tried- and-proven technology, preferably that with which the organization has some experience. If tool interfaces are needed, it may not be worth the trouble to create them. Vendors are very sensitive to what is saleable, and it is predictable that technology capable of performing needed functions will be plentifully available in the future.

For management and lesser-skilled customers, you must select technology which is simple, sturdy, bug-free and well proven in the field. The tools selected must be made easy to learn and easy to use if they are not that way to start with.

If the need to use new technology persists, it would be best to create a small pilot project. In this way some organizational learning will take place, and success is better assured. In such cases it is highly recommended to bring in outside expertise, which will be available for at least a pilot project. Although this appears more costly in the short run, the results will include a finished project and increased confidence in the technology employed. It will also allow proper allocation of resources so that existing personnel can capitalize on their current knowledge while learning a new tool.

PROBLEM NO. 6 - EXCESSIVE RELIANCE ON TOOLS

Excessive reliance on tools - any tools - is caused by technophiles usually within the IT department. Somehow, an expectation that tools are magic is never far from peoples' minds, especially those of technical professionals. This is not to say that tools are not needed. Developing CRM does require some functions on a large scale. For instance, the back-end integration of data, cleansing or scrubbing data, bulk movement of data as well as user-friendly GUI interfaces for data delivery are demanding technical issues even with the best tools.

Unfortunately the level of integration among products of various vendors is still not high. The result is that the project team could become fixated on the tools issues and, as a result, get nothing done while waiting for the right tool or use up valuable resources in making the tool work. The team may also try to collect data and do everything the tool demands without even understanding why. This could lead to imposing a tool's limitations on the CRM solution.

Solution

Put the entire tool issue in perspective by not building the CRM project around tools. Establish a sound methodology and tailor it to the scope and deliverables of the project. Let the methodology guide the use of the tool, not the other way around Then, either look for appropriate tools or use tools available within the organization that are known, well proven and serviceable. Capitalize on the strength of the tool and work around its weaknesses. Remember that the most important activities are the up-front analysis tasks, which may not require the most sophisticated tools. These tasks involve understanding customer needs, defining data architecture, educating users and obtaining their buy-in. If necessary, build extra time into the project schedule to allow for the use of"archaic" tools.

PROBLEM NO. 7 – THE CRM TEAM MAY UNDERESTIMATE THE NEED FOR DATA QUALITY

Underestimation of the complexities in integrating CRM data from disparate sources is very common. More challenging is the quality issue. Most of the legacy systems suffer from poor quality and when you try to integrate them across systems and databases, the problem is compounded severely. A majority of business intelligence and CRM projects that have failed did so because of the lack of data quality and inability to improve it.

If current systems, which may feed the CRM project, are not documented properly, or if a lack of expertise exists in extracting data from these operational systems, the difficulties of transformation and scrubbing data may be grossly underestimated. Oftentimes, customer and product codes used within different systems may not be common or compatible.

In addition, extracting, transforming and scrubbing data from proprietary software can be a time bomb. Not fully understanding the architecture of an accounting package, for instance, can easily cause a delay. Proprietary packages may also cause other unforeseen problems. One small CRM project, for instance, was bogged down for months simply for lack of a data extraction facility from a simple package with a proprietary architecture.

A more subtle type of problem is identifying data that is required by the CRM project but does not currently exist in any automated or legacy data source within the organization. Such data must be acquired from the outside and may be very difficult or expensive to find.

Solution

Detailed knowledge of the systems feeding the CRM project is essential to avoiding undesired effects in loading data. If adequate systems documentation does not exist, then allow extra time during the analysis phase to create documentation. In addition, it is important also to analyse the data very carefully to anticipate the nature and level of scrubbing that will be necessary. A simple case involves date formats. The CRM project must present dates that are consistent even if the dates come from different sources. If your organization has not standardized on a single date format for all systems, you must take this into account in planning the project and designing the extraction process.

The solution to potential problems raised by proprietary software is simply to know its architecture and limitations. If documentation or in-house knowledge is not sufficient, it will be necessary to work with the vendor to determine whether data may be extracted, exactly how it appears when extracted and what is necessary to perform extraction. This will avoid unpleasant surprises and additional work during the design and implementation of scrubbing, transforming and loading procedures.

These activities should be part of up-front planning when considering a CRM project. Indeed, if you are considering purchasing a package and at the same time implementing CRM, it is imperative that these questions be answered during package evaluation and selection. It is essential, for instance, to assess the degree of compatibility involved in the data interface between the legacy systems and the CRM project. The cost of building and maintaining such an interface should be included in package evaluation criteria.

The issue of dealing with business changes lies at the heart of systems maintenance. The CRM project too must be maintained, but the question is more critical, since the data is historical. During analysis and requirements definition, it is very important to ascertain how sensitive each type of data may be to business changes, and what acceptable limits are for responses to queries for changed data. At this point, it may be necessary to communicate to management some of the limitations in dealing with historical data and possible costs that would be incurred in a conversion mechanism.

In the case of data that is required but does not exist, it is first necessary to ascertain that this is the case, which, again, will be done by careful analysis of the sources of data required by CRM users. At that point, it may be necessary to design a mechanism or possibly even a system to introduce that data into the CRM project at the appropriate time and in the appropriate format. For instance, if your organization purchases competitive sales data from external sources but desires to compare this data with your sales districts, it will be necessary to create a mechanism, perhaps using ZIP codes, that does the necessary mapping and integrates the two kinds of data. Or, it may be quite possible to pay your source vendors for this service and simply transmit data to them via a simple spreadsheet.

PROBLEM NO. 8 – THE CRM PROJECT MAY BE IMPLEMENTED IN ONE BIG STEP

If a sound project methodology, especially involving phasing, is not followed, many of the problems noted elsewhere in this object would be magnified out of proportion. For instance, the size and physical design of a CRM database, which are major factors in performance, cannot possibly be known until the types of queries have been thoroughly defined and the level of summarization determined. Lack of experience in integrating different kinds of data could also cause dislocations in a project schedule.

Solution

Many of the management issues – and technical problems as well – can be addressed and minimized by phasing the project based on the type of data required.

Manageable phases in a typical CRM project are outlined below. You can pick, choose or combine, according to your needs and management priority.

- Bring into the CRM project relatively stable, less- volatile customer master data for all customer entities.
- Load more volatile data, but that which is easily scrubbed or requires less effort to define and create consistency
- Populate with data that is more problematic or less clearly defined, that may require significant scrubbing and transformation
- Implement with data that does not exist in legacy systems, and may need to be created in order to respond to CRM needs.
- Incorporate externally supplied data, for instance news services from commercial sources, such as business partners.

It will not always be easy to proceed in this manner. However, recognition that some kinds of data will be easier to work with than others can serve as a guide in planning the project. In this way the risk is minimized during the initial stages and credibility is established. In addition, adequate time can be allocated for dealing with more difficult or problematic data at a later stages once a basic system is implemented and in use.

PROBLEM NO. 9 – THE CRM PROJECT TEAM MAY NEGLECT SECURITY ISSUES

Finally, you must remember that the CRM project is an open facility – normally a Web-based system – that will store and deliver customer- sensitive data potentially open to many employees and customers. What is your exposure in storing this kind of data in the CRM project? Is the CRM project accessible via a public or private network? As the CRM project grows and becomes more visible and important as a corporate asset, this concern could grow.

Standard security controls or tools, particularly in a distributed environment, may not provide sufficient protection without precautions. In an operational system, security to the user may be affected via a transaction code or at the terminal or workstation level. However, in the CRM project, data in one column of a table not only can have a different source from the next column, it can also have a different security requirement. Customer's personal, medical, family and income oriented data calls for the highest level of privacy. One major global pharmaceutical firm released to Internet public their customers' private data by one wrong stroke of key. You can imagine the damage caused by one error by one employee.

Solution

Do not omit security from planning and implementation considerations. If necessary use a security specialist and try to use tools that provide column and value-level security. If a public network of any kind is used, consider encryption. In addition, a special programme of security education will pay dividends. In the age of globalization and the magic of the Internet, it is too easy for users to forget that an open facility has another side to it, and a few extra reminders on security issues and procedures will minimize the risk of data going to unintended and unauthorized destinations. The security should be implemented both within as well as without the automated system. Employees must be trained in the over all security system.

PROBLEM NO. 10 – THE CRM PROJECT MAY LACK ONGOING POST- IMPLEMENTATION FOLLOW-UP

To be of best use CRM must respond to continually changing customer service. Lack of a mechanism for addressing changes will rapidly cause the CRM project to stagnate and lose its utility. Just because the CRM project exists does not mean everyone will rush to use it, despite advance publicity and a strong sponsor. This will undercut the ultimate potential of the CRM project as a profitability tool.

The customer user base too is potentially problematic. We are dealing with at best a mixed bag of query formulation skills, possibly general computer skills, which could make individuals a bit shy in taking maximum advantage of the CRM project opportunities. Your salespeople may be on road most of the time. In addition, problems will always crop up with a new facility, and users, particularly high-ranking customer users, can easily become impatient in dealing with them. Some of them will make their unhappiness known, but others may simply not communicate the issues, and they will silently stop using the facility. This could cause the CRM project to die a quiet, gradual death.

Solution

The way to avoid long-term difficulties is to treat CRM as a retail business with many customer segments. You should keep in mind that you may have several hundred or thousand users of this centralized system and they may be geographically scattered. CRM must be included as a major item in your business strategy. This may be accomplished by several stratagems.

First, measure customer satisfaction. We are talking about two types of customer, internal as well as external. Internal customers are your employees who deal with employees. Initially measure the satisfaction of internal customers and then expand to the external. Customer satisfaction surveys should be started within a few weeks of putting the CRM project into production status and should then be carried out on a regular basis. A carefully constructed questionnaire will not only cover results, such as " are you getting the information you need" but also probe into potential problem areas, such as usability of data, ease of access, ease of use of end-user tools or the Web site. The survey should also be accompanied by visits with customers. Breadth and depth of customer satisfaction measurements will assure continuous improvement of the CRM project on a regular basis.

Establish a policy of continuous promotion of the CRM project, along with a mechanism to carry this out. A newsletter, for instance, will apprise customers of additions and changes. And while it is doing this, it will help shape the image of the CRM project as something significant. Speaking at departmental meetings staff meetings and publishing productivity-improvement testimonials about the CRM project are also useful measures.

Establish a routine education programme. Education does not stop with the initial introduction of the CRM project. On the contrary, "continuing CRM education" is a major means of keeping the CRM project in the centre of the business focus. Education should also not be restricted to concepts and general information. New directions and new tool education should be kept in the forefront, and CRM education should offer help in problem solving to increase the sophistication level of customers.

Offer one-on-one consulting. In working with higher- level managers, this may be the only means of training in query creation, end- user tools and similar facets of the facility. However, making house calls will generate favourable publicity and also provide a feedback mechanism from the customer community. Establish a help desk hot line. A repository and good meta data will help, but CRM is new and everyone has a learning curve. In addition, new hardware and software requires its own longer learning curve.

A separate help desk hot line, especially in the beginning, will help customers get over many of the teething problems that accompany the birth of a new approach. Create a CRM user group. The more input the CRM project has and the more feedback, the better. Since it requires different type of publicity and a forum for use, the CRM user group can maintain communication and contribute heavily to the development and acceptance of policies, procedures and standards for improved business operations.

This is a democratic way of developing and enforcing your standards and practices for CRM. Establish a change monitoring function. Involve the CRM users group in changes that affect all systems-related activities. This will require creating new administrative loops in such a way that the CRM project has advance notice of major changes, even if they are being planned.

The bigger CRM becomes, the more the CRM users group must be involved in technology and systems planning to anticipate the impact of changes. In conjunction with this, establish a coordinating mechanism with planned new development. Each of these activities is important in its own right. Taken as a whole, however, they will put the CRM project into the business mainstream and keep it there, so that it responds to and changes along with customer needs.

CUSTOMER INTEGRATION MANAGEMENT (CIM)

Customer Interaction Management helps organisations execute effective and efficient interactions with their customers and prospects. These interactions must be consistent and tailored to the customer needs, based on the segment of the customer, the service required and the used channel.

IMPORTANT

Today's competitive environment requires companies to ensure that the customer has a consistent experience across interactions and channels, giving him a clear sense of brand value and differentiation.

Customer Interaction specialists at Deloitte focus on the following offerings:

- *Customer Experience*: We support the organisation in describing and assessing the experience of its customer or prospect across their lifecycle, providing actionable recommendations for enriching the customer experience.
- *Multi-channel interaction management*: We provide advice regarding the ways the organisation can best reach its customers. By implementing right-channelling, we help companies maximize interaction value in a cost-efficient way.
- *Service Organisational design*: Our organisational design methods consider people and processes in order to put in place the right service models, contact flows and escalation rules.
- *Service request and SLA management*: We provide methods and tools to improve service request management and implement the appropriate service level agreements.
- *Contact Centre Implementation and Transformation*: Deloitte has a proven track-record in implementing multi-channel interaction centres, including integration with CRM processes and tools.

PREDICTIVE CUSTOMER INTERACTION MANAGEMENT

Introduction

Every business needs to efficiently manage outbound and inbound interactions with customers. These interactions can occur through many channels including the web, call centres branch offices, ATMs, and e-mail. With inbound interactions, customers offer their attention. They visit a web site, make a call, or access an ATM because they want something at that moment – information about a product or help with a problem.

These interactions usually present an opportunity to communicate with a customer who is engaged by choice and ready to share information regarding his or her wants and needs. Outbound interactions are typically used to target products to particular customer segments based on analysis of customer data. The success of these interactions – whether through e-mail, direct mail, or other channels – depends to a great extent on the organization's understanding of the customer's wants and needs at the time of the offer. This document describes an architecture that manages inbound and outbound interactions in a consistent manner to present a unified, real-time view of each customer.

Requirements for Effective Customer Interaction Management

The following list summarizes requirements for such an architecture:

- Provides consistent customer interaction management of outbound and inbound communications.
- Addresses the uniqueness and complexities of various inbound and outbound channels. For example, in an inbound call, the business logic might dictate that the CSR should not make an offer if the call time is greater than a given threshold.
- Allows businesses that are aligned along product lines to use both customer knowledge and data mining to publish product propensities.
- Allows customer data to be distributed across multiple systems.
- Combines rules, policies, inferencing, and analytics – both statistical and probabilistic – to produce complex models of reasoning via events, customer data, time, and analytics.
- Leverages existing investment in data mining tools such as SAS, SPSS, and others.
- Handles the low latency requirements of real-time customer interactions with sophisticated caching techniques.
- Provides flexibility, scalability, and high availability.

Key Aspects of Customer Interaction Management

How a business treats customers and manages customer relationships is a key differentiator and is critical to succeeding in highly competitive and dynamic environments.

The solution proposed in this document addresses three important aspects of customer interaction management:

1. Maintaining customer relationships using relationship events over time.
2. Driving up-sell and cross-sell opportunities using both inbound and outbound events.
3. Incorporating a feedback model to calculate the effectiveness of models over macro and micro dimensions.

Architecture

Effective customer interaction management requires an event-driven architecture that is application and database agnostic.

High-level components of such a solution include:

- Channel adapters.
- Customer interaction engine also referred to as a recomm-endation engine
  - Knowledge models maintained by business users.
  - Analytical models maintained by business users or reused from existing investments.
- Virtual data source
  - SOA platform to integrate customer and other information from various data sources. A typical implementation will require integration with customer and product data from operational stores and/or data warehouses

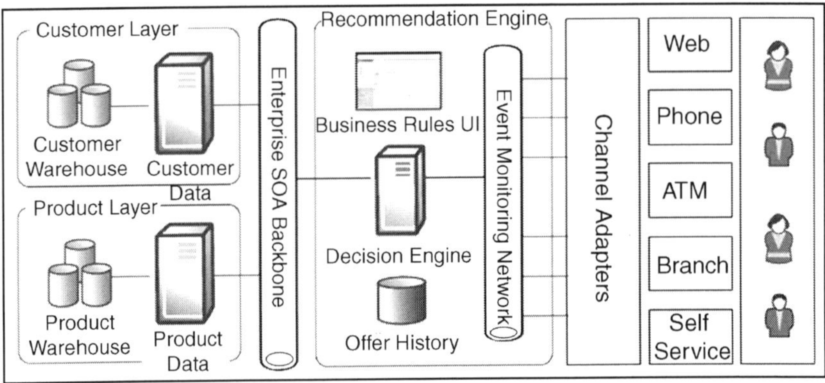

Channel Adapters

In the context of this solution, channel adapters have two key roles:

1. *Sense*: Channel adapters, either intrusively or non-intrusively, publish relevant events to the recommendation engine. The solution contains pre-defined adapters for various technologies used in the channels.
2. *Respond*: Channel adapters provide a mechanism to initiate a dialogue with the customer. The response is inferred and initiated by the recommendation engine to the channel adapters.

Recommendation Engine

The recommendation engine provides the following functions:

- A glossary of terms and vocabulary that form the basis of marketing strategies.
- Integration with channels using events.
- Pattern matching of a set of events with the policies, knowledge, and analytical models to generate a set of responses.

- Generic offers such as "Offer of the Day."
- Maintain history of offers and customer responses.
- A business user interface to create and represent marketing strategies or business "rules" based on the vocabulary of terms and events. TIBCO provides a recommendation engine based on TIBCO BusinessEvents™ software, a market-leading complex event processing application.

Virtual Data Source

The virtual data source integrates all relevant customer and product data. TIBCO BusinessWorks™ is an extensible SOA enablement platform that uses a no-coding approach to developing, deploying, and running integration projects and building serviceoriented architectures. It simplifies some of the more complex implementation issues that are critical for the glue and sequence between connected systems, such as process orchestration and transformation.

Customer Examples

Today's leading retail banks recognize that customers are their most important and strategic asset and are rapidly adopting customer-centric IT strategies to achieve competitive advantage. This part presents a number of practical examples showing how a real-time, event-driven, multi-channel, application-agnostic architecture delivers immediate value to the retail banking business and a unique banking experience to their customers.

Retail banks have traditionally used customer resource management systems to capture the inbound customer data stream and store the information in a central repository. Using a post-processing procedure, data mining tools are then used to analyse the data and apply rules to execute marketing campaigns.

TIBCO's approach to customer interaction management uses CEP software to enable:

- Real-time matching of customer profiles and product lines across all banking channels.
- Real-time, rules-based product recommendations based on statistical, relationship, or experience models per business line.

Example: Multi-Channel Customer Interaction

The following example shows how banks can use real-time information to provide more effective service:

- Mick and his wife have a new baby girl named Nora.
- While using the bank's internet portal, Mick updates his Personal Profile to include the new family member.
- Still using the portal, he checks the bank's mortgage packages and requests several brochures because he is thinking about renovating or buying a new home.

- The next day he and his wife get a present from the bank congratulating them on the new family member and offering a baby savings account especially tailored for them.
- One week later, while visiting the local branch, the local branch officer congratulates Nick on Nora's birth, offers him an informational appointment with the bank's mortgage advisor, and offers to increase the credit limit on the family credit card at no charge and with no paperwork. In the example, complex event processing software allows the bank to:

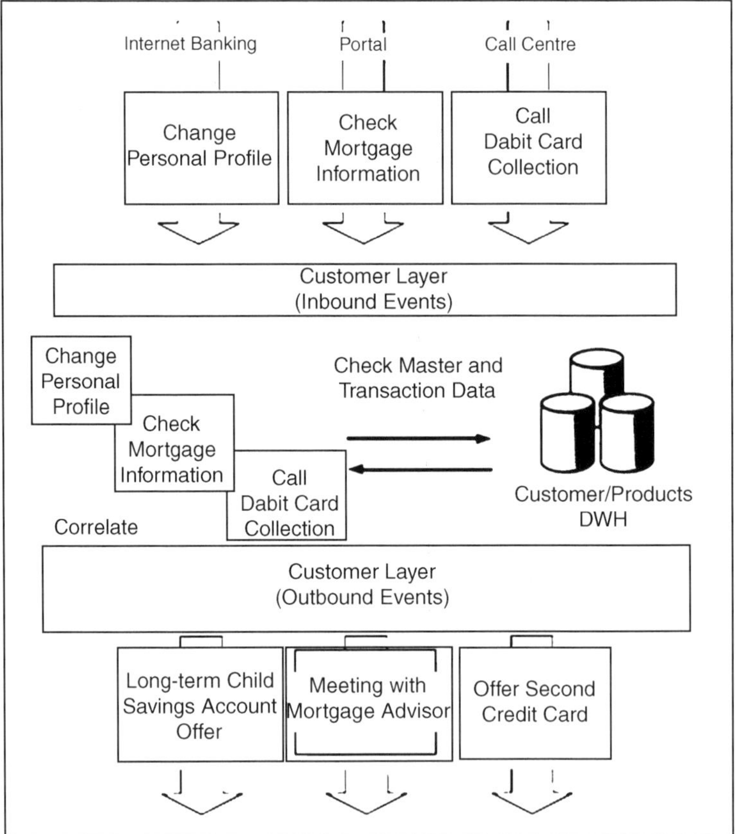

- Capture all events through all channels in real-time.
- Seek out patterns and correlate information with the goal of identifying important events, such as the birth of a child.
- Consult historical information to determine, for instance, the customer's demographic profile and to estimate the bank's share of wallet
- Apply different models, or rules, to assess which marketing campaign, if any, is most suited to the customer.
- Execute appropriate marketing strategies and recommend products

in real-time. By tracking customer interactions, capturing other vital, non-traditional customer events that help flesh out the customer profile – birth of a child, starting or ending school, landing a first job, getting married, renting a house, purchasing a new car, moving, changing a job, buying a house – and responding with relevant offers and services, banks have an opportunity to extend the customer relationship and demonstrate that the customer is the bank's most important asset.

ATTRACTING, RETAINING, AND GROWING CUSTOMERS

Markets can be characterized by their long-term buying dynamics and how easily and often customers can enter and leave:

- *Permanent capture markets*: Once a customer, always a customer.
- *Simple retention markets*: Customers can permanently be lost after each period.
- *Customer migration markets*: Customers can leave and come back

Some customers inevitably become inactive or drop out. The challenge is to reactivate dissatisfied customers through win-back strategies. It is often easier to re-attract ex-customers than to find new ones. The key is to analyse the causes of customer defection through exit interviews and lost-customer surveys. The aim is to win back only those customers who have strong profit potential. Customers are becoming harder to please. They are smarter, more price conscious, more demanding, less forgiving, and they are approached by many more competitors with equal or better offers. The challenge, according to Jeffrey Gitomer, is not necessarily to produce satisfied customers; several competitors can do this. The challenge is to produce delighted and loyal customers.

Mass Marketing ———————— One-to-One Marketing
Average customer ———————— Individual customer
Customer anonymity ———————- Customer profile
Standard product ——————— Customised market offering
Mass production ————————- Customised production.
Mass distribution ————————- Individualized distribution.
Mass advertising ————————- Individualized message
Mass Promotion ————————- Individualized incentives
One-Way message ——————— Two-way messages
Economies of scale ——————— Economies of scope
Share of market ————————- Share of customer
All Customers ———————— Profitable customers
Customer attraction ——————- Customer retention

Companies seeking to expand their profits and sales have to spend considerable time and resources searching for new customer. To generate leads, the company develops ads and places them in media that will reach new prospects; it sends direct mail and makes phone calls to possible new prospects; it salespeople participate in trade shows where they might find new leads; it purchases names from list brokers; and so on. All this activity produces a list of suspects.

Suspects are people or organizations who might conceivably have an interest in buying the companyâ€™s product or service, but may not have the means or real intention to buy. The next task is to identify which suspects are really good prospectsâ€"customer with the motivation, ability, and opportunity to make a purchaseâ€"by interviewing them, checking on their financial standing, and so on. Then it is time to send out the sales people.

It is not enough, however, to attract new customers; the company must keep them and increase their business. Too many companies suffer fro High customer churnâ€"high customer defection. It is like adding water to a leaking bucket. Cellular carriers, for example, are plagued with â€œspinners,â€? customers who switch carriers at least three times a year looking for the best deal. Many lose 25% of their subscribers each year at an estimated cost of $2 billion to $4 billion. Marketing practices instead of concentrating on the art of attracting new customers must ensure on retaining and cultivating the existing ones.

The emphasis is traditionally has been on making sales rather than building Relationships; on pre-selling and selling rather than caring for the customer afterward. There are two main ways to strengthen customer retention. One is to erect high switching barriers. Customers are less inclined to switch to another supplier when this would involve high capital costs, high search costs, or the loss of loyal-customer discounts. The better approach is to deliver high customer satisfaction. This makes it harder for competitors to offer lower prices or inducements to switch.

HOW TO HANDLE CUSTOMER COMPLAINTS

No matter how perfectly designed and implemented a marketing programme is, mistakes will happen. Given the potential downside of having an unhappy customer, it is critical that the negative experience be dealt with properly.

As with any marketing crisis large or small, swiftness and sincerity are the key watchwords. Customers must feel an immediate sense that the company truly cares.

Beyond that, the following procedures can help to recover customer goodwill:

- Set up a 7-day, 24-hour toll-free by phone, fax, or e-mail to receive and act on customer complaints.
- Contact the complaining customer as quickly as possible. The slower the company is to respond, the more dissatisfaction may grow and lead to negative word of mouth.

- Accept responsibility for the customer's disappointment; don't blame the customer.
- Use customer service people who are empathic.
- Resolve the complaint swiftly and to the customer's satisfaction. Some complaining customers are not looking for compensation so much as a sign that the company cares.

FORMING STRONG CUSTOMER BONDS

Berry & Parasuraman have identified 3 retention-building approaches:

1. *Adding financial benefits*: Frequency programmes and club marketing programmes
2. *Adding social benefits*: Individualising and personalising customer relationships.
3. *Adding structural ties*:
   - Create long term contracts
   - Charge a lower price to consumers who buy larger supplies
   - Turn the product into a long-term service

CRM DATABASE AND CRM

CRM DATABASE, THE MOST UTILIZED FEATURE IN CRM PROGRAMMES

One of the most utilized features of customer relationship management programmes is the CRM database. Companies use the CRM database to gather information and details about their customers, including their needs and purchasing history. The CRM database can also be used to track employee sales and success rates, as well as task lists and completion. Many companies incorporate their CRM database into their marketing and advertising plans. As the information entered into a CRM database is customizable to your own business, the uses of the data collected are only as limited as your imagination.

WHAT IS A CRM DATABASE

A CRM database is a programme of stored information that is relevant and useful to the success of your business. CRM database programmes can be used as standalone software, incorporated with existing databases, such as Outlook or Excel, or a combination of the two. What a CRM database may hold can vary greatly due to the type of business, the focus of marketing, and the direction in which the business is going. A CRM database can be used for customer information, employee tasks, marketing plans, and a variety of other daily business functions.

CRM DATABASE: CUSTOMER INFORMATION

The most often used information in a CRM database is the customer information. This can include personal information, such as contact addresses and phone numbers, as well as family size, location, and other demographic information. Many companies also use their CRM database to record purchase information, service calls, customer support needs, and even warranty information. Anything relative to customer interaction can be placed in a CRM database.

CRM DATABASE: EMPLOYEE INFORMATION

The CRM database can also be a hub for managing your employees. Vital information can be stored within the CRM database, such as employee ID files and commission information. Also, some employers and managers find it useful to assign tasks, check progress, and monitor the sales records of their employees through the CRM database. The CRM database can be a manager's second set of eyes, as to the productivity and motivation level of their employees.

CRM DATABASE: OTHER USES

Another popular use of a CRM database is within a business' marketing plan. Because of the detailed records kept on the customers and their buying habits, many businesses find their CRM database to be their best marketing tool. It is easy to create reports on buying trends and habits and focus marketing strategies to best fit these needs using the information in the CRM database. Other companies use the CRM database information to track sales and create goals for their sales team. Depending on the specific needs of an organization, there are plenty of different uses for the CRM database to discover or design.

CUSTOMIZING AND UTILIZING YOUR CRM DATABASE

One of the most useful things about a CRM database is the ability to customise it to the specific needs of a business. Adding and removing data fields to record the information about your company and customers that you want is a great feature of a CRM database. It is up to you as a business owner to decide what types of information are the most pertinent to the growth and profitability of your business.

Also creating specific reports on the items and information you need is easy with a CRM database. Analyzing your business has never been more efficient. Crate the perfect marketing plan and save money by focusing the advertising to the more receptive audience with the information you have stored. You will quickly discover that your business has grown tremendously in a short time once you begin using the CRM database to manage your business.

ADVANTAGES OF PROPHET CRM DATABASE

The Prophet CRM database allows you to accomplish all of the necessary tasks of your business, while streamlining these projects into one simple programme. Information can be imported from Outlook and Excel to make moving to the new CRM database fast and easy. You can customise the CRM database to suit your needs and create the perfect customer files and reports to stay ahead of the trends and needs of your consumers. The CRM database from Prophet will work with you to increase your sales and effectively grow your business beyond your wildest dreams.

4

Marketing Strategy

AN OVERVIEW

Marketing strategy is a process that can allow an organization to concentrate its limited resources on the greatest opportunities to increase sales and achieve a sustainable competitive advantage. A marketing strategy should be centred around the key concept that customer satisfaction is the main goal.

KEY PART OF THE GENERAL CORPORATE STRATEGY

Marketing strategy is a method of focusing an organization's energies and resources on a course of action which can lead to increased sales and dominance of a targeted market niche. A marketing strategy combines product development, promotion, distribution, pricing, relationship management and other elements; identifies the firm's marketing goals, and explains how they will be achieved, ideally within a stated timeframe. Marketing strategy determines the choice of target market segments, positioning, marketing mix, and allocation of resources. It is most effective when it is an integral component of overall firm strategy, defining how the organization will successfully engage customers, prospects, and competitors in the market arena. Corporate strategies, corporate missions, and corporate goals. As the customer constitutes the source of a company's revenue, marketing strategy is closely linked with sales. A key component of marketing strategy is often to keep marketing in line with a company's overarching mission statement.

Basic theory:

- Target Audience
- Proposition/Key Element
- Implementation

TACTICS AND ACTIONS

A marketing strategy can serve as the foundation of a marketing plan. A marketing plan contains a set of specific actions required to successfully implement a marketing strategy. For example: "Use a low cost product to attract consumers. Once our organization, via our low cost product, has established a relationship with consumers, our organization will sell additional, higher-margin products and services that enhance the consumer's interaction with the low-cost product or service." A strategy consists of a well thought out series of tactics to make a marketing plan more effective.

Marketing strategies serve as the fundamental underpinning of marketing plans designed to fill market needs and reach marketing objectives. Plans and objectives are generally tested for measurable results. A marketing strategy often integrates an organization's marketing goals, policies, and action sequences into a cohesive whole. Similarly, the various strands of the strategy, which might include advertising, channel marketing, internet marketing, promotion and public relations can be orchestrated. Many companies cascade a strategy throughout an organization, by creating strategy tactics that then become strategy goals for the next level or group. Each one group is expected to take that strategy goal and develop a set of tactics to achieve that goal. This is why it is important to make each strategy goal measurable. Marketing strategies are dynamic and interactive. They are partially planned and partially unplanned.

TYPES OF STRATEGIES

Marketing strategies may differ depending on the unique situation of the individual business. However there are a number of ways of categorizing some generic strategies.

A brief description of the most common categorizing schemes is presented below:

- *Strategies based on market dominance*: In this scheme, firms are classified based on their market share or dominance of an industry. *Typically there are four types of market dominance strategies*:
  1. Leader
  2. Challenger
  3. Follower
  4. Nicher
- *Porter generic strategies*: Strategy on the dimensions of strategic scope and strategic strength. Strategic scope refers to the market penetration while strategic strength refers to the firm's sustainable competitive advantage. The generic strategy framework comprises two alternatives each with two alternative scopes. These are Differentiation and low-cost leadership each with a dimension of Focus-broad or narrow.
  - Product differentiation
  - Cost leadership
  - Market segmentation
- *Innovation strategies*: This deals with the firm's rate of the new product development and business model innovation. It asks whether the company is on the cutting edge of technology and business innovation.

There are three types:

1. Pioneers
2. Close followers
3. Late followers

- *Growth strategies*: In this scheme we ask the question, "How should the firm grow?".

  There are a number of different ways of answering that question, but the most common gives four answers:

  1. Horizontal integration
  2. Vertical integration
  3. Diversification
  4. Intensification

A more detailed scheme uses the categories:

- Prospector
- Analyser
- Defender
- Reactor
- Marketing warfare strategies - This scheme draws parallels between marketing strategies and military strategies.

STRATEGIC MODELS

Marketing participants often employ strategic models and tools to analyse marketing decisions. When beginning a strategic analysis, the 3Cs can be employed to get a broad understanding of the strategic environment. An Ansoff Matrix is also often used to convey an organization's strategic positioning of their marketing mix. The 4Ps can then be utilized to form a marketing plan to pursue a defined strategy.

There are many companies especially those in the Consumer Package Goods market that adopt the theory of running their business centred around Consumer, Shopper & Retailer needs. Their Marketing departments spend quality time looking for "Growth Opportunities" in their categories by identifying relevant insights on their target Consumers, Shoppers and retail partners. These Growth Opportunities emerge from changes in market trends, segment dynamics changing and also internal brand or operational business challenges.The Marketing team can then prioritize these Growth Opportunities and begin to develop strategies to exploit the opportunities that could include new or adapted products, services as well as changes to the 7Ps.

REAL-LIFE MARKETING

Real-life marketing primarily revolves around the application of a great deal of common-sense; dealing with a limited number of factors, in an environment of imperfect information and limited resources complicated by uncertainty and tight timescales. Use of classical marketing techniques, in these circumstances, is inevitably partial and uneven. Thus, for example, many new products will emerge from irrational processes and the rational development process may be used to screen out the worst non-runners.

The design of the advertising, and the packaging, will be the output of the creative minds employed; which management will then screen, often by'gut-reaction', to ensure that it is reasonable. For most of their time, marketing managers use intuition and experience to analyse and handle the complex, and unique, situations being faced; without easy reference to theory. This will often be'flying by the seat of the pants', or'gut-reaction'; where the overall strategy, coupled with the knowledge of the customer which has been absorbed almost by a process of osmosis, will determine the quality of the marketing employed.

This, almost instinctive management, is what is sometimes called'coarse marketing'; to distinguish it from the refined, aesthetically pleasing, form favoured by the theorists.

PRODUCT

Product marketing deals with the first of the"7P"'s of marketing, which are Product, Pricing, Place, and Promotion, Packaging, Positioning & People. Product marketing, as opposed to product management, deals with more outbound marketing tasks. For example, product management deals with the nuts and bolts of product development within a firm, whereas product marketing deals with marketing the product to prospects, customers, and others. Product marketing, as a job function within a firm, also differs from other marketing jobs such as marketing communications, online marketing, advertising, marketing strategy, etc.

A Product market is something that is referred to when pitching a new product to the general public. The people you are trying to make your product appeal to is your consumer market.

For example: If you were pitching a new video game console game to the public, your consumer market would probably be the adult male Video Game market. Thus you would carry out market research to find out how best to release the game. Likewise, a massage chair would probably not appeal to younger children, so you would market your product to an older generation.

ROLE OF PRODUCT MARKETING

Product marketing in a business addresses five important strategic questions:

1. What products will be offered?
2. Who will be the target customers?
3. How will the products reach those?
4. At what price should the products be offered?
5. How will customers be introduced to the products?

PRODUCT MARKETING VS. PRODUCT MANAGEMENT

Product marketing frequently differs from product management in high-tech companies. Whereas the product manager is required to take a product's requirements from the sales and marketing personnel and create a product requirements document, which will be used by the engineering team to build the product, the product marketing manager can be engaged in the task of creating a Marketing Requirements Document which is used as source for the product management to develop the PRD.

In other companies the product manager creates both the MRDs and the PRDs, while the product marketing manager does outbound tasks like giving product demonstrations in trade shows, creating marketing collateral like hot-sheets, beat-sheets, cheat sheets, data sheets, and white documents. This requires the product marketing manager to be skilled not only in competitor analysis, market research, and technical writing, but also in more business oriented activities like conducting ROI and NPV analyses on technology investments, strategizing how the decision criteria of the prospects or customers can be changed so that they buy the company's product vis-a-vis the competitor's product, etc.

One issue that faces Product Marketers is that they are chartered with developing much of the content for the various constituents. Creating content tends to be given more value than the actual research and thinking that is behind all the content.

In smaller high-tech firms or start-ups, product marketing and product management functions can be blurred, and both tasks may be borne by one individual.

However, as the company grows someone needs to focus on creating good requirements documents for the engineering team, whereas someone else needs to focus on how to analyse the market, influence the "analysts", and understand longer term market direction. When such clear demarcation becomes visible, the former falls under the domain of product management, and the latter, under product marketing. In Silicon Valley, in particular, product marketing professionals have considerable domain experience in a particular market or technology or both. Some Silicon Valley firms have titles such as Product Marketing Engineer, who tend to be promoted to managers in due course.

The trend that is emerging in Silicon Valley is for companies to hire a team of a product marketing manager with a technical marketing manager. The Technical marketing role is becoming more valuable as companies become more competitive and seek to reduce costs and time to market. Another trend is to have one Product Marketing Manager per group of Product Managers. This is the model that leads to the issue of PMMs being pressured to write content instead of connecting with the market.

QUALIFICATIONS

The typical education qualification for this area of business is a high level Marketing or Business related degree, e.g. an BBA, MBA, not forgetting sufficient work experience in related areas. As a key skill is to be able to interact with technical staff, a background in engineering or computing is also an asset.

PRICE

Pricing is the process of determining what a company will receive in exchange for its products. Pricing factors are manufacturing cost, market place, competition, market condition, and quality of product. Pricing is also a key variable in microeconomic price allocation theory. Pricing is a fundamental aspect of financial modeling and is one of the four Ps of the marketing mix. The other three aspects are product, promotion, and place. Price is the only revenue generating element amongst the four Ps, the rest being cost centres. Pricing is the manual or automatic process of applying prices to purchase and sales orders, based on factors such as: a fixed amount, quantity break, promotion or sales campaign, specific vendor quote, price prevailing on entry, shipment or invoice date, combination of multiple orders or lines, and many others. Automated systems require more setup and maintenance but may prevent pricing errors. The needs of the consumer can be converted into demand only if the consumer has the willingness and capacity to buy the product. Thus pricing is very important in marketing.

QUESTIONS INVOLVED IN PRICING

Pricing involves asking questions like:

- How much to charge for a product or service? This question is that a typical starting point for discussions about pricing, however, a better question for a vendor to ask is - How much do customers value the products, services, and other intangibles that the vendor provides.
- What are the pricing objectives?
- Do we use profit maximization pricing?
- How to set the price?:
- Should there be a single price or multiple pricing?
- Should prices change in various geographical areas, referred to as zone pricing?
- Should there be quantity discounts?
- What prices are competitors charging?
- Do you use a price skimming strategy or a penetration pricing strategy?
- What image do you want the price to convey?
- Do you use psychological pricing?
- How important are customer price sensitivity and elasticity issues?

- Can real-time pricing be used?
- Is price discrimination or yield management appropriate?
- Are there legal restrictions on retail price maintenance, price collusion, or price discrimination?
- Do price points already exist for the product category?
- How flexible can we be in pricing?: The more competitive the industry, the less flexibility we have.
  - The price floor is determined by production factors like costs, economies of scale, marginal cost, and degree of operating leverage
  - The price ceiling is determined by demand factors like price elasticity and price points
- Are there transfer pricing considerations?
- What is the chance of getting involved in a price war?
- How visible should the price be? - Should the price be neutral? should it be highly visible? or should it be hidden?.
- Are there joint product pricing considerations?
- What are the non-price costs of purchasing the product?
- What sort of payments should be accepted?

WHAT A PRICE SHOULD DO

A well chosen price should do three things:

1. Achieve the financial goals of the company
2. Fit the realities of the marketplace
3. Support a product's positioning and be consistent with the other variables in the marketing mix
   - Price is influenced by the type of distribution channel used, the type of promotions used, and the quality of the product
     a. Price will usually need to be relatively high if manufacturing is expensive, distribution is exclusive, and the product is supported by extensive advertising and promotional campaigns
     b. A low price can be a viable substitute for product quality, effective promotions, or an energetic selling effort by distributors

From the marketer's point of view, an efficient price is a price that is very close to the maximum that customers are prepared to pay. In economic terms, it is a price that shifts most of the consumer surplus to the producer. A good pricing strategy would be the one which could balance between the price floor and the price ceiling.

TERMINOLOGY

There are numerous terms and strategies specific to pricing:

Effective Price

The effective price is the price the company receives after accounting for discounts, promotions, and other incentives.

Line Pricing

Line Pricing is the use of a limited number of prices for all product offerings of a vendor. This is a tradition started in the old five and dime stores in which everything cost either 5 or 10 cents. Its underlying rationale is that these amounts are seen as suitable price points for a whole range of products by prospective customers. It has the advantage of ease of administering, but the disadvantage of inflexibility, particularly in times of inflation or unstable prices.

Loss Leader

A loss leader is a product that has a price set below the operating margin. This results in a loss to the enterprise on that particular item in the hope that it will draw customers into the store and that some of those customers will buy other, higher margin items.

Promotional Pricing

Promotional pricing refers to an instance where pricing is the key element of the marketing mix.

Price/quality Relationship

The price/quality relationship refers to the perception by most consumers that a relatively high price is a sign of good quality. The belief in this relationship is most important with complex products that are hard to test, and experiential products that cannot be tested until used. The greater the uncertainty surrounding a product, the more consumers depend on the price/quality hypothesis and the greater premium they are prepared to pay.

The classic example is the pricing of Twinkies, a snack cake which was viewed as low quality after the price was lowered. Excessive reliance on the price/quantity relationship by consumers may lead to an increase in prices on all products and services, even those of low quality, which causes the price/quality relationship to no longer apply.

Premium Pricing

Premium pricing is the strategy of consistently pricing at, or near, the high end of the possible price range to help attract status-conscious consumers. Examples of companies which partake in premium pricing in the marketplace include Rolex and Bentley.

People will buy a premium priced product because:

- They believe the high price is an indication of good quality;

- They believe it to be a sign of self worth - "They are worth it;" it authenticates the buyer's success and status; it is a signal to others that the owner is a member of an exclusive group;
- They require flawless performance in this application - The cost of product malfunction is too high to buy anything but the best - example: heart pacemaker.

Goldilocks Pricing

The term Goldilocks pricing is commonly used to describe the practice of providing a "gold-plated" version of a product at a premium price in order to make the next-lower priced option look more reasonably priced; for example, encouraging customers to see business-class airline seats as good value for money by offering an even higher priced first-class option. Similarly, third-class railway carriages in Victorian England are said to have been built without windows, not so much to punish third-class customers as to motivate those who could afford second-class seats to pay for them instead of taking the cheaper option.

This is also known as a potential result of price discrimination. The name derives from the Goldilocks story in which Goldilocks chose neither the hottest nor the coldest porridge, but instead the one that was "just right". More technically, this form of pricing exploits the general cognitive bias of aversion to extremes. This practice is known academically as "framing". By providing three options you can manipulate the consumer into choosing the middle choice and thus, the middle choice should yield the most profit to the seller, since it is the one chosen most often.

Demand-based Pricing

Demand-based pricing is any pricing method that uses consumer demand - based on perceived value - as the central element. These include: price skimming, price discrimination and yield management, price points, psychological pricing, bundle pricing, penetration pricing, price lining, value-based pricing, geo and premium pricing. Pricing factors are manufacturing cost, market place, competition, market condition, quality of product.

Multidimensional Pricing

Multidimensional pricing is the pricing of a product or service using multiple numbers. In this practice, price no longer consists of a single monetary amount but rather consists of various dimensions. Research has shown that this practice can significantly influence consumers' ability to understand and process price information

NINE LAWS OF PRICE SENSITIVITY

The Strategy and Tactics of Pricing, Thomas Nagle and Reed Holden outlined 9

laws or factors that influence a buyer's price sensitivity with respect to a given purchase:

1. Reference Price Effect Buyer's price sensitivity for a given product increases the higher the product's price relative to perceived alternatives. Perceived alternatives can vary by buyer segment, by occasion, and other factors.
2. Difficult Comparison Effect Buyers are less sensitive to the price of a known/more reputable product when they have difficulty comparing it to potential alternatives.
3. Switching Costs Effect The higher the product-specific investment a buyer must make to switch suppliers, the less price sensitive that buyer is when choosing between alternatives.
4. Price-Quality Effect Buyers are less sensitive to price the more that higher prices signal higher quality. Products for which this effect is particularly relevant include: image products, exclusive products, and products with minimal cues for quality.
5. Expenditure Effect Buyers are more price sensitive when the expense accounts for a large percentage of buyers' available income or budget.
6. End-Benefit Effect The effect refers to the relationship a given purchase has to a larger overall benefit, and is divided into two parts: Derived demand: The more sensitive buyers are to the price of the end benefit, the more sensitive they will be to the prices of those products that contribute to that benefit. Price proportion cost: The price proportion cost refers to the per cent of the total cost of the end benefit accounted for by a given component that helps to produce the end benefit. The smaller the given components share of the total cost of the end benefit, the less sensitive buyers will be to the component's price.
7. Shared-cost Effect The smaller the portion of the purchase price buyers must pay for themselves, the less price sensitive they will be.
8. Fairness Effect Buyers are more sensitive to the price of a product when the price is outside the range they perceive as"fair" or"reasonable" given the purchase context.
9. The Framing Effect Buyers are more price sensitive when they perceive the price as a loss rather than a forgone gain, and they have greater price sensitivity when the price is paid separately rather than as part of a bundle.

APPROACHES

Pricing as the most effective profit lever. Pricing can be approached at three levels.The industry, market, and transaction level. Pricing at the industry level focuses on the overall economics of the industry, including supplier price changes and customer demand changes. Pricing at the market level focuses on the competitive position of the price in comparison to the value differential of the product to that of comparative competing products. Pricing at the transaction level focuses on managing the implementation of discounts away from the reference, or list price, which occur both on and off the invoice or receipt.

PRICING TACTICS

Micromarketing is the practice of tailoring products, brands, and promotions to meet the needs and wants of microsegments within a market. It is a type of market customization that deals with pricing of customer/ product combinations at the store or individual level.

PRICING MISTAKES

Many companies make common pricing mistakes.

Bernstein's object "Supplier Pricing Mistakes" outlines several which include:

- Weak controls on discounting
- Inadequate systems for tracking competitor selling prices and market share
- Cost-Up pricing
- Price increases poorly executed
- Worldwide price inconsistencies
- Paying sales representatives on dollar volume vs. addition of profitability measures

PLACE

Marketing experts know that the best product in the world will never make an impact in the business world if no one can locate and obtain it. Keeping this simple, yet vital brick in the house of marketing, McDonald's gives careful consideration to the placement of its restaurants. Within their marketing research, they take into consideration the population of a given area, major roadways in the vicinity of the proposed restaurant site, traffic that passes by the restaurant site, and the demographics of the area, as they know a great deal about their customers.

The construction of a McDonald's restaurant costs millions of dollars, and in order for the operation to be profitable, placement must be in an area that maximizes the customer exposure, therefore increasing the chance of generating business. However, please keep in mind that McDonald's leaves nothing to chance. They do their marketing homework, and it shows. The fact that McDonald's always seems to be "right around the corner" is due to a great deal of extensive marketing research, planning and execution. If you really give this idea a great deal of thought, take into consideration the very low number of McDonald's restaurants that go out of business in a given community. This is not sheer luck, nor is it just something that has happened by chance. It only looks like a coincidence! While other fast food chains come and go, McDonald's is always there for you, right around the corner in most cases.

PROMOTION

Promotion is one of the four elements of marketing mix. It is the communication link between sellers and buyers for the purpose of influencing, informing, or persuading a potential buyer's purchasing decision.

The following are two types of Promotion:

1. The line promotion: Promotion in the media in which the advertiser pays an advertising agency to place the ad
2. Below the line promotion: All other promotion. Much of this is intended to be subtle enough for the consumer to be unaware that promotion is taking place. E.g. sponsorship, product placement, endorsements, sales promotion, merchandising, direct mail, personal selling, public relations, trade shows

The specification of five elements creates a promotional mix or promotional plan. These elements are personal selling, advertising, sales promotion, direct marketing, and publicity. A promotional mix specifies how much attention to pay to each of the five subcategories, and how much money to budget for each. A promotional plan can have a wide range of objectives, including: sales increases, new product acceptance, creation of brand equity, positioning, competitive retaliations, or creation of a corporate image. Fundamentally, however there are three basic objectives of promotion.

These are:

1. To present information to consumers as well as others
2. To increase demand
3. To differentiate a product.

There are different ways to promote a product in different areas of media. Promoters use internet advertisement, special events, endorsements, and newspapers to advertise their product. Many times with the purchase of a product there is an incentive like discounts, free items, or a contest. This is to increase the sales of a given product. The term "promotion" is usually an "in" expression used internally by the marketing company, but not normally to the public or the market - phrases like "special offer" are more common. An example of a fully integrated, long-term, large-scale promotion are My Coke Rewards and Pepsi Stuff.

ADVERTISING

Advertising is a form of communication intended to persuade an audience to purchase or take some action upon products, ideals, or services. It includes the name of a product or service and how that product or service could benefit the consumer, to persuade a target market to purchase or to consume that particular brand. These brands are usually paid for or identified through sponsors and viewed via various media. Advertising can also serve to communicate an idea to a large number of people in an attempt to convince them to take a certain action.

Commercial advertisers often seek to generate increased consumption of their products or services through branding, which involves the repetition of an image or product name in an effort to associate related qualities with the brand in the minds of consumers. Non-commercial advertisers that spend money to advertise items other than a consumer product or service include political parties, interest groups, religious organizations and governmental agencies. Nonprofit organizations may rely on free modes of persuasion, such as a public service announcement.

Modern advertising developed with the rise of mass production in the late 19th and early 20th centuries. Mass media can be defined as any media meant to reach a mass amount of people. Different types of media can be used to deliver these messages, including traditional media such as newspapers, magazines, television, radio, outdoor or direct mail; or new media such as websites and text messages. Advertising may be placed by an advertising agency on behalf of a company or other organization.

Industry

In 2007, spending on advertising was estimated at more than $150 billion in the United States and $385 billion worldwide. Internationally, the largest advertising conglomerates are Interpublic, Omnicom, Publicis, and WPP.

Backdrop

Egyptians used papyrus to make sales messages and wall posters. Commercial messages and political campaign displays have been found in the ruins of Pompeii and ancient Arabia. Lost and found advertising on papyrus was common in Ancient Greece and Ancient Rome. Wall or rock painting for commercial advertising is another manifestation of an ancient advertising form, which is present to this day in many parts of Asia, Africa, and South America. The tradition of wall painting can be traced back to Indian rock art paintings that date back to 4000 BC. History tells us that Out-of-home advertising and billboards are the oldest forms of advertising.

As the towns and cities of the Middle Ages began to grow, and the general populace was unable to read, signs that today would say cobbler, miller, tailor or blacksmith would use an image associated with their trade such as a boot, a suit, a hat, a clock, a diamond, a horse shoe, a candle or even a bag of flour. Fruits and vegetables were sold in the city square from the backs of carts and wagons and their proprietors used street callers to announce their whereabouts for the convenience of the customers. As education became an apparent need and reading, as well as printing, developed advertising expanded to include handbills. In the 17th century advertisements started to appear in weekly newspapers in England. These early print advertisements were used mainly to promote books and newspapers, which became increasingly affordable with advances in the printing press; and medicines, which were increasingly sought after as disease ravaged Europe. However, false advertising and so-called "quack" advertisements became a problem, which ushered in the regulation of advertising content.

As the economy expanded during the 19th century, advertising grew alongside. In the United States, the success of this advertising format eventually led to the growth of mail-order advertising.

In June 1836, French newspaper La Presse was the first to include paid advertising in its pages, allowing it to lower its price, extend its readership and increase its profitability and the formula was soon copied by all titles. Around 1840, Volney B. Palmer established a predecessor to advertising agencies in Boston.

Around the same time, in France, Charles-Louis Havas extended the services of his news agency, Havas to include advertisement brokerage, making it the first French group to organize. At first, agencies were brokers for advertisement space in newspapers. N. W. Ayer & Son was the first full-service agency to assume responsibility for advertising content. N.W. Ayer opened in 1869, and was located in Philadelphia.

At the turn of the century, there were few career choices for women in business; however, advertising was one of the few. Since women were responsible for most of the purchasing done in their household, advertisers and agencies recognized the value of women's insight during the creative process. In fact, the first American advertising to use a sexual sell was created by a woman – for a soap product. Although tame by today's standards, the advertisement featured a couple with the message "The skin you love to touch".

In the early 1920s, the first radio stations were established by radio equipment manufacturers and retailers who offered programmes in order to sell more radios to consumers. As time passed, many non-profit organizations followed suit in setting up their own radio stations, and included: schools, clubs and civic groups. When the practice of sponsoring programmes was popularised, each individual radio programme was usually sponsored by a single business in exchange for a brief mention of the business' name at the beginning and end of the sponsored shows. However, radio station owners soon realised they could earn more money by selling sponsorship rights in small time allocations to multiple businesses throughout their radio station's broadcasts, rather than selling the sponsorship rights to single businesses per show.

This practice was carried over to television in the late 1940s and early 1950s. A fierce battle was fought between those seeking to commercialise the radio and people who argued that the radio spectrum should be considered a part of the commons – to be used only non-commercially and for the public good. The United Kingdom pursued a public funding model for the BBC, originally a private company, the British Broadcasting Company, but incorporated as a public body by Royal Charter in 1927.

In Canada, advocates like Graham Spry were likewise able to persuade the federal government to adopt a public funding model, creating the Canadian Broadcasting Corporation. However, in the United States, the capitalist model prevailed with the passage of the Communications Act of 1934 which created the Federal Commu-nications Commission. To placate the socialists, the U.S. Congress did require commercial broadcasters to operate in the "public interest, convenience, and necessity". Public broadcasting now exists in the United States due to the 1967 Public Broadcasting Act which led to the Public Broadcasting Service and National Public Radio.

In the early 1950s, the DuMont Television Network began the modern practice of selling advertisement time to multiple sponsors. Previously, DuMont had trouble finding sponsors for many of their programmes and compensated by selling smaller blocks of advertising time to several businesses. This eventually became the standard for the commercial television industry in the United States. However, it was still a common practice to have single sponsor shows, such as The United States Steel Hour. In some instances the sponsors exercised great control over the content of the show—up to and including having one's advertising agency actually writing the show. The single sponsor model is much less prevalent now, a notable exception being the Hallmark Hall of Fame.

The 1960s saw advertising transform into a modern approach in which creativity was allowed to shine, producing unexpected messages that made advertisements more tempting to consumers' eyes. The Volkswagen ad campaign—featuring such headlines as "Think Small" and "Lemon"—ushered in the era of modern advertising by promoting a "position" or "unique selling proposition" designed to associate each brand with a specific idea in the reader or viewer's mind. This period of American advertising is called the Creative Revolution and its archetype was William Bernbach who helped create the revolutionary Volkswagen ads among others. Some of the most creative and long-standing American advertising dates to this period.

The late 1980s and early 1990s saw the introduction of cable television and particularly MTV. Pioneering the concept of the music video, MTV ushered in a new type of advertising: the consumer tunes in for the advertising message, rather than it being a by-product or afterthought. As cable and satellite television became increasingly prevalent, specialty channels emerged, including channels entirely devoted to advertising, such as QVC, Home

Shopping Network, and ShopTV Canada. Marketing through the Internet opened new frontiers for advertisers and contributed to the "dot-com" boom of the 1990s. Entire corporations operated solely on advertising revenue, offering everything from coupons to free Internet access. At the turn of the 21st century, a number of websites including the search engine Google, started a change in online advertising by emphasizing contextually relevant, unobtrusive ads intended to help, rather than inundate, users. This has led to a plethora of similar efforts and an increasing trend of interactive advertising.

The share of advertising spending relative to GDP has changed little across large changes in media. For example, in the US in 1925, the main advertising media were newspapers, magazines, signs on streetcars, and outdoor posters. Advertising spending as a share of GDP was about 2.9 per cent. By 1998, television and radio had become major advertising media. Nonetheless, advertising spending as a share of GDP was slightly lower—about 2.4 per cent.

A recent advertising innovation is "guerrilla marketing", which involve unusual approaches such as staged encounters in public places, giveaways of products such as cars that are covered with brand messages, and interactive advertising where the viewer can respond to become part of the advertising message.Guerrilla advertising is becoming increasing more popular with a lot of companies. This type of advertising is unpredictable and innovative, which causes consumers to buy the product or idea. This reflects an increasing trend of interactive and "embedded" ads, such as via product placement, having consumers vote through text messages, and various innovations utilizing social network services such as Facebook.

Public Service Advertising

The same advertising techniques used to promote commercial goods and services can be used to inform, educate and motivate the public about non-commercial issues, such as HIV/AIDS, political ideology, energy conservation and deforestation. Advertising, in its non-commercial guise, is a powerful educational tool capable of reaching and motivating large audiences. "Advertising justifies its existence when used in the public interest—it is much too powerful a tool to use solely for commercial purposes." Attributed to Howard Gossage by David Ogilvy.

Public service advertising, non-commercial advertising, public interest advertising, cause marketing, and social marketing are different terms for the use of sophisticated advertising and marketing communications techniques on behalf of non-commercial, public interest issues and initiatives. In the United States, the granting of television and radio licenses by the FCC is contingent upon the station broadcasting a certain amount of public service advertising. To meet these requirements, many broadcast stations in America air the bulk of their required public service announcements during the late night or early morning when the smallest percentage of viewers are watching, leaving more day and prime time commercial slots available for high-paying advertisers. Public service advertising reached its height during World Wars I and II under the direction of more than one government.

Marketing Mix

The marketing mix has been the key concept to advertising. The marketing mix was suggested by Jeremy McCarthy, professor at Harvard Business School, in the 1960s. The marketing mix consists of four basic elements called the four P's Product is the first P representing the actual product. Price represents the process of determining the value of a product. Place represents the variables of getting the product to the consumer like distribution channels, market coverage and movement organization. The last P stands for Promotion which is the process of reaching the target market and convincing them to go out and buy the product.Geana, Mugur Valentin.

Types of Advertising

Virtually any medium can be used for advertising. Commercial advertising media can include wall paintings, billboards, street furniture components, printed flyers and rack cards, radio, cinema and television adverts, web banners, mobile telephone screens, shopping carts, web popups, skywriting, bus stop benches, human billboards, magazines, newspapers, town criers, sides of buses, banners attached to or sides of airplanes, in-flight advertisements on seatback tray tables or overhead storage bins, taxicab doors, roof mounts and passenger screens, musical stage shows, subway platforms and trains, elastic bands on disposable diapers,doors of bathroom stalls,stickers on apples in supermarkets, shopping cart handles the opening part of streaming audio and video, posters, and the backs of event tickets and supermarket receipts. Any place an "identified" sponsor pays to deliver their message through a medium is advertising.

Digital Advertising

Television Advertising/Music in Advertising

The TV commercial is generally considered the most effective mass-market advertising format, as is reflected by the high prices TV networks charge for commercial airtime during popular TV events. The annual Super Bowl football game in the United States is known as the most prominent advertising event on television. The average cost of a single thirty-second TV spot during this game has reached US$3 million. The majority of television commercials feature a song or jingle that listeners soon relate to the product.

Virtual advertisements may be inserted into regular television programming through computer graphics. It is typically inserted into otherwise blank backdrops or used to replace local billboards that are not relevant to the remote broadcast audience. More controversially, virtual billboards may be inserted into the background where none exist in real-life. This technique is especially used in televised sporting events Virtual product placement is also possible.; Infomercials: An infomercial is a long-format television commercial, typically five minutes or longer. The word "infomercial" combining the words "information" & "commercial". The main objective in an infomercial is to create an impulse purchase, so that the consumer sees the presentation and then immediately buys the product through the advertised toll-free telephone number or website. Infomercials describe, display, and often demonstrate products and their features, and commonly have testimonials from consumers and industry professionals.

Radio Advertising

Radio advertising is a form of advertising via the medium of radio. Radio advertisements are broadcast as radio waves to the air from a transmitter to an antenna and a thus to a receiving device. Airtime is purchased from a station or network in exchange for airing the commercials. While radio has the obvious limitation of being restricted to sound, proponents of radio advertising often cite this as an advantage.

Online Advertising

Online advertising is a form of promotion that uses the Internet and World Wide Web for the expressed purpose of delivering marketing messages to attract customers. Examples of online advertising include contextual ads that appear on search engine results pages, banner ads, in text ads, Rich Media Ads, Social network advertising, online classified advertising, advertising networks and e-mail marketing, including e-mail spam.

Product Placements

Covert advertising, also known as guerrilla advertising, is when a product or brand is embedded in entertainment and media. For example, in a film, the main character can use an item or other of a definite brand, as in the movie Minority Report, where Tom Cruise's character John Anderton owns a phone with the Nokia logo clearly written in the top corner, or his watch engraved with the Bulgari logo.

Another example of advertising in film is in I, Robot, where main character played by Will Smith mentions his Converse shoes several times, calling them "classics," because the film is set far in the future. I, Robot and Spaceballs also showcase futuristic cars with the Audi and Mercedes-Benz logos clearly displayed on the front of the vehicles. Cadillac chose to advertise in the movie The Matrix Reloaded, which as a result contained many scenes in which Cadillac cars were used. Similarly, product placement for Omega Watches,

Ford, VAIO, BMW and Aston Martin cars are featured in recent James Bond films, most notably Casino Royale. In "Fantastic Four: Rise of the Silver Surfer", the main transport vehicle shows a large Dodge logo on the front. Blade Runner includes some of the most obvious product placement; the whole film stops to show a Coca-Cola billboard.

Physical Advertising

Press Advertising

Press advertising describes advertising in a printed medium such as a newspaper, magazine, or trade journal. This encompasses everything from media with a very broad readership base, such as a major national newspaper or magazine, to more narrowly targeted media such as local newspapers and trade journals on very specialized topics. A form of press advertising is classified advertising, which allows private individuals or companies to purchase a small, narrowly targeted ad for a low fee advertising a product or service. Another form of press advertising is the Display Ad, which is a larger ad that typically run in an object part of a newspaper.

Billboard advertising: Billboards are large structures located in public places which display advertisements to passing pedestrians and motorists. Most often, they are located on main roads with a large amount of passing motor and pedestrian traffic; however, they can be placed in any location with large amounts of viewers, such as on mass transit vehicles and in stations, in shopping malls or office buildings, and in stadiums.

Mobile Billboard Advertising

Mobile billboards are generally vehicle mounted billboards or digital screens. These can be on dedicated vehicles built solely for carrying advertisements along routes preselected by clients, they can also be specially equipped cargo trucks or, in some cases, large banners strewn from planes. The billboards are often lighted; some being backlit, and others employing spotlights. Some billboard displays are static, while others change; for example, continuously or periodically rotating among a set of advertisements. Mobile displays are used for various situations in metropolitan areas throughout the world, including: Target advertising, One-day, and long-term campaigns, Conventions, Sporting events, Store openings and similar promotional events, and Big advertisements from smaller companies.

In-store Advertising

In-store advertising is any advertisement placed in a retail store. It includes placement of a product in visible locations in a store, such as at eye level, at the ends of aisles and near checkout counters, eye-catching displays promoting a specific product, and advertisements in such places as shopping carts and in-store video displays.

Celebrity Branding

This type of advertising focuses upon using celebrity power, fame, money, popularity to gain recognition for their products and promote specific stores or products. Advertisers often advertise their products, for example, when celebrities share their favourite products or wear clothes by specific brands or designers. Celebrities are often involved in advertising campaigns such as television or print adverts to advertise specific or general products. The use of celebrities to endorse a brand can have its downsides, however. One mistake by a celebrity can be detrimental to the public relations of a brand. For example, following his performance of eight gold medals at the 2008 Olympic Games in Beijing, China, swimmer Michael Phelps' contract with Kellogg's was terminated, as Kellogg's did not want to associate with him after he was photographed smoking marijuana.

Sales Promotions

Sales promotions are another way to advertise. Sales promotions are double purposed because they are used to gather information about what type of customers you draw in and where they are, and to jumpstart sales. Sales promotions include things like contests and games, sweepstakes, product giveaways, samples coupons, loyalty programmes, and discounts. The ultimate goal of sales promotions is to stimulate potential customers to action.

Media and Advertising Approaches

Increasingly, other media are overtaking many of the "traditional" media such as television, radio and newspaper because of a shift towards consumer's usage of the Internet for news and music as well as devices like digital video recorders such as TiVo.

Advertising on the World Wide Web is a recent phenomenon. Prices of Web-based advertising space are dependent on the "relevance" of the surrounding web content and the traffic that the website receives.

Digital signage is poised to become a major mass media because of its ability to reach larger audiences for less money. Digital signage also offer the unique ability to see the target audience where they are reached by the medium. Technology advances has also made it possible to control the message on digital signage with much precision, enabling the messages to be relevant to the target audience at any given time and location which in turn, gets more response from the advertising. Digital signage is being successfully employed in supermarkets. Another successful use of digital signage is in hospitality locations such as restaurants. and malls.

E-mail advertising is another recent phenomenon. Unsolicited bulk E-mail advertising is known as "e-mail spam". Spam has been a problem for e-mail users for many years. Some companies have proposed placing messages or corporate logos on the side of booster rockets and the International Space

Station. Controversy exists on the effectiveness of subliminal advertising and the pervasiveness of mass messages. Unpaid advertising can provide good exposure at minimal cost. Personal recommendations, spreading buzz, or achieving the feat of equating a brand with a common noun— these can be seen as the pinnacle of any advertising campaign. However, some companies oppose the use of their brand name to label an object. Equating a brand with a common noun also risks turning that brand into a genericized trademark - turning it into a generic term which means that its legal protection as a trademark is lost.

As the mobile phone became a new mass media in 1998 when the first paid downloadable content appeared on mobile phones in Finland, it was only a matter of time until mobile advertising followed, also first launched in Finland in 2000. By 2007 the value of mobile advertising had reached $2.2 billion and providers such as Admob delivered billions of mobile ads.

More advanced mobile ads include banner ads, coupons, Multimedia Messaging Service picture and video messages, advergames and various engagement marketing campaigns. A particular feature driving mobile ads is the 2D Barcode, which replaces the need to do any typing of web addresses, and uses the camera feature of modern phones to gain immediate access to web content. 83 per cent of Japanese mobile phone users already are active users of 2D barcodes. A new form of advertising that is growing rapidly is social network advertising. It is online advertising with a focus on social networking sites. This is a relatively immature market, but it has shown a lot of promise as advertisers are able to take advantage of the demographic information the user has provided to the social networking site. Friendertising is a more precise advertising term in which people are able to direct advertisements towards others directly using social network service.

From time to time, The CW Television Network airs short programming breaks called "Content Wraps," to advertise one company's product during an entire commercial break. The CW pioneered "content wraps" and some products featured were Herbal Essences, Crest, Guitar Hero II, CoverGirl, and recently Toyota.

Recently, there appeared a new promotion concept, "ARvertising", advertising on Augmented Reality technology.

Current Trends

Rise in New Media

With the dawn of the Internet came many new advertising opportunities. Popup, Flash, banner, Popunder, advergaming, and e-mail advertisements are now commonplace. Particularly since the rise of "entertaining" advertising, some people may like an advertisement enough to wish to watch it later or show a friend. In general, the advertising community has not yet made this easy, although some have used the Internet to widely distribute their ads to anyone willing to see or hear them. In the last three quarters of 2009 mobile and internet advertising grew by 18.1% and 9.2% respectively. Older media advertising saw declines: "10.1% (TV), "11.7% (radio), "14.8% (magazines) and "18.7% (newspapers).

Niche Marketing

Another significant trend regarding future of advertising is the growing importance of the niche market using niche or targeted ads. Also brought about by the Internet and the theory of The Long Tail, advertisers will have an increasing ability to reach specific audiences. In the past, the most efficient way to deliver a message was to blanket the largest mass market audience possible.

However, usage tracking, customer profiles and the growing popularity of niche content brought about by everything from blogs to social networking sites, provide advertisers with audiences that are smaller but much better defined, leading to ads that are more relevant to viewers and more effective for companies' marketing products. Among others, Comcast Spotlight is one such advertiser employing this method in their video on demand menus. These advertisements are targeted to a specific group and can be viewed by anyone wishing to find out more about a particular business or practice at any time, right from their home. This causes the viewer to become proactive and actually choose what advertisements they want to view.

Crowdsourcing

The concept of crowdsourcing has given way to the trend of user-generated advertisements. User-generated ads are created by consumers as opposed to an advertising agency or the company themselves, most often they are a result of brand sponsored advertising competitions.

For the 2007 Super Bowl, the Frito-Lays division of PepsiCo held the Crash the Super Bowl contest, allowing consumers to create their own Doritos commercial. Chevrolet held a similar competition for their Tahoe line of SUVs. Due to the success of the Doritos user-generated ads in the 2007 Super Bowl, Frito-Lays relaunched the competition for the 2009 and 2010 Super Bowl. The resulting ads were among the most-watched and most-liked Super Bowl ads. In fact, the winning ad that aired in the 2009 Super Bowl was ranked by the USA Today Super Bowl Ad Metre as the top ad for the year while the winning ads that aired in the 2010 Super Bowl were found by Nielsen's BuzzMetrics to be the "most buzzed-about".

This trend has given rise to several online platforms that host user-generated advertising competitions on behalf of a company. Founded in 2007, Zooppa has launched ad competitions for brands such as Google, Nike, Hershey's, General Mills, Microsoft, NBC Universal, Zinio, and Mini Cooper. Crowdsourced advertisements have gained popularity in part to its cost effective nature, high consumer engagement, and ability to generate word-of-mouth. However, it remains controversial, as the long-term impact on the advertising industry is still unclear.

Global Advertising

Advertising has gone through five major stages of development: domestic, export, international, multi-national, and global. For global advertisers, there are four, potentially competing, business objectives that must be balanced when developing worldwide advertising: building a brand while speaking with one voice, developing economies of scale in the creative process, maximising local effectiveness of ads, and increasing the company's speed of implementation.

Born from the evolutionary stages of global marketing are the three primary and fundamentally different approaches to the development of global advertising executions: exporting executions, producing local executions, and importing ideas that travel. Advertising research is key to determining the success of an ad in any country or region. The ability to identify which elements and/or moments of an ad that contributes to its success is how economies of scale are maximised. Once one knows what works in an ad, that idea or ideas can be imported by any other market. Market research measures, such as Flow of Attention, Flow of Emotion and branding moments provide insight into what is working in an ad in any country or region because the measures are based on the visual, not verbal, elements of the ad.

Diversification

In the realm of advertising agencies, continued industry diversification has seen observers note that "big global clients don't need big global agencies any more". This is reflected by the growth of non-traditional agencies in various global markets, such as Canadian business TAXI and SMART in Australia and has been referred to as "a revolution in the ad world".

New Technology

The ability to record shows on digital video recorders allow users to record the programmes for later viewing, enabling them to fast forward through commercials. Additionally, as more seasons of pre-recorded box sets are offered for sale of television programmes; fewer people watch the shows on TV. However, the fact that these sets are sold, means the company will receive additional profits from the sales of these sets. To counter this effect, many advertisers have opted for product placement on TV shows like Survivor.

Advertising Education

Advertising education has become widely popular with bachelor, master and doctorate degrees becoming available in the emphasis. A surge in advertising interest is typically attributed to the strong relationship advertising plays in cultural and technological changes, such as the advance of online social networking. A unique model for teaching advertising is the student-run advertising agency, where advertising students create campaigns for real companies. Organizations such as American Advertising Federation and AdU Network partner established companies with students to create these campaigns.

Criticisms

While advertising can be seen as necessary for economic growth, it is not without social costs. Unsolicited Commercial E-mail and other forms of spam have become so prevalent as to have become a major nuisance to users of these services, as well as being a financial burden on internet service providers. Advertising is increasingly invading public spaces, such as schools, which some critics argue is a form of child exploitation. In addition, advertising frequently uses psychological pressure on the intended consumer, which may be harmful.

Regulation

In the US many communities believe that many forms of outdoor advertising blight the public realm. As long ago as the 1960s in the US there were attempts to ban billboard advertising in the open countryside. Cities such as São Paulo have introduced an outright ban with London also having specific legislation to control unlawful displays.

There have been increasing efforts to protect the public interest by regulating the content and the influence of advertising. Some examples are: the ban on television tobacco advertising imposed in many countries, and the total ban of advertising to children under 12 imposed by the Swedish government in 1991. Though that regulation continues in effect for broadcasts originating within the country, it has been weakened by the European Court of Justice, which had found that Sweden was obliged to accept foreign programming, including those from neighbouring countries or via satellite. Greece's regulations are of a similar nature, "banning advertisements for children's toys between 7 am and 10 pm and a total ban on advertisement for war toys".

In Europe and elsewhere, there is a vigourous debate on whether advertising to children should be regulated. This debate was exacerbated by a report released by the Kaiser Family Foundation in February 2004 which suggested fast food advertising that targets children was an important factor in the epidemic of childhood obesity in the United States.

In New Zealand, South Africa, Canada, and many European countries, the advertising industry operates a system of self-regulation. Advertisers, advertising agencies and the media agree on a code of advertising standards that they attempt to uphold. The general aim of such codes is to ensure that any advertising is 'legal, decent, honest and truthful'. Some self-regulatory organizations are funded by the industry, but remain independent, with the intent of upholding the standards or codes like the Advertising Standards Authority in the UK.

In the UK most forms of outdoor advertising such as the display of billboards is regulated by the UK Town and County Planning system. Currently the display of an advertisement without consent from the Planning Authority is a criminal offense liable to a fine of £2,500 per offence. All of the major outdoor billboard companies in the UK have convictions of this nature.

Naturally, many advertisers view governmental regulation or even self-regulation as intrusion of their freedom of speech or a necessary evil. Therefore, they employ a wide-variety of linguistic devices to bypass regulatory laws. The advertisement of controversial products such as cigarettes and condoms are subject to government regulation in many countries. For instance, the tobacco industry is required by law in most countries to display warnings cautioning consumers about the health hazards of their products. Linguistic variation is often used by advertisers as a creative device to reduce the impact of such requirements.

Advertising Research

Advertising research is a specialized form of research that works to improve the effectiveness and efficiency of advertising. It entails numerous forms of research which employ different methodologies. Advertising research includes pre-testing and post-testing of ads and/or campaigns—pre-testing is done before an ad airs to gauge how well it will perform and post-testing is done after an ad airs to determine the in-market impact of the ad or campaign on the consumer. Continuous ad tracking and the Communicus System are competing examples of post-testing advertising research types.

Evidence-based Advertising

Evidence-based advertising refers to advertising principles, which have been proven through experimental studies. They can be applied to an advertising campaign with high confidence of increasing persuasiveness regardless of time and place. Principles are usually accompanied with various conditions, which must be taken into consideration when applying them. According to Professor J. Scott Armstrong from The Wharton School, evidence-based principles "draw upon typical practice, expert opinion, factual evidence and empirical evidence."

UNDERWRITING SPOT

An underwriting spot is an announcement made on public broadcasting outlets, especially in the United States, in exchange for funding. These spots usually mention the name of the sponsor, and can resemble traditional advertising in commercial broadcasting. However, there are legal restrictions, such as a prohibition of making product claims, announcing prices, or providing an incentive to buy a product or service. In the U.S., these restrictions apply to all non-commercial educational stations, and even for non-sponsoring companies and products.

Donors who contribute funding can include corporations, small businesses, philanthropic organizations, charitable trusts, and individuals. Criticism has emerged that these spots are a corrupting influence on the operations of public broadcasting, and introduce the same biases into non-commercial radio and television that allegedly exist on for-profit outlets. These include inhibiting influences on public affairs programmes where investigative journalism is featured and tendencies towards the use of non-artistic criteria in determining the selection of programmes, such as symphony broadcasts on radio and theatrical productions on television.

PBS Policy

The Public Broadcasting Service defines its "Programme Underwriting Policy" in its PBS Redbook.

As of 2007[update] its provisions include the following:

- Underwriters are defined as third parties that voluntarily contribute cash to partially or fully finance the production or acquisition of a programme by a PBS station. Underwriters do not include investment or licensing partners or distribution entities providing cash for other purposes.
- The block of time containing underwriter credits is called the "underwriting credit pod"; it can be no longer than 60 seconds, with no more than 15 seconds allocated per underwriter. If any underwriter is mentioned, then all must be acknowledged.
- Underwriting credit pods must "mirror the production values of the programme and flow smoothly with programme content and other packaging elements."
- Underwriting credit pods must appear at the end of the programme and may appear at the beginning. In news and public affairs programmes, underwriting credits must be included in both places. The end underwriting pod can be either before or after the program's production credits; if an underwriting pod is including in the beginning, it must start within the program's first three minutes and should be placed after the program's opening or tease.
- When PBS partially funds the production, the underwriting credit pod must end with "...from Viewers Like You. Thank you"; when funding is received from the Corporation for Public Broadcasting,

they are credited with a voiceover and a "visual treatment" consisting of the CPB logo, the tag line "a private corporation funded by the American people" and the CPB's website.

Sponsorship underwriting and advertising are essentially the same thing when linked by the exchange of something of value such as cash, goods or services. The underwriter receives a number of informational messages about their business which are broadcast in exchange for a dollar amount. Individuals, Foundations, and nonprofit donors may underwrite programming without the need for an underwriting informational advertising contract. PBS and CPB rules permit underwriting commercial use for broadcast stations with certain speech limits that are only available to broadcast stations because of the nature of the non-profit license.

Cable television does not mention or permit this underwriting use as there are no speech restrictions permitted by cable law. Title 47. U.S.C.. Cable television is pay for play programming purchased by the cable subscriber. Underwriting is found on cable "must carry" PBS stations.

Only Public, Educational, and Governmental cable channels have commercial use restrictions and are created to be free from all underwriting informational messages permitted for PBS channels. Commercial underwriting considerations have limited 1st Amendment protections as the paid underwriting message is bias in nature.

DIRECT MARKETING

Direct marketing is a form of advertising that reaches its audience without using traditional formal channels of advertising, such as TV, newspapers or radio. Businesses communicate straight to the consumer with advertising techniques such as fliers, catalogue distribution, promotional letters, and street advertising.

Direct Advertising is a sub-discipline and type of marketing. There are two main definitional characteristics which distinguish it from other types of marketing. The first is that it sends its message directly to consumers, without the use of intervening commercial communication media. The second characteristic is the core principle of successful Advertising driving a specific "call to action." This aspect of direct marketing involves an emphasis on trackable, measurable, positive responses from consumers regardless of medium.

If the advertisement asks the prospect to take a specific action, for instance call a free phone number or visit a Web site, then the effort is considered to be direct response advertising.

Direct marketing is predominantly used by small to medium-size enterprises with limited advertising budgets that do not have a well-recognized brand message. A well-executed direct advertising campaign can offer a positive return on investment as the message is not hidden with overcomplicated branding. Instead, direct advertising is straight to the point; offers a product, service, or event; and explains how to get the offered product, service, or event.

The term direct marketing is believed to have been first used in 1967 in a speech by Lester Wunderman, who pioneered direct marketing techniques with brands such as American Express and Columbia Records. The term junk mail, referring to unsolicited commercial ads delivered via post office or directly deposited in consumers' mail boxes, can be traced back to 1954. The term spam, meaning "unsolicited commercial e-mail," can be traced back to March 31, 1993, although in its first few months it merely referred to inadvertently posting a message so many times on UseNet that the repetitions effectively drowned out the normal flow of conversation.

Although Wunderman may have been the first to use the term direct marketing, the practice of mail order selling essentially began in the U.S. upon invention of the typewriter in 1867. The first modern mail-order catalog was produced by Aaron Montgomery Ward in 1872. The Direct Mail Advertising Association, predecessor of the present-day Direct Marketing Association, was first established in 1917. Third class bulk mail postage rates were established in 1928. Direct marketing's history in Europe can be traced to the 15th century. Upon Gutenberg's invention of movable type, the first trade catalogs from printer-publishers appeared sometime around 1450.

Benefits and Drawbacks

Direct marketing is attractive to many marketers, because in many cases its positive effect can be measured directly. For example, if a marketer sends out 1,000 solicitations by mail, and 100 respond to the promotion, the marketer can say with confidence that campaign led directly to 10% direct responses. The number of recipients who are offended by junk mail/spam, however, is not easily measured. By contrast, measurement of other media must often be indirect, since there is no direct response from a consumer. Measurement of results, a fundamental element in successful direct marketing.

The Internet has made it easier for marketing managers to measure the results of a campaign. This is often achieved by using a specific Web site landing page directly relating to the promotional material, a call to action will ask the consumer to visit the landing page, and the effectiveness of the campaign can be measured by taking the number of promotional messages distributed and dividing it by the number of responses.

Another way to measure the results is to compare the projected sales for a given term with the actual sales after a direct advertising campaign. While many marketers recognize the financial benefits of increasing targeted awareness, some direct marketing efforts using particular media have been criticized for generating unwanted solicitations, not due to the method of communication but because of poorly compiled demographic databases, advertisers do not wish to waste money on communicating with consumers not interested in their products. For example, direct mail that is irrelevant to the recipient is considered "junk mail," and unwanted e-mail messages are considered "spam."

Some consumers are demanding an end to direct marketing for privacy and environmental reasons, which direct marketers are able to do to some extent by using "opt-out" lists, variable printing, and more-targeted mailing lists. In response to consumer demand and increasing business pressure to increase the effectiveness of reaching the right consumer with direct marketing, companies such as Ireland Advertising specialize in targeted direct advertising to great effect, reducing advertising budget waste and increasing the effectiveness of delivering a marketing message with better geodemography information, delivering the advertising message to only the consumers interested in the product, service, or event on offer.

Channels

Direct Mail

The most common form of direct marketing is direct mail, sometimes called junk mail, used by advertisers who send document mail to all postal customers in an area or to all customers on a list.

Any low-budget medium that can be used to deliver a communication to a customer can be employed in direct marketing. Probably the most commonly used medium for direct marketing is mail, in which marketing communications are sent to customers using the postal service.

The term direct mail is used in the direct marketing industry to refer to communication deliveries by the Post Office, which may also be referred to as "junk mail" or "admail" or "crap mail" and may involve bulk mail.

Junk mail includes advertising circulars, catalogs, free trial CDs, pre-approved credit card applications, and other unsolicited merchandising invitations delivered by mail or to homes and businesses, or delivered to consumers' mailboxes by delivery services other than the Post Office. Bulk mailings are a particularly popular method of promotion for businesses operating in the financial services, home computer, and travel and tourism industries.

In many developed countries, direct mail represents such a significant amount of the total volume of mail that special rate classes have been established. In the United States and United Kingdom, for example, there are bulk mail rates that enable marketers to send mail at rates that are substantially lower than regular first-class rates. In order to qualify for these rates, marketers must format and sort the mail in particular ways – which reduces the handling required by the postal service. Advertisers often refine direct mail practices into targeted mailing, in which mail is sent out following database analysis to select recipients considered most likely to respond positively. For example a person who has demonstrated an interest in golf may receive direct mail for golf related products or perhaps for goods and services that are appropriate for golfers. This use of database analysis is a type of database marketing. The United States Postal Service calls this form of mail "advertising mail".

Telemarketing

Another common form of direct marketing is telemarketing, in which marketers contact consumers by phone. The unpopularity of cold call telemarketing has led some US states and the US federal government to create "no-call lists" and legislation including heavy fines. This process may be outsourced to specialist call centres. In the US, a national do-not-call list went into effect on October 1, 2003. Under the law, it is illegal for telemarketers to call anyone who has registered themselves on the list. After the list had operated for one year, over 62 million people had signed up. The telemarketing industry opposed the creation of the list, but most telemarketers have complied with the law and refrained from calling people who are on the list. Canada has passed legislation to create a similar Do Not Call List. In other countries it is voluntary, such as the New Zealand Name Removal Service.

E-mail Marketing

E-mail Marketing is a third type of direct marketing. A major concern is spam. As a result of the proliferation of mass spamming, ISPs and e-mail service providers have developed increasingly effective E-Mail Filtering programmes. These filters can interfere with the delivery of e-mail marketing campaigns, even if the person has subscribed to receive them, as legitimate e-mail marketing can possess the same hallmarks as spam. There are a range of e-mail service providers that provide services for legitimate opt-in e-mailers to avoid being classified as spam.

Door-to-Door Leaflet Marketing

Leaflet distribution services are used extensively by the fast food industries, and many other business focussing on a local catchment Business to consumer business model, similar to direct mail marketing, this method is targeted purely by area, and costs a fraction of the amount of a mailshot due to not having to purchase stamps, envelopes or having to buy address lists and the names of home occupants.

Broadcast Faxing

A fourth type of direct marketing, broadcast faxing, is now less common than the other forms. This is partly due to laws in the United States and elsewhere which make it illegal.

Voicemail Marketing

A fifth type of direct marketing has emerged out of the market prevalence of personal voice mailboxes, and business voicemail systems. Due to the ubiquity of e-mail marketing, and the expense of direct mail and telemarketing, voicemail marketing presented a cost effective means by which to reach people directly, by voice.

Abuse of consumer marketing applications of voicemail marketing resulted in an abundance of "voice-spam", and prompted many jurisdictions to pass laws regulating consumer voicemail marketing.

More recently, businesses have utilized guided voicemail to accomplish personalized business-to-business marketing formerly reserved for telemarketing. Because guided voicemail is used to contact only businesses, it is exempt from Do Not Call regulations in place for other forms of voicemail marketing.

Couponing

Couponing is used in print media to elicit a response from the reader. An example is a coupon which the reader cuts out and presents to a super-store check-out counter to avail of a discount. Coupons in newspapers and magazines cannot be considered direct marketing, since the marketer incurs the cost of supporting a third-party medium; direct marketing aims to circumvent that balance, paring the costs down to solely delivering their unsolicited sales message to the consumer, without supporting the newspaper that the consumer seeks and welcomes.

Direct-response Television Marketing

Direct marketing on TV has two basic forms: long form and short form, which refers to typical 30-second or 60-second commercials that ask viewers for an immediate response. TV-response marketing—i.e. infomercials—can be considered a form of direct marketing, since responses are in the form of calls to telephone numbers given on-air. This both allows marketers to reasonably conclude that the calls are due to a particular campaign, and allows the marketers to obtain customers' phone numbers as targets for telemarketing. Under the Federal Do-Not-Call List rules in the US, if the caller buys anything, the marketer would be exempt from Do-Not-Call List restrictions for a period of time due to having a prior business relationship with the caller. Firms such as QVC, Thane Direct, and Interwood Marketing Group then cross-sell and up-sell to these respondents. One of the most famous DRTV commercials was for Ginsu Knives by Ginsu Products, Inc. of RI. Several aspects of ad, such as its use of adding items to the offer and the guarantee of satisfaction were much copied and came to be considered part of the formula for success with short-form direct-response TV ads

Direct Selling

Direct selling is the sale of products by face-to-face contact with the customer, either by having salespeople approach potential customers in person, or through indirect means such as Tupperware parties.

Popularity of Direct Advertising

A report produced by the Direct Marketing Association found that 57% of the campaigns studied were employing integrated strategies. Of those, almost half launched with a direct mail campaign, typically followed by e-mail and then telemarketing.

SALES

A sale is the pinnacle activity involved in the selling products or services in return for money or other compensation. It is an act of completion of a commercial activity.

The seller - the provider of the goods or services - completes a sale in response to an acquisition or to an appropriation or to a request. There follows the passing of title in the item, and the application and due settlement of a price, the obligation for which arises due to the seller's requirement to pass ownership. Ideally, a seller agrees upon a price at which he willingly parts with ownership of or any claim upon the item. The purchaser, though a party to the sale, does not execute the sale, only the seller does that. To be precise the sale completes prior to the payment and gives rise to the obligation of payment. If the seller completes the first two stages of the sale prior to settlement of the price, the sale remains valid and gives rise to an obligation to pay.

Sales Techniques

A sale can take place through:

- Direct sales, involving person to person contact
- Pro forma sales
- Agency-based
  - Sales agents
  - Sales outsourcing through direct branded representation
  - Transaction sales
  - Consultative sales
  - Complex sales
  - Consignment
  - Telemarketing or telesales
  - Retail or consumer
- Traveling salesman
  - Door-to-door methods
  - Hawking
- *Request for proposal*: An invitation for suppliers, through a bidding process, to submit a proposal on a specific product or service. An

RFP usually represents part of a complex sales process, also known as "enterprise sales".

- *Business-to-business*: Business-to-business sales are much more relationship-based owing to the lack of emotional attachment to the products in question. Industrial/professional sales involves selling from one business to another
- Electronic
  - *Web*: Business-to-business and business-to-consumer
  - *Electronic Data Interchange*: A set of standard for structuring information to be electronically exchanged between and within businesses
- Indirect, human-mediated but with indirect contact
  - Mail-order
  - Vending machine
- Sales methods:
  - Selling technique
  - IMPACT Selling
  - SPIN Selling
  - Consultative selling
  - Sales enablement
  - Solution selling
  - Conceptual Selling
  - Strategic Selling
  - Transactional Selling
  - Sales Negotiation
  - Reverse Selling
  - Paint-the-Picture
  - The take away

Sales Agents

Agents in the sales process can represent either of two parties in the sales process; for example:

1. *Sales broker or Seller agency or seller agent*: This is a traditional role where the salesman represents a person or company on the selling end of a deal
2. *Buyers broker or Buyer brokerage*: This is where the salesman represents the consumer making the purchase. This is most often applied in large transactions.
3. *Disclosed dual agent*: This is where the salesman represents both parties in the sale and acts as a mediator for the transaction. The role of the salesman here is to oversee that both parties receive an honest and fair deal, and is responsible to both.
4. *Transaction broker*: This is where the salesperson doesn't represent

either party, but handles the transaction only. The seller owes no responsibility to either party getting a fair or honest deal, just that all of the documents are handled properly.

5. Sales outsourcing involves direct branded representation where the sales reps are recruited, hired, and managed by an external entity but hold quotas, represent themselves as the brand of the client, and report all activities back to the client. It is akin to a virtual extension of a sales force.
6. *Sales managers*: Qualified and talented sales managers aim to implement various sales strategies and management techniques in order to facilitate improved profits and increased sales volume. They are also responsible for coordinating the sales and marketing department as well as oversight concerning the fair and honest execution of the sales process by their agents.
7. *Salesmen*: The primary function of professional sales is to generate and close leads, educate prospects, fill needs and satisfy wants of consumers appropriately, and therefore turn prospective customers into actual ones. Questioning - to understand a customer's goal and requirements relevant to the product - and the creation of a valuable solution by communicating the necessary information that encourages a buyer to achieve their goal at an economic cost comprise the functions of the salesperson or of the sales engine. A good salesman should never mis-sell or over-evaluate the customer's requirements.

Inside Sales vs. Outside Sales

Since the advent of the telephone a distinction has been made between "inside sales" and "outside sales", although it is generally agreed that these terms do not have hard-and-fast definitions. In the United States, the Fair Labour Standards Act defines outside sales representatives as "employees sell their employer's products, services, or facilities to customers away from their employer's place(s) of business, in general, either at the customer's place of business or by selling door-to-door at the customer's home" while defining those who work "from the employer's location" as inside sales. Inside sales generally involves attempting to close business primarily over the phone via cold calling or telemarketing, while outside sales will usually involve initial phone work to book sales calls at the potential buyer's location to attempt to close the deal in person. Some companies have an inside sales department that works with outside representatives and book their appointments for them. Inside sales sometimes refers to upselling to existing customers.

The Relationships between Sales and Marketing

Marketing and sales differ greatly, but have the same goal. Marketing improves the selling environment and plays a very important role in sales. If the marketing department generates a list of potential customers, that can benefit sales. A marketing department in an organization has the goal increasing the number of interactions between potential customers and the organization.

Achieving this goal may involve the sales team using promotional techniques such as advertising, sales promotion, publicity, and public relations, creating new sales channels, or creating new products, among other things. It can also include bringing the potential customer to visit the organization's website(s) for more information, or to contact the organization for more information, or to interact with the organization via social media such as Twitter, Facebook and blogs.

The relatively new field of sales process engineering views "sales" as the output of a larger system, not just as the output of one department. The larger system includes many functional areas within an organization. From this perspective, "sales" and "marketing" label for a number of processes whose inputs and outputs supply one another to varying degrees. In this context, improving an "output" involves studying and improving the broader sales process, as in any system, since the component functional areas interact and are interdependent.

Most large corporations structure their marketing departments in a similar fashion to sales departments and the managers of these teams must coordinate efforts in order to drive profits and business success. For example, an "inbound" focused campaign seeks to drive more customers "through the door", giving the sales department a better chance of selling their product to the consumer. A good marketing programme would address any potential downsides as well.

The sales department would aim to improve the interaction between the customer and the sales facility or mechanism and/or salesperson. Sales management would break down the selling process and then increase the effectiveness of the discrete processes as well as the interaction between processes. For example, in many out-bound sales environments, the typical process includes out-bound calling, the sales pitch, handling objections, opportunity identification, and the close. Each step of the process has sales-related issues, skills, and training needs, as well as marketing solutions to improve each discrete step, as well as the whole process.

One further common complication of marketing involves the inability to measure results for a great deal of marketing initiatives. In essence, many marketing and advertising executives often lose sight of the objective of sales/revenue/profit, as they focus on establishing a creative/innovative programme, without concern for the top or bottom lines - a fundamental pitfall of marketing for marketing's sake. Many companies find it challenging to get marketing and sales on the same page. The two departments, although different in nature, handle very similar concepts and have to work together for sales to be successful. Building a good relationship between the two that encourages communication can be the key to success - even in a down economy.

Marketing Potentially Negates the Need for Sales

Some sales authors and consultants contend that an expertly planned and executed marketing strategy may negate the need for outside sales entirely. They suggest that by effectively bringing more customers"through the door" and enticing them into contact, sales organizations can dramatically improve their results, efficiency, profitability, and allow salespeople to provide a drastically higher level of customer service and satisfaction, instead of spending the majority of their working hours searching for someone to sell to.

Industrial Marketing

The idea that marketing can potentially eliminate the need for sales people depends entirely on context. For example, this may be possible in some B2C situations; however, for many B2B transactions this is mostly impossible. Another dimension is the value of the goods being sold. Fast-moving consumer-goods require no sales people at the point of sale to get them to jump off the supermarket shelf and into the customer's trolley. However, the purchase of large mining equipment worth millions of dollars will require a sales person to manage the sales process - particularly in the face of competitors.

Sales and Marketing Alignment and Integration

Another area of discussion involves the need for alignment and integration between corporate sales and marketing functions. According to a report from the Chief Marketing Officer Council, only 40 per cent of companies have formal programmes, systems or processes in place to align and integrate the two critical functions. Traditionally, these two functions have operated separately, left in siloed areas of tactical responsibility. Glen Petersen; The Profit Maximization Paradox sees the changes in the competitive landscape between the 1950s and the time of writing as so dramatic that the complexity of choice, price and opportunities for the customer forced this seemingly simple and integrated relationship between sales and marketing to change forever. Petersen goes on to highlight that salespeople spend approximately 40 per cent of their time preparing customer-facing deliverables while leveraging less than 50 per cent of the materials created by marketing, adding to perceptions that marketing is out of touch with the customer and that sales is resistant to messaging and strategy. Internet applications, commonly referred to as Sales 2.0 tools, have also increasingly been created to help align the goals and responsibilities of marketing and sales departments.

PRODUCT PLACEMENT

Product placement, or embedded marketing, is a form of advertisement, where branded goods or services are placed in a context usually devoid of ads, such as movies, the story line of television shows, or news programmes. The product placement is often not disclosed at the time that the good or service is featured. Product placement became common in the 1980s.

In April 2006, Broadcasting & Cable reported,"Two thirds of advertisers employ'branded entertainment' - product placement - with the vast majority of that in commercial TV programming." The story, based on a survey by the Association of National Advertisers, said"Reasons for using in-show plugs varied from'stronger emotional connection' to better dovetailing with relevant content, to targeting a specific group."

Product placement dates back to the nineteenth century in publishing. By the time Jules Verne published the adventure novel Around the World in Eighty Days he was a world-renowned literary giant to the extent transport and shipping companies lobbied to be mentioned in the story as it was published in serial form; however if he was actually paid to do so remains unknown. Product placement is still used in books to some extent, particularly in novels.

Placement in Movies

Although recognizable brand names probably had appeared in movies prior to the 1920s, the weekly trade periodical Harrison's Reports published its first denunciation of that practice with respect to Red Crown gasoline appearing in the comedy film The Garage, directed by and co-starring Fatty Arbuckle.

During the next four decades, Harrison's Reports frequently cited cases of on-screen brand-name products, always condemning the practice as harmful to movie theaters. Publisher P. S. Harrison's editorials strongly reflected his feelings against product placement in films. An editorial in Harrison's Reports criticized the collaboration between the Corona Typewriter company and First National Pictures when a Corona typewriter appeared in the film The Lost World. Harrison's Reports published several incidents about Corona typewriters appearing in films of the mid-1920s.

Among the famous silent films to feature product placement was Wings, the first film to win the Academy Award for Best Picture. It contained a plug for Hershey's chocolate.

Another early example in film occurs in Horse Feathers where Thelma Todd's character falls out of a canoe and into a river. She calls for a life saver and Groucho Marx's character tosses her a Life Savers candy.

In the film Love Happy, Harpo Marx's character cavorts on a rooftop among various billboards and at one point escapes from the villains on the old Mobil logo, the "Flying Red Horse". Harrison's Reports severely criticized this scene in its film review and in a front-page editorial of the same issue. The film It's a Wonderful Life, directed by Frank Capra, depicts a young boy with aspirations to be an explorer, displaying a prominent copy of National Geographic. In the film noir Gun Crazy, the climactic crime is the payroll robbery of the Armour meat-packing plant, where a Bulova clock is prominently seen.

In other early media, e.g., radio in the 1930s and 1940s and early television in the 1950s, programmes were often underwritten by companies. "Soap operas" are called such because they were initially underwritten by consumer, packaged-goods companies such as Procter & Gamble or Unilever. When television began to displace radio, DuMont's Cavalcade of Stars television show was, in its era, notable for not relying on a sole sponsor in the tradition of NBC's Texaco Star Theater and similar productions. Sponsorship exists today with programmes being sponsored by major vendors such as Hallmark Cards. The conspicuous display of Studebaker motor vehicles in the television series Mr. Ed, which was sponsored by the Studebaker Corporation from 1961 to 1963, is another example of product placement. Incorporation of products into the actual plot of a film or television show is generally called "brand integration".

An early example of such "brand integration" was by Abercrombie & Fitch when one of its stores provided the notional venue for part of the romantic-comedy film Man's Favourite Sport? starring Rock Hudson and Paula Prentiss. A recent example is HBO's Sex and the City, where the plot revolved around, among other things, Absolut Vodka, a campaign upon which one of the protagonists was working, and a billboard in Times Square, where a bottle prevented an image of the model from being pornographic. Knight Rider, a television series featuring a talking Pontiac Trans Am, is another example of brand integration. The earliest example of product placement in a computer or video game occurs in Action Biker for Skips crisps, a product by KP Snacks. Video games, such as Crazy Taxi, feature real retail stores as game destinations. However, sometimes the economics are reversed and video-game makers pay for the rights to use real sports teams and players. Today, product placement in online video is also becoming common. Online agencies are specializing in connecting online video producers, which are usually individuals, with brands and advertisers.

Self Promotion

Twentieth Century Fox, a subsidiary of News Corporation, has promoted its parent company's own Sky News channel through including it as a plot device when characters are viewing news broadcasts of breaking events. The newscaster or reporter in the scene will usually state that the audience is viewing Sky News, and reports from other channels are not shown. One notable example is the film Independence Day.

Sports

Product placement has long been prevalent in sports as well, from professional sports to college sports, and even on the local level with high school sports. This can be attributed to sports being prevalent on television, which increases exposure to these products.

The Green Monster at Fenway Park in Boston, Massachusetts, was originally built to have such advertisements, but since 1947 has largely been devoid of such advertisements. The Citgo sign overlooking Fenway Park can also be considered a form of product placement, despite the Boston Red Sox having a sponsorship deal with Gulf Oil.

Outside of baseball product placement in sports began to rise in the 1970s, when NASCAR began to allow sponsors to cover the cars they were sponsoring with their logos. This has subsequently followed with the uniforms the drivers themselves wear having sponsor logos. The Arena Football League, NFL Europe, and several association football leagues eventually allowed sponsors of the uniforms. The National Hockey League began allowing sponsors to line along the interior walls of the ice rinks in the early 1980s. This, combined with new rules mandating players to wear helmets, arguably gave the NHL a different look in the 1980s than compared with the 1970s.

NFL

While the now-defunct NFL Europe allowed liberal use of sponsors with the team's uniforms, the main National Football League has long been more stringent. For instance, the league prohibits logos of sponsors painted onto the fields, although Gillette Stadium in Foxborough, Massachusetts, does have a disposable razor painted onto the field in honour of naming-rights sponsor Gillette. In 2008, the league allowed sponsors on the practice jerseys of the uniforms, but not the game-worn uniforms.

The NFL's strict policy contradicts several other policies on the uniforms. In 1991, the league allowed the individual uniform suppliers to display their logo on the products they made in conjunction with the rest of the sports world, and since 2002, Reebok has been the official uniform supplier for the entire league. In addition, two of the league's flagship teams — the Green Bay Packers and the Pittsburgh Steelers — adopted some form of their identity from corporate sponsors. The Packers adopted the nickname "Packers" because they were sponsored by the Indian Packing Company, and later had "ACME PACKERS" written on their uniforms in the early 1920s after the Acme Packing Company bought Indian Packing.

The Steelers adopted their current logo in 1962 as a product-placement deal with the American Iron and Steel Institute, which owned the rights to the Steelmark logo. The Steelers later were allowed to add "-ers" to the Steelmark logo the following year so that they could own a trademark on the logo.

Categories and Variations

Actual product placement falls into two categories: products or locations that are obtained from manufacturers or owners to reduce the cost of production, and products deliberately placed into productions in exchange for fees.

Sometimes, product usage is negotiated rather than paid for. Some placements provide productions with below-the-line savings, with products such as props, clothes and cars being loaned for the production's use, thereby saving them purchase or rental fees. Barter systems and service deals are also common practices. Producers may also seek out companies for product placements as another savings or revenue stream for the movie, with, for example, products used in exchange for help funding advertisements tied-in with a film's release, a show's new season or other event.

A variant of product placement is advertisement placement. In this case an advertisement for the product is seen in the movie or television series. Examples include a Lucky Strike cigarette advertisement on a billboard or a truck with a milk advertisement on its trailer.

Another variant is the widespread use of promotional consideration in which a television game show would award an advertiser's product as a prize or consolation prize in return for a subsidy from the product's manufacturer.

Product-placement companies work to integrate their client company brands with film and television productions. Jay May, president of Feature This!, a branded entertainment company, explains the process: "The studio sends us the script. We break it down. We look for our clients' demographics and then we tell our client this movie is available with this actor, with this director, with this producer, do you want it?"

Measuring Effectiveness

Quantification methods track brand integrations, with both basic quantitative and more demonstrative qualitative systems used to determine the cost and effective media value of a placement. Rating systems measure the type of placement and on-screen exposure is gauged by audience recall rates. Products might be featured but hardly identifiable, clearly identifiable, long or recurrent in exposure, associated with a main character, verbally mentioned and/or they may play a key role in the storyline. Media values are also weighed over time, depending on a specific product's degree of presence in the market.

Consumer Response and Economic Impact

As with any advertising, its effectiveness tends to be assumed because advertisers continue to use product placement as a marketing strategy. However, some consumer groups such as Commercial Alert object to the practice as "an affront to basic honesty" that they claim is too common in today's society. Commercial Alert asks for full disclosure of all product-placement arrangements, arguing that most product placements are deceptive and not clearly disclosed. It advocates notification before and during television programmes with embedded advertisements. One justification for this is to allow greater parental control for children, whom it claims are easily influenced by product placement.

The Writers Guild of America, a trade union representing authors of television scripts, had raised objections in 2005 that its members are forced to write ad copy disguised as storyline on the grounds that "the result is that tens of millions of viewers are sometimes being sold products without their knowledge, sold in opaque, subliminal ways and sold in violation of government regulations."

According to PQMedia, a consulting firm that tracks the product-placement market, 2006 product placement was estimated at $3.1 billion rising to $5.6 billion in 2010. However, these figures are somewhat misleading in PQMedia's view in that today, many product-placement and brand-integration deals are a combination of advertising and product placement.

In these deals, the product placement is often contingent upon the purchase of advertising revenues. When the product placement that is bundled with advertising is allocated to part of the spending, PQMedia estimates that product placement is closer to $7 billion in value, rising to $10 billion by 2010.

A major driver of growth for the use of product placement is the increasing use of digital video recorders such as TiVO, which enable viewers to skip advertisements. This ad-skipping behaviour increases in frequency the longer a household has owned a DVR.

Radio, Television and Publishing

Reality Television

Product-placement advertisements can be common in reality television shows. For example the well-known Russian television show Dom-2 often features one of the participants stating something along the lines of: "Oh, did you check out the new product X by company Y yet?" after which the camera zooms in onto the named product. It has been claimed that the participants get paid for it. Recently in the United States series The Real World Road Rules Challenge participants often state a similar line, usually pertaining to the mobile device and carrier a text message has been received. "Extreme Makeover has several sponsors with prominent placement deals: Sears, Ford and Pella Windows to name three. Seeing the designers go off to Sears every episode and deck out the house with Kenmore appliances, is not just a sponsorship, it's integral to the subject family getting their lives back.".

Public and Educational Television

In the United States, most educational television operates under a funding model in which local stations receive donations from "Viewers Like You" but do not interrupt programming directly with spot advertising. While the use of underwriting as a form of indirect advertisement is permissible and common on non-commercial educational stations, price comparisons or calls to action of the form used by commercial television are expressly prohibited as a condition of the station's license.

It may therefore make good business sense for an underwriter of an educational programme to obtain greater visibility through a form of promotional consideration in which a manufacturer of woodworking tools could, instead of merely donating money to fund production of a popular home-improvement show, go one step further by also providing the tools used on-air to build the individual projects.

This approach is suitable both for commercial and non-commercial television, but requires very careful targeting to match a product to a show that naturally would already use that product. A programme-like commercial The Learning Channel's Trading Spaces is an ideal fit for a vendor such as Home Depot. Non-commercial broadcasts such as PBS's The New Yankee Workshop would represent an ideal fit for power tool makers Porter-Cable, Delta Machinery and Vermont-American while a programme like The Red Green Show could represent an once-in-a-lifetime opportunity for a manufacturer of duct tape.

One unusual placement is American Public Television's Classical Stretch, a long-running series of physical fitness sessions hosted by Montréal's Miranda Esmonde-White with the first three seasons distributed by New York PBS flagship station WPBS-TV. As the market for physical-fitness advice is largely saturated, Classical Stretch endeavours to differentiate itself from the many existing programmes in its genre by having everything take place outdoors, on a tropical beach, with unobtrusive classical music in the background. In theory, this could prohibitively increase a non-commercial program's production costs; in reality, the costs of relocating production and constructing necessary facilities are readily borne by the show's underwriters, a travel company and a luxury resort in Riviera Maya, Mexico.

Television Programmes

List of television shows with the most instances of product placement:

- *The Biggest Loser*: 6,248
- *American Idol*: 4,636
- *Extreme Makeover*: Home Edition — 3,371
- *America's Toughest Jobs*: 2,807
- *One Tree Hill*: 2,575
- *Deal or No Deal*: 2,292
- *America's Next Top Model*: 2,241
- *Last Comic Standing*: 1,993

- *Kitchen Nightmares*: 1,853
- *Hell's Kitchen*: 1,807

Advertiser-produced Programming

In 2010 Wal-Mart teamed with Procter & Gamble to produce Secrets of the Mountain and The Jensen Project, both family-oriented, television films which feature the characters using Wal-Mart and Procter & Gamble- branded products. The Jensen Project also features a preview of a not-then-released Kinect, a computing input device.

Comic Publishing

South African football comic Supa Strikas uses product placement within its pages to promote a variety of brands, and allow for the comic's free distribution to its readers around the world. Product placement occurs throughout the publication; on the players' shirts, through placed billboards and signage, and through the branding of locations or scenarios. Globally, Supa Strikas receives the majority of its support from Chevron, which sponsors the comic series through its Caltex and Texaco brands. These brands are displayed as the shirt sponsors for the Supa Strikas team across Southern Africa, Central America, Egypt and Malaysia.

In other markets — where Chevron lacks a presence — other headline brands sponsor the team's kit, including Visa in Kenya, Uganda and Tanzania; GTBank in Nigeria; and Henkel's Loctite brand in Brazil. In addition, other brands also receive advertising in the comics and animation, with their logos included as both billboard and background advertising, and through the branding of locations and scenarios. These companies include Metropolitan Life, Nike, Spur Steak Ranches and the South African National Roads Agency, among others.

This innovative approach to comic publication has seen the brand grow dramatically over the last few years, with Supa Strikas now reaching an estimated ten million readers a week worldwide. Today, the comic is available across Africa Botswana, Cameroon, Egypt, Ghana, Kenya, Mauritius, Namibia, Nigeria, Reunion, South Africa, Tanzania, Uganda and Zambia; in Latin America Brazil, Colombia, El Salvador, Guatemala, Honduras and Panama; in Europe Finland, Norway and Sweden; and Asia Malaysia.

The Supa Strikas model has shown considerable successes, leading to the creation of a number of other titles which use the same system. These include cricket comic Supa Tigers, which is distributed in India and Pakistan, and Strike Zone, a baseball comic based in Panama.

Music and Recording Industries

While radio and television stations are at least in theory strictly regulated by national governments, producers of printed or recorded works are not, leading marketers in some cases to attempt to get advertisers' brands mentioned in lyrics of popular songs. A recent popularity of product placement in music videos and actual song lyrics can be accredited to The Kluger Agency. Due to the repetitive nature of a popular song and its effects on pop culture as a whole, Product Placement or what the music industry calls "Brand Partnerships" are becoming a more effective way to create a trend practically overnight.

In January 2009, an album Migra Corridos with five songs including accordion ballad "El Mas Grande Enemigo" had received airplay on twenty-five Mexican radio stations. The tune purports to be the lament of a would-be immigrant left to die in the Arizona desert by coyotes. No disclosure was made to the radio stations that the U.S. Border Patrol had commissioned the compact disc with content devised by Elevación, a Hispanic advertising agency based in Washington, D.C. and New York City.

Payola and Legal Considerations

Much of the current body of broadcast law pertaining to the obligation of licensed broadcasters to disclose to audiences when they receive money or valuables in return for on-air promotion of a product dates to the payola scandals of 1950s broadcast radio.

An investigation launched in November 1959 into allegations that some radio disc jockeys had accepted bribes in return for radio airplay led to the indictment of disc jockey Alan Freed on May 9, 1960; he would be fined for accepting $2,500 to play certain songs, a violation of commercial bribery laws, and would ultimately lose his employment in commercial radio. On September 13, 1960, the U.S. government acted to ban payola in broadcasting.

Under current U.S. law, Section 317 of the Communications Act states that "All matter broadcast by any radio station for which money, service, or other valuable consideration is directly or indirectly paid, or promised to or charged or accepted by, the station so broadcasting, from any person, shall, at the time the same is so broadcast, be announced as paid for or furnished, as the case may be, by such person. With similar and related provisions reflected in Federal Communications Commission regulations as CFR 47, Section 73.1212.

While these provisions have been taken into legal consideration in subsequent payola investigations, including one 2005 investigation by New York State Attorney General Eliot Spitzer into Sony BMG and other major record companies, it is probable that a regulation requiring advertisements and advertisers to be clearly identified has far broader implications in many areas, including that of the use of product placement by advertisers in broadcast programming.

Often, a broadcaster will claim to have complied with the regulation by placing some form of acknowledgement of promotional consideration in an inconspicuous place in a broadcast - such as embedded within a portion of a programme's closing credits. The question of whether adequate disclosure is being provided, however, remains open; the issue was raised in 2005 by FCC commissioner Jonathan Adelstein, on the grounds that "some will tell you that if broadcasters and cable companies insist on further commercialising new and other shows alike, that is their business. But if they do so without disclosing it to the viewing public, that is payola, and that is the FCC's business." In 2008, the Federal Communications Commission gave notice of proposed rulemaking, in which it proposed to require more disclosure of product placement. According to Adelstein, "You shouldn't need a magnifying glass to know who's pitching you... A crawl at the end of the show shrunk down so small the human eye can't read it isn't really in the spirit of the law."

Within the United Kingdom, product placement is currently banned. A recent EU directive would have allowed it, however culture secretary Andy Burnham refused to accept it, and for a time it appeared likely that the UK would introduce laws to fully outlaw it, whereas in the past it was only regulated by OFCOM. However in September 2009 it was announced that the OFCOM ban would be lifted in an effort to raise funds for commercial broadcasters, but will remain in force in children's TV and on the BBC. This news has been greeted with enthusiasm by British media companies like Independent Vision who are looking to further enhance the current business model for Advertiser Funded Programming.

Product Displacement

According to Danny Boyle, director of film Slumdog Millionaire the makers had to resort to something he calls "product displacement" when companies such as Mercedes-Benz refused to allow their products to be used in non-flattering settings. While they did not mind having a gangster driving their cars, they objected to their products been shown in a slum setting. This forced the makers in post-production to remove logos digitally, costing "tens of thousands of pounds". Boyle did not, however, comment on the disproportionately common on-screen reference to the cigarette brand Marlboro Lights in the same film, leading some commentators to question whether there was significant funding from the said company for the film.

Similarly, in the film The Blues Brothers, portions of the defunct Dixie Square Mall in Harvey, Illinois, were reconstructed in façade and used as the scene of an indoor car chase. Signage belonging to tenants of the mall when it was operational was in some cases removed and replaced with that of other vendors; for instance, a Walgreens would become a Toys "ß" Us.

PUBLICITY

Publicity is the deliberate attempt to manage the public's perception of a subject. The subjects of publicity include people goods and services, organizations of all kinds, and works of art or entertainment. From a marketing perspective, publicity is one component of promotion which is one component of marketing. The other elements of the promotional mix are advertising, sales promotion, and personal selling. Promotion But the publicist cannot wait around for the news to present opportunities. They must also try to create their own news.

Examples of this include:

- Art exhibitions
- Event sponsorship
- Arrange a speech or talk
- Make an analysis or prediction
- Conduct a poll or survey
- Issue a report
- Take a stand on a controversial subject
- Arrange for a testimonial
- Announce an appointment
- Invent then present an award
- Stage a debate
- Organize a tour of your business or projects
- Issue a commendation

The advantages of publicity are low cost, and credibility. New technologies such as weblogs, web cameras, web affiliates, and convergence are changing the cost-structure. The disadvantages are lack of control over how your releases will be used, and frustration over the low percentage of releases that are taken up by the media. Publicity draws on several key themes including birth, love, and death. These are of particular interest because they are themes in human lives which feature heavily throughout life. In television serials several couples have emerged during crucial ratings and important publicity times, as a way to make constant headlines. Also known as a publicity stunt, the pairings may or may not be according to the fact.

Publicists

A publicist is a person whose job is to generate and manage publicity for a product, public figure, especially a celebrity, or for a work such as a book or movie or band. Publicists usually work at large companies handling multiple clients.

Effectiveness of Publicity

The theory, Any press is good press, has been coined to describe situations where bad behaviour by people involved with an organization or brand has actually resulted in positive results, due to the fame and press coverage accrued by such events. One example would be the Australian Tourism Board's "So where the bloody hell are you?" advertising campaign that was initially banned in the UK, but the amount of publicity this generated resulted in the official website for the campaign being swamped with requests to see the banned ad. The popular sitcom, Married... with Children, achieved skyrocketing ratings after moralist Terry Rakolta attempted to have it removed from the air.

SALES PROMOTION

Sales promotion is one of the four aspects of promotional mix. Media and non-media marketing communication are employed for a pre-determined, limited time to increase consumer demand, stimulate market demand or improve product availability.

Examples include:

- Contests
- Point of purchase displays
- Rebate
- Free travel, such as free flights

Sales promotions can be directed at either the customer, sales staff, or distribution channel members. Sales promotions targeted at the consumer are called consumer sales promotions. Sales promotions targeted at retailers and wholesale are called trade sales promotions. Some sale promotions, particularly ones with unusual methods, are considered gimmick by many.

Consumer Sales Promotion Techniques

- *Price deal*: A temporary reduction in the price, such as happy hour
- *Loyal Reward Programme*: Consumers collect points, miles, or credits for purchases and redeem them for rewards. Two famous examples are Pepsi Stuff and AAdvantage.
- *Cents-off deal*: Offers a brand at a lower price. Price reduction may be a percentage marked on the package.
- *Price-pack deal*: The packaging offers a consumer a certain percentage more of the product for the same price.
- *Coupons*: coupons have become a standard mechanism for sales promotions.
- *Loss leader*: the price of a popular product is temporarily reduced in order to stimulate other profitable sales
- *Free-standing insert*: A coupon booklet is inserted into the local newspaper for delivery.
- *On-shelf couponing*: Coupons are present at the shelf where the product is available.
- *Checkout dispensers*: On checkout the customer is given a coupon based on products purchased.
- *On-line couponing*: Coupons are available on line. Consumers print them out and take them to the store.

- *Mobile couponing*: Coupons are available on a mobile phone. Consumers show the offer on a mobile phone to a salesperson for redemption.
- *Online interactive promotion game*: Consumers play an interactive game associated with the promoted product.
  Example Ad For Online Games 7'UP Dancing Allu Arjun.
- *Rebates*: Consumers are offered money back if the receipt and barcode are mailed to the producer.
- *Contests/sweepstakes/games*: The consumer is automatically entered into the event by purchasing the product.
- *Point-of-sale displays*:
  - *Aisle interrupter*: A sign that juts into the aisle from the shelf.
  - *Dangler*: A sign that sways when a consumer walks by it.
  - *Dump bin*: A bin full of products dumped inside.
  - *Glorifier*: A small stage that elevates a product above other products.
  - *Wobbler*: A sign that jiggles.
  - *Lipstick Board*: A board on which messages are written in crayon.
  - *Necker*: A coupon placed on the 'neck' of a bottle.
  - *YES unit*: "your extra salesperson" is a pull-out fact sheet.
- Kids eat free specials: Offers a discount on the total dining bill by offering 1 free kids meal with each regular meal purchased.

Trade Sales Promotion Techniques

- *Trade allowances*: Short term incentive offered to induce a retailer to stock up on a product.
- *Dealer loader*: An incentive given to induce a retailer to purchase and display a product.
- *Trade contest*: A contest to reward retailers that sell the most product.
- *Point-of-purchase displays*: Extra sales tools given to retailers to boost sales.
- *Training programmes*: Dealer employees are trained in selling the product.
- *Push money*: Also known as "spiffs". An extra commission paid to retail employees to push products.

Trade discounts: These are payments to distribution channel members for performing some function.

Political Issues

Sales promotions have traditionally been heavily regulated in many advanced industrial nations, with the notable exception of the United States. For example, the United Kingdom formerly operated under a resale price maintenance regime in which manufacturers could legally dictate the minimum resale price for virtually all goods; this practice was abolished in 1964.

Most European countries also have controls on the scheduling and permissible types of sales promotions, as they are regarded in those countries as bordering upon unfair business practices. Germany is notorious for having the most strict regulations. Famous examples include the car wash that was barred from giving free car washes to regular customers and a baker who could not give a free cloth bag to customers who bought more than 10 rolls.

SEX IN ADVERTISING

Sex in advertising is the use of sexual or erotic imagery in advertising to draw interest to a particular product, for purpose of sale. A feature of sex in advertising is that the imagery used, such as that of a pretty woman, typically has no connection to the product being advertised.

The purpose of the imagery is to attract the attention of the potential customer or user. The type of imagery that may be used is very broad, and would include nudity, cheesecake, and beefcake, even if it is often only suggestively sexual.

Sex has been employed in advertising since the beginning of advertising. At the beginning, wood carvings and illustrations of attractive women adorned posters, signs, and ads for saloons, tonics, and tobacco. In several notable cases, sex in advertising has been claimed as the reason for increased consumer interest and sales. In 1885, W. Duke & Sons inserted trading cards into cigarette packs that featured sexually provocative starlets. Duke grew to become the leading cigarette brand by 1890. Woodbury's Facial Soap, a woman's beauty bar, was almost discontinued in 1910. The soap's sales decline was reversed, however, with ads containing images of romantic couples and promises of love and intimacy for those using the brand. Jovan Musk Oil, introduced in 1971, was promoted with sexual entendre and descriptions of the fragrance's sexual attraction properties. As a result, Jovane, Inc.'s revenue grew from $1.5 million in 1971 to $77 million by 1978.

The use of sex in advertising can be highly overt or extremely subtle. It ranges from relatively explicit displays of sexual acts, to the use of basic cosmetics to enhance attractive features.

Over the past two decades, the use of increasingly explicit sexual imagery in consumer-oriented print advertising has become almost commonplace. Sexuality is considered one of the most powerful tools of marketing and particularly advertising. Post-advertising sales response studies have shown it can be very effective for attracting immediate interest, holding that interest, and, in the context of that interest, introducing a product that somehow correlates with that interest. Gallup & Robinson, an advertising and marketing research firm, has reported that in more than 50 years of testing advertising effectiveness, it has found the use of the erotic to be a significantly above-average technique in communicating with the marketplace, "...although one of the more dangerous for the advertiser. Weighted down with taboos and volatile attitudes, sex is a Code Red advertising technique... handle with care... seller beware; all of which makes it even more intriguing." This research has led to the popular idea that "sex sells". In contemporary mainstream consumer advertising, sex is present in promotional messages for a wide range of branded goods. Ads feature provocative images of well-defined women in revealing outfits and postures selling clothing, alcohol, beauty products, and fragrances. Advertisers such as Calvin Klein, Victoria's Secret, and Pepsi use these images to cultivate a ubiquitous sex-tinged media presence. Also, sexual information is used to promote mainstream products not traditionally associated with sex. For example, the Dallas Opera recent reversal of declining ticket sales has been attributed to the marketing of the more lascivious parts of its performances.

The Concept

Sex in advertising builds on the premise that people are curious about sexuality and that experience in marketing has been that sexuality sells products. From a marketing point of view, sexuality can have biological, emotional/physical or spiritual aspects. The biological aspect of sexuality refers to the reproductive mechanism as well as the basic biological drive that exists in all species, which is hormonally controlled.

The emotional or physical aspect of sexuality refers to the bond that exists between individuals, and is expressed through profound feelings or physical manifestations of emotions of love, trust, and caring. There is also a spiritual aspect of sexuality of an individual or as a connection with others. Advertisers may and do use the various aspects of sexuality in advertisements.

When sexuality is used in advertising, certain values and attitudes towards sex are necessarily 'sold' along with a product. In advertising terms, this is called "the concept". The message may be that "innocence is sexy" or that link pain and violence with sexiness and glamour or that women enjoy being dominated, or that women come with a product or that the use of a certain product is naughty but legal, or that use of a certain product will make the user more attractive to the opposite sex, and many other messages.

Historically, advertising has used women in erotic roles more often than men. However, in recent years young men have increasingly been used in a similar manner, though women continue to be depicted in sexualized roles disproportionately. When couples are used in an advertisement, the sex-roles played by each also sends out messages. The interaction of the couple may send out a message of relative dominance and power, and may stereotype the roles of one or both partners. Usually the message would be very subtle, and sometimes advertisements attract interest by changing stereotypical roles.

Criticism

Use of sexual imagery in advertising has been criticized on various grounds. Religious Conservatives often consider it obscene. Some feminists and masculists claim it reinforces sexism by objectifying the individual. Increasingly, this argument has been complicated by growing use of androgynous and homoerotic themes in marketing.

Calvin Klein has been at the forefront of this movement, having himself declared:

- "Jeans are about sex. The abundance of bare flesh is the last gasp of advertisers trying to give redundant products a new identity."

Calvin Klein's first controversial jeans advertisement was when a 15 year old Brooke Shields, in Calvin Klein jeans, remarks -

- "Want to know what gets between me and my Calvin's? Nothing."

Later in 1995 Klein's advertising campaign showed teenage models in provocative poses wearing Calvin Klein underwear and jeans. The ads were withdrawn when parents and child welfare groups threatened to protest and Hudson stores did not want their stores associated with the ads. It was reported that the Justice Department was investigating the ad campaign for possible violations of federal child pornography and exploitation laws. In recent years ads for jeans, perfumes and many other products have featured provocative images that were designed to elicit sexual responses from as large a cross section of the population as possible, to shock by their ambivalence, or to appeal to repressed sexual desires, which are thought to carry a stronger emotional load. Increased tolerance, more tempered censorship, emancipatory developments and increasing buying power of previously neglected appreciative target groups in rich markets have led to a marked increase in the share of attractive flesh 'on display'.

PROCESS STRATEGIES

INTRODUCTION

The world keeps changing. It always has and always will. This is the fundamental importance of strategic management, for the use of strategic planning is to make decisions now to guide an organization's future directions. In terms of future directions, the basic problem of any company is survival. And to survive over the long term, as Lowell Steele of General Electric succinctly summarized, a company must have two strategic capabilities: the ability to prosper and the ability to change.

Prosperity

The failure to prosper imperils survival because when expenses exceed income over a long enough period a company fails in bankruptcy. Moveover, prosperity now requires not only profitability but long-term growth. Modern stock markets often value long-term asset growth over short-term dividends.

In these days of corporate takeovers, continual corporate growth in earnings and sales is necessary for management to retain control. Together, this combination of continuing profitability and continual growth presents a tough strategic problem because all markets eventually mature and growth in a company's business is limited by the growth of its markets.

In the second half of the twentieth century, this need for continual corporate growth not only created both the driving force for corporate diversification but was also a major cause of the dissolution of large companies. Successful management of a portfolio of different businesses in the same company became a major top corporate leadership challenge. An illustration of this was the successful growth of General Electric in the last two decades of the twentieth century. The CEO who provided strategic management for GE during that time, Jack Welch, became well known in the business world growing GE in two decades from a market value of $12 billion to $500 billion—then a rare corporate feat. In his intended last year at GE,Welch bought more growth for GE by acquiring Honeywell:

- "It was vintage Jack Welch. At the Oct. 23 press conference announcing General Eletric Co.'s $45 billion acquisition of the aeospace and industrial conglomerate Honeywell International Inc, the GE chairman and CEO strutted around the stage, boasting of the promise of the deal... Welch spoke bullishly of the acquisition—'It's exciting.... ' "

In the fall of the year before Welch's intended retirement, Welch had learned that the Honeywell was agreeing to be acquired by United Technologies, and Welsh rushed in with a higher offer to buy Honeywell. Honeywell would add 7% growth to GE's earnings. GE had revenues of $131 billion with operating profits of $19 billion. Honeywell had $25 billion revenue and $4 billion profits. Growth was important to GE to maintain a high stock value— through continuing growth.

Then Welch's business fame was so extensive that he had earlier received a $ 7.1 million advance for his projected memoirs. It was one of the highest book advances in publishing history; and the publisher, Time Warner's Doubleday, would have to sell at least 1.6 million copies in North America to make a profit:

- Executives of Doubleday had prepared a complete book jacket and marketing plan to pitch to Mr. Welch. Sitting in his shirt sleeves at a conference table, Mr. Welch preferred discussing his ideas about management over marketing details... At one point, the conversation turned to Lee Iacocca, the legendary chairman of Chrysler Motors whose autobiography sold 2.6 million copies in hardcover and 3.5 million in document back in North America. Mr. Welch told them that he would consider a book like Mr. Iacocca's a failure, because it was about a personality rather than ideas. Mr.Welch said he preferred the 1964 book by Alfred P. Sloan, MyYears with General Motors...

Strategic management is about ideas. Worth magazine asked several successful CEOs about what they thought was important in the job of the CEO.

Two of them, Koichi Nishimura of Solectron and Eric Schmidt of Novell, responded:

1. *Nishimuara*: Four things, I think, are important. First, communicate a vision of where the company is and what you are doing. The second is that when you communicate, you want to be able to motivate people. Third, you want feedback. And fourth, you want to take action.
2. *Schmidt*: I think the job breaks down into three parts. First, setting a strategic vision that is implementable. That's number one. Second is recruiting and leading great human beings. The third is worrying about shareholder value. If you follow those three rules, then everything else sort of works.... I think the question from an investor should be, Does the CEO have a strategy that you believe can win?

Strategic vision, communicating vision, recruiting and motivating good people, obtaining feedback, and taking action that creates shareholder prosperity—these are essential elements in corporate leadership. Strategy is ideas about the longterm future.

Change

Attaining the kind of growth and prosperityWelch had achieved atGErequired him to make great changes within the company. On taking office back in 1981,Welch first sold off a hundred of GE's businesses and then consolidated the rest into 14 business groups.

This massive restructuring gaveWelch a tough reputation:

- Neutron Jack, as he is sometimes called, is widely regarded as one of the world's most ruthless managers. The truth is more complex. Some of his actions are indeed harsh, and he antagonized people inside the company and out by fixing something they didn't think was broke. What is becoming clear only now is how those moves fit into a larger plan to strengthen the enterprise and to make its remaining employees more secure.

Welch's success at GE was to strategically change GE from primarily manufacturing businesses into primarily financial service businesses. In 1980, manufacturing produced 70% of GE's revenues, with services contributing 30%. By 1999, manufacturing produced only 26% of revenues, with services having grown to 74%. Welch's strategy was to retain only a selective group of manufacturing businesses and grow financial services: "ChairmanWelch unloaded the consumer electronics division and built financial services into a powerhouse, while keeping GE dominant in turbines and jet engines." Periodic change in a large organization is necessary to help the firm adapt to new times, for new times keep on occurring.

One of Jack Welch's most widely quoted strategic precepts was:

- "Control your own destiny, or someone else will."

The failure to make appropriate changes at the right time, imperials survival because the company may become competitively obsolete in its products, services, and value to customers. Change requires an ability to anticipate the external dynamics of the environments in which a company operates—markets, competition, innovation, government regulation, economic conditions, globalization, and so on. Change also requires an ability to alter a company's directions.

Lowell Steele nicely summarized the emphasis of change as the focus of strategic thinking:

- Strategy is concerned overwhelmingly with questions of change. How much must the enterprise change in order to survive and to continue to prosper? How much change can it finance and manage? How fast can it change? These are profoundly difficult questions.

Strategic management is about the difficult questions of future business—whether it should go and how should it change—a particularly risky set of questions for a large business that is already successful. In many of the older books on strategy, it was presumed that the logic of strategy should begin with a "mission and vision" statement. A mission statement is a statement of what kind of business is the organization; and a vision statement is what kind of business the organization would like to become. However, this older kind of "strategic logic" is not really useful for an ongoing organization, unless the mission changes.

What is useful in vision for an organization is foresight on change to the mission. The "vision thing" is: how should the mission change to take advantage of future market opportunities and meet future competitive threats? Strategic thinking is not about the mission of the business but changes to the mission.

Strategic Thinking

CEOs like Jack Welch become successful and famous because of their ability to think and act strategically. And because of the fundamental importance of strategy to long-term corporate survival, this ability to think strategically became recognized as an important leadership skill for executives.

For example, one can often see specifications for the ability to strategize in common recruitment advertisements for executive positions, such as the following ad, which appeared in The New York Times in May 2000:

- ... Corporation, a publicly traded manufacturer of products... has an excellent opportunity in its Engineered Products headquarters office.... The successful candidate will have hands-on experience in

> sourcing components. The position will report to Group VP and be responsible for purchasing in (5) divisions.... The individual must thrive on multitasking, have outstanding negotiating skills, be a good manager of people and projects, and be a strategic thinker. Highly competitive compensation package. For confidential consideration, forward resume and salary requirements to..

This is the fundamental management skill which we address in this book. What is a strategic thinker? How can hands-on experience improve a manager's ability to think strategically? Which practical techniques facilitate effective strategic planning in a large organization? What important strategic concepts used by successful leaders such as Sloan and Welch? Change in a company environment always forces strategic redirection. Changes in automobile technology provided the strategic ground for Sloan's successful management of General Motors, and changes in services and medical technologies provided some of the impetus for Welch's successful strategic management of General Electric.

Information Technology

By the end of the twentieth century, progress in information technology had become the strongest and most pervasive force for strategic change in businesses throughout the world.

One example of IT's impact was Thomas Middelhoff's strategic exhortation to his company in 2000:

- We have to reach every brain to explain that we have nothing less than an industrial revolution. That makes it necessary to change how we see and run our business. That means speed is king. That means we have to be decentralized on the one hand and also more corporate. We have without any question a generational change at Bertelsmann.

The growth of the Internet was a rapid phenomena. For example, in the United States, 14% of the population used the Internet in 1996, jumping to 22% in 1997, 31% in 1998, 38% in 1999, and 44% in 2000. In 2000, the average monthly hours a user spent on line was 19 hours. U.S. consumer spending online had grown from a few million in 1996 to $3 billion dollars in 1997, $7 billion in 1998, $19 billion in 1999, and $36 billion in 2000. Of the $36 billion spent in 2000, $11.0 billion was for travel, $7.7 billion for PCs, $2.4 billion for clothes, $13.4 billion for books, and $13.4 billion for other merchandise. In October 2000, advertising revenues of the Internet in the U.S. totaled $600 million. In business history, the decade of the 1990s will likely be called the decade of the Internet. Its innovation and rapid impact on business made it an interesting and challenging time—that brought to everyone's immediate attention the great importance of progress in information technology upon all business strategy.

The dramatic experience of that decade was nicely summarized by Joseph Nocera and Time Carvell:

- The Internet decade has seen the unscrupulous rewarded, the dimwitted suckered, the ill-qualified enriched at a pace greater than at any other time in history. The Internet has been a gift to charlatans, hypemeisters, and merchants of vapour... and despite all that, it still changes everything.

The Internet was an example of a larger class of phenomena in business history called pervasive innovations. William Abernathy and Kim Clark even introduced a new term to strategic management—transilience of innovation—to emphasize the importance of a pervasiveness of an innovation upon the operations of a firm. Transilience means the ability to pass through a system, and it emphasizes the range of business impacts that a transilient innovation may have upon the value-adding capabilities of a firm, passing through its activities to make changes in:

- The kinds of products and way the firm produces products
- The kinds of customers and markets the business serves

Abernathy and Clark classified the types of transilient innovation impacts upon a firm by the innovation's potential to alter either product/production or market/customer competencies:

- In product/production competency, innovations may alter
  - Product design
  - Production systems
  - Technical skills and knowledge base
  - Materials and capital equipment
- Under market/customer competency, innovations may alter
  - Customer bases
  - Customer applications
  - Channels of distribution and service
  - Customer knowledge and modes of communication

  For any of these factors the impact of innovation may range from strengthening existing competencies to making existing competencies obsolete. Accordingly, Abernathy and Clark also classified innovations:

  a. A technological innovation that conserved both existing production and market competencies was called a regular innovation.
  b. A technological innovation that conserved existing production competency but altered market competency was called a niche-creation innovation.
  c. A technological innovation that made an existing production competency obsolete but preserved existing market competency was called a revolutionary innovation.

d. A technological innovation that obsoleted both existing production and market competencies was called an architectural innovation.

The innovation of the Internet was an architectural innovation. Historically, many firms have usually successfully exploited regular or niche creation innovations, for they sustain current operations. But many large firms have perished during revolutionary or architectural innovations. For example, Clayton Christensen examined reasons why large U.S. firms historically have often failed to profit from revolutionary or architectural innovations:

- Resource dependence in large firms, influenced by investors and current customers.
- The emergent markets of radical innovations are early-on perceived as too small for big firm growth needs.
- The ultimate use of radical innovations are often not known early.
- The performance and features of radical new innovations are often not attractive to current markets.

The architectural impact information technology made on business strategy was summarized by Bill Miller who spent a long career and argued that IT was:

- Altering the competitive dynamics of both products and services, leading to the new importance of dominant designs and platforms in product/service strategy
- Flattening organizational hierarchy or even dissolving boundaries into networked forms, such as "virtual enterprises"
- Impacting management styles through introducing both a "transparency" of the business model to all levels of employees and making their jobs more complex, through the increased need for teaming and direct attention to the bottom-lines of business goals.

Information technologies could strategically impact businesses in different ways:

- A business can be in the information technology business, providing information technology goods and services
- A business can use information technology as a core technology in its production of goods and delivery of services
- A business can use information technology as a supporting technology in its design of products/services;
- A business can use information technology as a marketing tool to attract customers to its product/services.

As suggested, address this new challenge of IT to strategic management, using a strategy process in which information technology integrates with business strategy.

Strategic Management

Strategy, planning, budgeting, and knowledge are the four forward-looking activities of management, and it is important that they be clearly distinguished. Budgeting is the allocation of resources for the future operations of an organization. Budgeting is neither planning nor strategy. All organizations budget, but they do not necessarily plan nor strategize. Organizations annually budget in order to allocate the resources for continuing operations. Thus the managers of all organizations do formulate budgets; but not all managers plan or formulate strategy. Planning is thinking out of tactics for the continuing operations of an organization. Planning is not strategy but the implementation of strategy. Managers plan when the tactics of operations change from year to year. Organizations that need to annually plan are those with significant changes in tactics and operations from one year to the next.

Strategy is neither planning nor budgeting. Strategy is the perspective for long term change. Many organizations do not even begin to formulate strategy until an immediate emergency requires change; but by then, it may be too late to formulate effective strategy. Effective strategy requires looking out ahead, anticipating the need for change and preparing for it. A strategy is a change in the direction of the objectives of the operations over a course of years.

Few organizations do strategy when external conditions, markets, and competition all are stable. Strategy is needed when external conditions change—change in technology, change in markets, change in competitors. Knowledge is the basis for improving and controlling the future value-adding operations of a business enterprise. Progress in information technology provides new tools for managing the development of the knowledge assets of the business. Knowledge has been and continues to be the major force in strategic changes in business.

Thus in a modern theory of strategy:

- Strategy is change in direction,
- Planning is future tactics,
- Budgeting is allocation of resources,
- Strategic knowledge is future innovation.

Case Study: Merger of AOL and Time Warner

The first historical case as suggested, examine happened just as the twenty-first century began. It is important in illustrating the rapid advance of new forms of business practice due to progress in information technology. One of the new companies in what then was called the "new economy" took over an older and larger business in the "old economy". The case shows how innovation that creates rapid market growth can be exceedingly highly valued by a stock market.

In this case, the market valued the new markets being created by AOL over the older markets then being served by Time Warner. The historical setting was when the then-new electronic commerce, or e-commerce, had spawned a whole new raft of companies and media industry. The booming U.S. stock market of that decade had priced most of these new companies exceedingly high. America Online was one of these, providing service access to the Internet to subscribers. In January, it used its very high market value to merge with an older media company, Time Warner. The business community took this merger as the first sign that e-commerce companies were beginning to mature.

For example, Richard Siklow and Catherine Yang of Business Week wrote:

- On the surface, it looked like just another awesome megadeal... America Online is the acquirer. The trading symbol for the new company, tellingly, is AOL. Given the realities of the New Economy, it could hardly be otherwise. By now, the pattern is clear: the digital will prevail over the analog, new media will grow faster than old, and the leaders of the Net economy will become the 21st century Establishment.

On December 10, 1999, the market capitalization of America Online was about $250 billion dollars, whereas the market capitalization of Time Warner was about $85 billion. The difference was in the stock markets multiplication of their relative price-to-earnings ratios. In the last 12 months, AOL had earnings of about $1 billion, so that its P/E ratio was 250/1. TimeWarner's earnings were about $1.3 billion, so that its P/E ratio was about 65 to 1. Thus AOL's P/E was being valued over TimeWarner's P/E at a multiple of 250/65.

This was the heart of the deal. AOL's vast P/E ratio gave it the leverage to take over Time Warner, and Time Warner was willing to be acquired, hoping the resulting company would have a PE ratio more like AOL's than Time Warner's. Time Warner had a major debt load, which AOL did not have. Moreover, AOL was in a rapidly growing new market, e-commerce, into which Time Warner had tried to enter but failed. Yet in terms of assets-valuable products and steady, proved earnings- Time Warner had a much larger asset base. For example, TimeWarner had 73 million consumer subscriptions compared to AOL's 24 million.

Time Warner product brands included:

- Time, People, Sports showed, Fortune, Money magazines
- The cable companies of HBO, Cinemax, CNN, TNT,
- The movie and music production companies of Warner Bros.

In contrast, America Online had AOL, Netscape Navigator, and stakes in several companies. Time Warner brought to the merger a powerhouse of media contentproducing companies, whereas America Online principally brought success in the new electronic businesses of the time. Barry Schuler, then president of AOL Interactive Services, characterized AOL's strengths:"We are good at aggregating eyeballs and delivering services".

AOL purchased Time Warner for $183 billion, but with AOL having just one-fifth TimeWarner's revenue and only 15% of its employees. TimeWarner, an upstart in the 1920s, had become a major media establishment company by the 1990s. The deal was to have AOL shareholders receive one share in the new company for current AOL shares, and for TimeWarner shareholders to receive 1.5 shares for each of theirs. AOL shareholders ended up with 55% of the new company, and Time Warner shareholders with 45% of the new company.

At the time, the Time Warner shareholders expected a market premium of 70% for their shares. What were the strategies of the two CEOs of AOL and Time Warner in creating the merger? Steven Case, founder and then CEO of AOL, had two major strategies. The first was to transmute AOL's high trading multiple of the booming market stock market of 1999 into assets and revenue stream, which would survive any drop in the high-tech companies valuation of that time:

- TimeWarner stood out as the only company with the content, distribution, global reach and customers. Case wants it all: The branded content fromWarner Music, Turner cable networks, and Time Inc. Magazines that can be digitized and sold online. The cable pipes to speed delivery of AOL. A global promotional platform that will save AOL a fortune in ad spending. Relationships with about 73 million subscribers to Time Warner cable systems, HBO, and Time Inc. Magazines.... Time Warner's old-fashioned media properties deliver a stable stream of revenues, about $27.1 billion in 1999, and cash flow, about $6 billion... that are shielded from the vagaries of the Internet world.

From a bottom-up kind of strategic perspective, Case's strategic perspective on the cash-flows of Time-Warner's major publication and television empire would provide AOL a steady and major source of income over the long term. Also from a bottom-up strategic perspective, the acquisition of Time Warner's businesses would provide a step in the direction solving AOL's bandwidth problem. AOL had been providing Internet service of connection through existing copper telephone lines of customers—slow and technically limited to 54 Kbit modem connections. The market demand for Internet connections was broadband. Time Warner owned a major cable company that could provide a much faster broadband connection to its cable customers. Through the merger Time Warner gave AOL access to a market of 20 million cable customers. The CEO of TimeWarner before the merger was Gerald Levin. His strategic perspective for Time Warner also involved kinds of top-down and bottom-up perspectives of strategy. From the top-down—looking out on the growing importance of the Internet and electronic commerce—Levin saw the need to continue moving TimeWarner into the digital world:

- Levin can empathize as a cable and tech guy stuck atop a content giant.... Before Ted Turner dreamed up CNN, Levin made his reputation by putting HBO onto a satellite in 1975. He's also been burned by technology, notably when Time Warner spent upwards of $100 million on a prototype interactive TV network in Orlando. But his biggest tech bet, on the potential of two-way cable lines, paid off handsomely... TimeWarner's stock a so-so performer for much of the 1990s, surged... during the period since Levin took over in 1993.

From the bottom-up perspective of Time Warner's recent business capabilities, Levin saw a strategic advantage for immediately merging Time Warner into one of the biggest successful players in electronic commerce.

Levin's ventures for Time Warner into the Internet world had not been strategically successful:

- But Levin's hard-won reputation as a tech-savvy executive has faded since then. He passed up the opportunity to buy a portal like Lycos or Excite, and Time Warner's own Internet hub, called Pathfinder, flopped.... So when Case called to offer him the chance to be CEO of AOL Time Warner—the biggest game in cyberspace and media!—why, how could Levin resist?

In July 2000, shareholders of both companies approved the merger, but its success was still not certain.

As Gretchen Morgenson, of The New York Times commented:

- For months, if not years, the virtual has trounced the real in the stock market valuations of Internet concerns vastly exceed the values that investors assigned to companies unlucky enough to own tangible assets... Last week... thetables turned... and investors are about to experience the Great Internet Shakeout... A big indication that the tectonic plates of the virtual world were shifting was the bid of the high flying America Online to acquire the landlocked TimeWarner... 'If calendar 1999 was one of discovery of the internet, 2000 is going to be characterized by much more rigorous scrutiny of the business models... ' "

Before the stock market bubble of dot.com burst, Case had transformed equity of AOL into more equity by acquiring Time Warner.

Case Analysis

In this case, we see two important theoretical ideas about strategy. The first is the importance of information strategy to business strategy. Both AOL and Timer Warner were in the businesses of information. AOL was in the business of being an information channel provider as an Internet service provider. TimeWarner was both in the business of providing information channels and creating information content in these channels. Progress in information technology was bringing both firms into similar business strategies— channels and content. The second idea about strategy is how strategy was formulated by both C¸ EOs, using two kinds of perspectives on their company's future—a top-down perspective from the big picture of the Internet innovation and from a bottom-up perspective of the little picture of the companies' businesses future operations.

Strategic thinking by both CEO's required two kinds of views on the future:

1. A perspective on changes in the larger environment of the business and
2. A perspective on future business operations about their current strengths and weaknesses to changes in operations for future strengths.

TOP-DOWN AND BOTTOM-UP PERSPECTIVE

Let us first examine the idea that there are two basic perspectives in strategic thinking—strategic views from the top of the organization and strategic views from the bottom.

As showed in Figure, these different perspectives create different views and even different kinds of logics in stratregic thinking:

- A big-picture view with a logic of proceeding from the general to the specific changes of the future
- An operational-reality view with a logic of proceeding from the specific to the general changes of the future

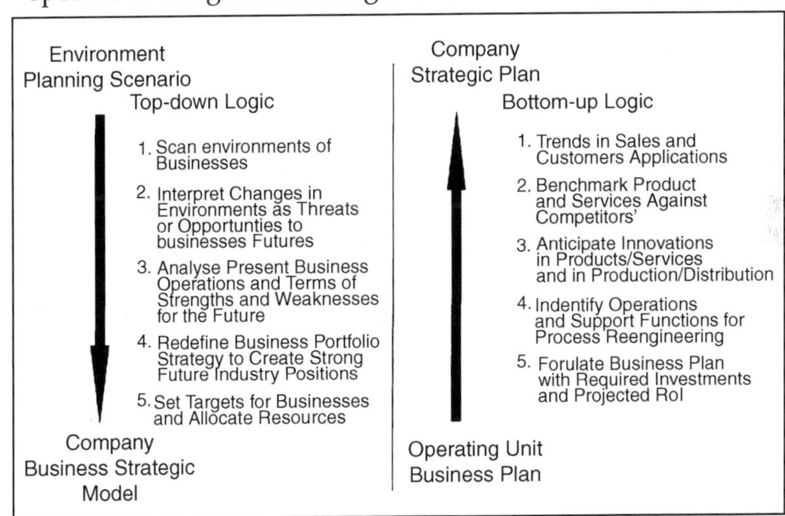

In the logic of strategic thinking, one can always look to the future by describing the big picture of everything and then deducing how changes there can impact upon the particular situation of one's own future action. For example, in this way one can see oneself as a member of a general economic class, cultural class, or generation and ask how one's particular life is impacted by trends and changes happening to these general categories of people and life.

This is the deductive approach to strategy—going from the general trends to the particular descriptions of future life. Also and conversely in the logic of strategic thinking, one can always look at changes in the particular situation of one's future and then generalize that similar changes are happening to others like oneself. For example, in this way one can generalize changes in one's own life as an exemplar of the kinds of general categories of other people and lives. This is the inductive approach to strategy—going from the particular examples to the general descriptions of future life. At the top of an organization, information to see the big picture is more readily available there than at the bottom of an organization. Conversely, at the bottom of an organization, information to see the reality of operations is more readily available there than at the top of the organization.

A famous and bitter example of these differences in information between the big-picture-of-the-world and the reality-of-operations was the difference in perspective between the generals and the soldiers in the First World War in Europe in the early twentieth century. From 1914 to 1918, the war stagnated into trench warfare, with the generals on both sides planning one more great battle to win the war. Each battle resulted in thousands of deaths with no substantial gain in territory or weakening of the ability of the other army to fight.

The view from the general's perspective was the massing of artillery and soldiers for an attack. But the view from the soldier's perspective was that the new machine gun and artillery made every attack impossible to win, resulting only in the slaughter of the attackers. From the big picture, the view of the war was simply the massing of the attack forces.

But from the reality of the trenches, the view of the war was simply devastation and destruction under the sustained and withering fire of machine guns, which would finally halt all attacks. After four years of trench war, both the German/Austrian armies and the British/French armies were too exhausted to win, and a new fresh army of Americans was brought into battle to finish the war. But throughout that war, the perspective of the generals in all armies was that the failure of their massed attacks was due to lack of spirit in their soldiers. Not only is the experiential base of the two perspectives of top-down and bottom-up different, so too are the logics appropriate to top-down and bottom-up strategy. Figure also summarizes the differences as deductive and inductive kinds of logic of the two perspectives. The top-down perspective of strategy uses a deductive logic that begins with the great and goes down towards the small.

In formulating strategy, top leadership should look around at the environments of the firm and its businesses to:

- Scan the environments of a firm to identify major future trends and changes in government, the economy, territorial markets and competitors, and in the scientific and technological culture.

- Interpret the changes as threats and opportunities to the businesses of the firm.
- Analyse the present firm's activities in terms of strengths and weaknesses to face such threats or seize such opportunities.
- Redefine the missions of the firm's businesses to match the future operations to future threats and opportunities.
- Set goals and targets for businesses to meet in a proper time horizon.

In contrast, at the operating levels of businesses in a firm, managers should look to the strategic immediacy of the business's markets, competitors, operations, and knowledge:

- Examine the trends in sales in the markets of the businesses of the firm and identify innovations that can alter these markets.
- Benchmark a firm's products and processes against competitors' products and processes and identify changes needed to maintain or surpass any competitor's current advantages.
- Investigate progress in information technology and in the knowledge bases of the business's product and production processes.
- Reexamine current operations and control, and identify innovations in operations and control of operations needed to adapt to changes in market, competition, and new information and knowledge capabilities.
- Formulate a business plan, with targets for market-share and profits along with required investments and resources needed to achieve the plan.

These different perspectives of the big-picture and trench-reality are both vital to a good strategy process. Therefore, what is critical to good strategy formulation is the interaction of these perspectives. Now, although the top-down and bottomup perspectives in strategic thinking are important to formulating good strategy, coordinating them is extremely difficult to pull off in a large organization because of the hierarchy of authority. In large organizations, these perspectives become quite different because of the hierarchical nature of authority.

For example in a diversified firm, there are usually at least four levels of management hierarchy:

1. *Firm level*: Board, CEO and firm executive team
2. *Business level*: President and business executive team
3. *Department level*: Department head and staff
4. *Office level*: Office manager and assistant

The hierarchical levels of authority in a firm usually begin at the top of the firm level with a board of directors and a chief executive officer. The CEO and his or her executive team are responsible for the strategy of the whole firm. This strategy includes what businesses are and should be within the firm and the overall financial performance of the firm. The planning scenario needed at this level should include anticipation of change in all the industries of the firm's businesses. The bottom-up input to the firm's strategy should be provided by the participation of the business's presidents to the CEO in the strategy process. At the next organizational level, below that of the firm, is the business unit, and its president is responsible for strategy for the business as a whole.

Part of the business's planning scenario is the industrial context of the firm as well as the territories and cultures in the markets to which the business sells. Another part of its planning scenario are goals and targets specified for it by the firm-level strategy, the strategic firm model. The outcome of strategic planning for the business will be a strategic business model specifying changes for its future policies.

The final two levels within a company, department and office, are levels in which managers should provide bottom-up information to the business level in formulating the strategic business model. Policies of this model then provide the guidance for planning and improving operations and activities of the departments and offices.

Since it is organizationally natural for the bottom of the organization to listen more closely to the top than for the top to listen to the bottom, two kinds of misunderstandings are common in strategic thinking in large organizations:

1. The managers of operating units frequently do not think that the top executives understand the strategic problems and challenges in operations.
2. The top executives frequently do not believe the operating units are trying hard enough to implement the strategic goals they formulate.

This is the first challenge of strategic thinking in large organizations, to encourage real and accurate communication of strategic perspectives between the top and the bottom. Therefore, in a good strategy process, one needs to formalize these two perspectives as two views of a firm's totalities, those of the environments of the firm and those of the operations of the firm. The top-to-down perspective looks at the big picture and formulates strategic policies for long-term direction. The bottomto- top perspective looks at the specific nuts and bolts of the company's operations to try to carry out the desirable long-term direction.

- The critical problem in the strategy process of any organization is to facilitate a positive, constructive, and creative interaction between the two perspectives in strategic thinking.

Moreover, this problem is exacerbated by the periodic and noncontinuous requirements of strategic thinking. The actual process of formulating strategy is infrequent but recurrent, exploratory and interactive with the different experiential bases of the top management and of lower management levels.

While the results of strategic planning may look as if created by a linear process, the strategic process is nonlinear and recursive and interactive with different experiential bases of the company top and bottom. For example, Arthur A.

Thompson and A. J. Strickland nicely summarized the recurrent nature of the strategy process:

- The march of external and internal events guarantees that a company's vision, objectives, strategy, and implementation approaches will have to be revisited, recon sidered, and eventually revised. This is why the task of evaluating performance and initiating corrective adjustments is both the end and the beginning of the strategic management cycle.

Since the strategic management process is interactive and cyclic, the information flow must be recurrently both bottom-up and top-down between the views of the environment and the business. The cyclic nature of strategic planning is also coupled into the budget cyclic of any business, going from yearly planning to yearly planning.

Furthermore, in a multibusiness firm, there are two kinds of the top-down and bottom-up perspectives:

1. Firm-to-business perspectives
2. Businesses-to-business divisions perspectives

This makes the top-down and bottom-up communications in a multibusiness firm even more challenging than in a single business firm. Using an interactive approach to the strategy process is important in the practice of strategic management because the principle cause of failure in the strategy of large organizations has often been due to a lack of proper internal interaction between the two strategic perspectives:

- Inadequate top-down perspective of innovative changes in environments
- Inadequate bottom-up perspectives of the need for new business models for innovative change
- Inadequate communication between executive levels and operational levels about needed strategic change

How can leadership in a large organization avoid these common kinds of mistakes in strategy processes? Good interactions between the strategic perspectives from the top and from the bottom are necessary to create a potentially profitable vision of the future—a strategic vision of the challenges, opportunities, and direction of the future business and how operations need to change to succeed in that future.

The planning process in a large organization can use two kinds of strategic techniques to assist this:

1. A strategic technique for effectively summarizing the changes in the environment's future is called a "planning scenario."
2. A strategic technique for effectively summarizing the desirable changes in operations for such a future environment is called a "strategic business model."

PLANNING SCENARIOS AND STRATEGIC BUSINESS MODELS

It is always important to strategically think about the big picture of changes in the environments of business. It is equally important to strategically think about the smaller picture of how a particular business can exploit the business opportunities in that change. For strategic thinking in a large organization, we need to consider what kinds of techniques can formally assist groups of managers reach to consensus about what is important:

- About changes of the future and
- Their implications for future operations.

To help a group to strategically think about the big picture, the technique of the planning scenario is effective. To help a group strategically think about operational realities of the future, the technique of a strategic business model is effective. These two techniques can help a large organization describe the two key totalities of strategic thinking—future environments of the company and the future company itself.

Planning Scenario

Strategic thinking needs to grasp the big picture of changes in the environments of a company. For example two of the CEOsWorth interviewed in 2000, Raymond Gilmartin CEO of Merck and Koichi Nishimura CEO of Solectron, commented:

- *Gilmartin*: Part of leadership is saying in touch with what's going on outside your company.... You need to gather information to see the patterns, to tell if you're on the wrong track, to take risks and make decisions that go against the grain.
- *Nishimura*: Getting it right comes from pattern recognition.You integrate information and you go "humm."

Gathering information and constructing patterns of trends and changes in the environments of business is the purpose of scenario planning in the strategy process. To systematically gather information and create insightful "humm patterns," the strategy technique of scenario narrative is very useful. All strategy is based upon assumptions about the future and its business opportunities and challenges. A modern technique for exploring and expressing these pictures of the future is called a scenario, and when used for planning, a planning scenario. Scenario planning uses scenario narratives and societal models.

Scenario narratives provide a method for describing and thinking about the possible impacts of the future upon a current business. Strategic stories envision adventures of the business in the future. The future will be an adventure that will challenge business. Experience is always of the present, with memories and stories of the past. The future consists of anticipations and/or surprises and plans for the future conceived in the present.

All existence is always in the present:

- In the mind only exists intelligent perception of the past and imagination of the future.

As we saw in the case of Rakuten, the major changes in the environments of a business are changes in structures of the society in which the business operates. To build a planning scenario that captures this kind of complexity and completeness of possible future change, one needs to use a general classification of all the societal environments of a business. In all human societies, traditional or modern, there have been general classes of social patterns that create societal structures. These include categories of territory, culture, economy, government.

Planning scenarios should address issues of change in the large patterns of society, such as:

- Will there be changes in how the control of territory is decided in the future?
- Will there be changes in the culture of the nation?
- Will there be changes in the economy of the nation, world?
- Will there be changes in government of a nation?

Strategic Business Model

Strategic thinking also needs to think about what kind of business model can meet the challenges and exploit the future opportunities in the environments of the company. So the second strategic totality to be considered in the planning process is the future of the business of the corporation. The strategic technique effective for this is a model of how one's company now operates but should change in the future, a strategic business model. Strategic models of the business of a corporate summarize the future policies of the company which will prepare it to perform in the future.

The strategic importance of the concept of a 'business model' was nicely expressed by Geoffrey Colvin, commenting on the troubles Xerox was having in 2000:

- "The quote of the year for 2000 comes from Xerox CEO Paul Allaire... He gets the Distinguished Service Cross for extraordinary executive heroism because he told analysts in a conference call, 'We have an unsustainable business model.' In the past CEOs of big, established companies didn't say things like that. They didn't tell the people who rate their stock that the way they make money doesn't work anymore... The largest fact of life in business today is that virtually every company... has to change its business model to make it sustainable in the Internet worked, infotech-based world."

A business model is an abstraction of a business identifying how that business makes money. Business models are abstracted about how inputs to an organization are transformed to value-adding outputs. All models of organizations are models of kinds of open systems. One important version of this was the now famous value-added model of Michael Porter. As a value-adding open-system model, an organization is described as taking resources from its environment and transforming them to value-added outputs sold back into its market environment. The transformation of input resources into output products/services is performed by the processes and operations of the business. The Porter model is only one of several kinds of business models, one can use in strategic planning.

- A strategic business model abstracts the basic value-adding transformation that describes how a business makes its money.

Strategic thinking about how a business now makes money and how it must change to continue making money is the 'bottom-line' for strategic management. For example, in thinking about the future capabilities of an organization, Clayton Christensen and Michael Overdorf emphasized the need to consider resources, processes, and values in an existing organization compared to the challenge of needed change.

The resources of a business consist of tangible resources and intangible resources. The processes of a business consist of the activities and procedures with which a business procures resources, adds value, and produces and sells products and services. Thus dealing with change also requires determining what changes in processes and procedures are necessary to produce new kinds of value and/or address the needs of new kinds of customers. The value dimension of an organization are the standards by which management and other employees set priorities and judge the importance of activities and results.

Values are standards about how resources are used and how processes are run, as Christensen and Overdorf comment:

- An organization's values the standards by which employees set priorities.... A company's values reflect its cost structure or its business model because they define the rules its employees must follow for the company to prosper.
- A strategic business model is a systematic list of the policies that will guide the future specification of inputs, outputs, processes and values of the complete operations of the business of the corporation.

The importance of conceiving of a good business model was emphasized by the experience of the many new companies begun in the Internet growth years of 1996–2000. Then hundreds of these dot.coms were begun with extensive venture capital funding, and many without having a viable business model. Next in the year 2000, over 125 of these companies folded as they ran out of capital and had not yet become profitable.

The often repeated moral then was that a good business model was necessary for profitability and survival. Strategic business models need to be constructed around strategic issues of change in markets and innovation, competition and structure, operations and control, information and knowledge, asking strategic questions such as:

- What are likely to be the changes in the markets that a business will serve and innovations that will impact these markets?
- What are likely to be changes in competition against which a business will compete and in the structure of the industrial sectors in which competition occurs?
- What is likely to be the progress in information technologies that a business can strategically exploit and how can this improve the knowledge assets of a business?
- What must be the changes in operations and control of business processes that the business needs to implement to be efficient and effective in its future value-adding processes?

STRATEGIC VISION

In a large organization, strategic vision needs to arise from strategic thinking exercises of constructing planning scenarios of the future environments of the company and a strategic business model of the company's business(es). The reason this is so important in a large organization is that the experiences of being at the top and at the bottom are so different that both top and bottom perspectives are severely limited.

From the top, it is really hard to see the real problems in the trenches; and from the experiences at the bottom, it is equally hard to see the pressures of control on the organization. A good strategic vision is essential in strategic planning because strategic change cannot occur without top leadership's having a vision of and a commitment to change.

The relationship of leadership to strategic vision and change is critical in the strategy process:

- Strategic vision is the fundamental responsibility of leadership since only top management has the authority to make major changes in operating organizations.
- Strategic change is only periodically necessary; but to be effective such change must be envisioned, anticipated, and planned.
- Sources for strategic vision are either external in the environments of the organization or internal as opportunities developed within the organization.

For example, Worth magazine interviews with some successful CEOs in 2000 also showed their concern with the importance of providing visionary leadership, such as in comments by Koici Nishimura of Solectron and Raymond Gilmartin of Merck and by Eric Schmidt of Novell:

- *Nishimura*: When you are leading a company, you have to figure out, conceptually, what you are trying to do. Once you have decide that, and you think it's okay, the second thing you have to figure out is: What tactics are you going to use... ?You continually have to ask: Are the assumptions I made still good? My job is to continually reassess the assumptions or the foundation that the company is built on.

- *Gimartin*: You need to have a vision that is the anchor point for what you're doing.... There needs to be some form of overarching statement that makes sense and on which the ECO stakes his or her job.
- *Schmidt*: Leadership is defined about perception, not just reality. So there's always this tension in leadership to overhype. And to make promises that you can't keep and articulate things that can't happen.... You want to do some level of overselling, but the problem is that the people you're communicating to are smart. If they think you're a snake-oil salesman, then your whole credibility goes to zero. So leadership is also defined by credibility.

Why leadership in large organizations often fails to envision and prepare for change arises from the nature of leadership in large organizations. In large organizations, leaders are usually selected as those who are committed to doing more of the same. Managers often rise to leadership because they embody a vision of the organization's past. The vision of the past represented a tested story of success. Past leadership built organizational structures and culture that evolved into a successful company.

Later when the business environment changes, the earlier structures and cultures and leadership became ineffectual in the new conditions. Yet despite the tendency for management not to make changes, still the need for long-term change is indigenous in organizations because organizations have little control over change in their environments—and thus they may be forced by competition to change or die. Many students of strategy and organization have argued that instability is a periodic experience for all organizations.

For example, Michael Tushman and Elaine Romanelli argued that organizations experience periods of relative stability interrupted by sharp strategic reorientations. They and others have seen organizational change as a kind of evolution, stimulated by responding to change in business and economic structures. Michael Tushman and Elaine Romanelli with Beverly Virany nicely summarized the connection between strategic vision, environmental change and organizational decline:

- At least part of the reason for substantial organization decline in the face of environmental change lies with the executive team. A set of executives who have been historically successful may become complacent with existing systems and/or be less vigilant to environmental changes. Or, even if an executive team registers external threat, they may not have the energy and/or competence to effectively deal with fundamentally different competitive conditions.

> The importance of an effective executive team is accentuated in industries where the rate of change in underlying technologies is substantial.

Also students of innovation have documented that a major source of changes in the business environment and within the economic structure consists of applied knowledge discontinuities, which Tushman called "technology discontinuities" and later Clayton Christensen called "disruptive change". Progress in information technology has created many disruptive changes.

As an example, Tushman and his colleagues looked at the mini computer industry, focusing on fifty-nine firms started between 1967 and 1971. They compared firm records of success and failure over a subsequent 14-year period. In their analysis of the reasons some firms survived and many failed, they argued that one must understand how the conduct of the firm in the context of the changing economic structure affected the performance of the firm. The conduct of firms consists of the strategic, tactical and organizational activities guided by the executive team.

Conduct must alter as the context of the firm changes when alterations in the economic structure affect competition.

Changes can arise from:

- Technological changes
- Market changes
- Resource changes
- Regulation changes
- Competitive changes

Successful leadership performance depends upon the executive team's ability to envision, anticipate a correct future and formulate a correct strategy and organization for the future operations of the business. Such vision, strategy and organization correctly anticipates technological opportunities for new products, market changes for new needs and applications, resource changes that affect the availability and cost of materials and energy, and changes in government regulations that affect safety, monopolies, taxes, and so on. When industries faced changes, Tushman et al. found that those firms whose executive teams lacked vision and made no changes in strategy and organization and product failed after the change occurred. Even those firms with correct visionbut whose executives constantly made changes in strategy, organization, and product failed.

The firms that survived and prospered through a competitive discontinuity, a disruptive change, were those whose executive teams:

- Envision and correctly anticipate the discontinuity and prepare for it with appropriate product strategy and reorganization
- After making the appropriate strategic change, hold a steady course to produce proper products/services with quality and low costs.

It is particularly difficult for a company to formulate a new product strategy when it hits a competitive discontinuity generated by new applied knowledge.

The principal reasons in the difficulty of formulating a new product strategy in a competitive discontinuity are:

- The technical uncertainties of a new applied knowledge vision
- The differing perspectives among the different product-group managers and the technical staff about that vision

For a company to develop a new next-generation product-line strategy, the whole company must fight out different visions about the product plans in a new applied knowledge situation. To formulate a next-generation product plan for an applied-knowledge competitive-discontinuity, it is necessary for a high-level executive to envision and force the strategic issue and to organize the effort necessary to formulate and implement a new strategy for the whole company. Competitive discontinuities are a common problem for a firm initially successful in a radically new industry because applied knowledge in the industry continues to progress for a time.

The reason for the crisis is that competitive discontinuities due to rapid progress in applied knowledge force not only changes in product strategy but changes in business strategy to exploit the changing market. This is why competitive discontinuities are strategically challenging. And this is why strategic vision that foresees discontinuities and strategic planning that prepares for discontinuities are the key challenges of strategic thinking.

PLANNING

Strategic plans need to be formulated as guided by the direction in a strategic vision.Yet the actual implementation of a strategic plan will require that it be put into action through a sequence of operational plans.

Accordingly, we next need to review the differences between strategic and operational plans:

- Strategic planning is a concern for and laying out of the directions for the long-term future.
- Operational planing is a concern for and laying out of the directions for the short-term future.

The conceptual duality of controlling both long-term and short-term events makes strategic planning and operational planning complementary cognitive functions of management. In the case of HP, it had good operational planning capability but not good long-term strategic planning capability. The ink-jet product success was a result of good short-term product development and planning.

Stasis and Change in Operations

Operational planning is aimed at controlling the steadiness of organizational operations, or stasis. Stasis in management attention attends to the immediate efficiency of operations, for it is efficiency that in the short term determines profitability in a commercial organization. Efficient repetition of operations, as the production and sales of a large volume of products, creates economies of scale, and upon such economies rests profitability of operations. In the long-term performance, management practice additionally needs to focus upon making desirable changes for future operations, strategy. Strategy focuses on the long-term, mediate effectiveness of operations—not to the shortterm, immediate efficiency of operations.

- Efficiency of business operations produces profits in the short term, but effectiveness of business operations creates survivability in the long term.

It is the effectiveness of business strategy in the long term that creates the right kinds of products and services for market share and dominance. It is in market share and dominance that a business survives over time.

Thus both stasis of current operations and change in future operations are essential to strategic management thinking. Stasis produces the short-term, immediate benefits of organizations, whereas change produces the long-term, benefits mediated through intervening events.

Stasis and change are complementary. Few steady-state operations can go on forever without needing change because many aspects of an organization are not static—markets, technology, competition, politics, etc. Thus periodically—at the beginning of an organization, through the growth of an organization, and at subsequent critical periods of an organization—operations need to change for the organization's long-term effectiveness and survival.

Planning needs both to continually optimize stasis and periodically change stasis:

- Operational planning focuses upon optimization of stasis in operations in the immediate, short-time horizon.
- Strategic planning focuses upon change in future operations for survival in the mediate, long-term horizon.

Both operational planning and strategic planning become integrated in the annual budgeting activity of organizations. But conceptually they are different. Thus in the planning and implementation procedures of strategic management, the procedures need to facilitate both short-term and long-term planning.

Implementing Operational and Strategic Plans

How is operational planning implemented? How is strategic planning implemented? To answer these questions, we need to remind ourselves of the levels of decision logic in the control of an organization's activities. Organizations conduct repetitive activities in their operations to add value—such as manufacturing and selling products or providing and delivering services. Thus the ground logical level of any organization is its repetitive activities that directly transform inputs of resources into value-added outputs of products/services. The scheme, or order, of how repetitive activities are to be carried out in an organization is called its "operations." Operations are the patterns of order that govern, or control, activities. For example, in automobile manufacturing operations it is the order of the assembly line, where engines are first assembled in parallel with chassis and body assemblies and then engines are mounted onto chassis and then bodies are attached. In a large organization, precisely how these operations are to be conducted are specified as organizational "procedures." Procedures are the instructions on how to carry out an operation.

For example, in automobile manufacturing, there are designs which specify the tooling for production and standards for performing operations. Procedures as designs and standards control operations. The next decision-logic level in organizations is "policies," which specify the purpose of procedures. For example, in automobile manufacturing, policies determine the types of autos to be designed, the extent of annual model change, the markets to be targeted for the auto designs, the cost targets for production, and so on. Policies control procedures.

The highest decision-logic level in organizations is "strategies," which provide the directions of change for policies. For example, in automobile manufacturing, strategies determine the product lines to be produced, acquisition of new brands, extent of vertical integration of production, and so on. Strategies control changes in policies.

In summary, the hierarchy of decision logic in an organization consists of the following control levels:

- Activities that transform inputs to outputs
- Operations that control activities
- Procedures that control operations
- Policies that control procedures
- Strategies that control policies

The relationship of operational and strategic planning can now be seen in how their implementation affects differently these levels of decision-control in organizations. Operational planning is implemented by changing the lower-two levels of operations and procedures, whereas strategic planning is implemented by changing the upper two levels of policies and strategy: 0perational planning specifies operations and procedures and strategic planning specifies policies and strategy:

- Operational plans are implemented through targets of operations and changes of procedures.
- Strategic plans are implemented through targets of strategy and changes in polices.

Furthermore, when we look in detail at these two kinds of planning as suggested, find that their logics and processes are really very different:

1. Operations planning uses the logics of known action and specific

directions to specify how to achieve specific goals of repetitive types of action.

2. Strategic planning uses the logics of unknown action and preparation to launch exploration into action never previously experienced.

The logic of planning is the logic of operations—knowing how to get to someplace we have gone before.

The logic of strategy is the logic of exploration— preparing to go someplace we have never gone before. In the logic of an operational plan, one can clearly state the ends and means of action—goals and tactics— since we have performed this operational action before, repetitively, and we understand what it takes to do it.

Thus operations plans can be summarized in bullet form, for everyone involved can fill in the story's details—been there, done that—know how to do it again.

An operations plan just says how much we are going to do again. However, in the logic of a strategic plan, one is going exploring, rather that repeating an action previously performed. The logic of strategy consists—not of spelling out the means and ends of known action—but of refining perception, creating commitments, preparing for action. Together—perception, commitment, and preparation—constitute the real logic of strategic exploration.

Strategy is not planning:

- Strategy is change in long-term direction
- Strategic planning lays out the sequence of steps to implement long-term change
- Operational planning details the immediate steps of implementing long-term change and of continuing stasis

STRATEGY PROCESS

Now we can put these ideas together and depict an effective modern strategy process. We recall that strategic thinking is a process, and a strategic plan is a result of the process.

The problem of a strategy process in a large organization is how to have planning procedures that:

- Focuses management thinking on long-term prosperity
- Anticipates relevant change
- Stimulates constructive interaction between top-down and bottom-up perspectives
- Creates effective strategic vision
- Transforms strategy into action

Strategic Planning Teams

Look at the first step in Figure, which shows that the first two steps in creating a strategic thinking process in an organization is to establish a planning process that encourages the interaction of top-down and bottom-up perspectives by,

- Forming top-down and bottom-up strategic-planning teams
- Scheduling interactions between teams

The composition of a top-down strategy team needs to consist of a firm-level planning staff and executives of the businesses or divisions that compose the company. A bottom-up strategy team should consist of managers of the businesses in the firm. Since there are hierarchical differences in the authority positions in these teams, it is important to formally schedule interactive presentations of their planning work to one another as the planning efforts proceed to stimulate appropriate interaction of perspectives.

PlanningScenario and Strategic Business Model

Look again at Figure, which shows that the next step is to focus the strategy teams upon creating formal descriptions of the environments and the businesses as outputs of the interactions:

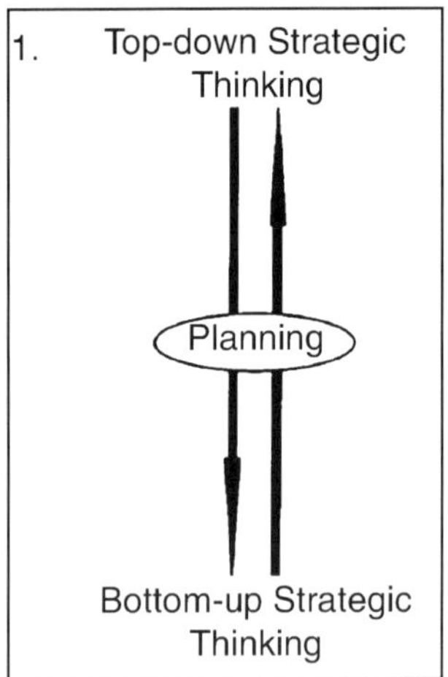

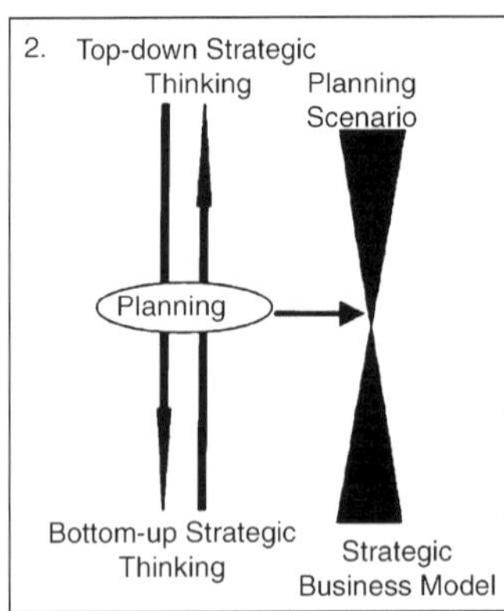

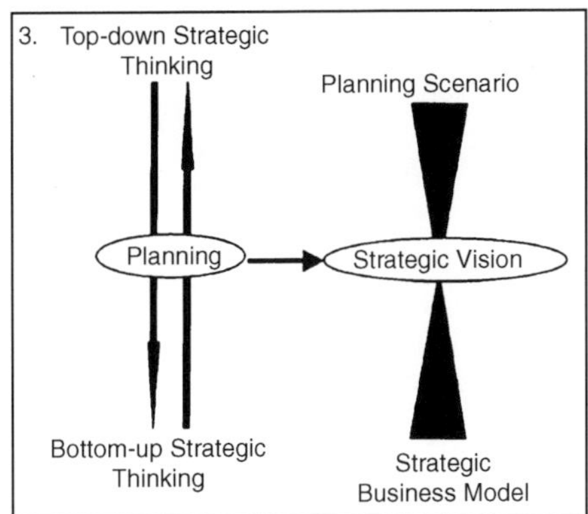

A planning scenario anticipates from the top-down perspective the future environments of the company. Formulating such a scenario requires anticipating changes in the structures of the societies in which a company operates. In industrialized societies, four general structures exist, economic structures, governmental structures, territorial structures, and cultural structures. The technique of scenario planning provides a systematic way of examining trends and forecasts of possible and likely changes in the future in these structures. A strategic model of a business summarizes from the bottom-up perspective the intended future policies of the business.

- The kind of strategic business model one uses to depict future business policies depends upon which kind of corporate performance one wishes to optimize.

In formulating any strategic business model, important strategic issues are those of markets and innovation competition and structure, operations and control, and information and knowledge.

Strategic Vision

The procedures for creating a planning scenario and strategic business models facilitate the two perspectives on the future from the general to the particular and from the particular to the general; and from this interaction the third step to add in the planning process is an integrative picture of the future:

- Formulate an intuitive strategic vision.

A strategic vision is an intuitive view of the future. For example, in the merger of AOL and Time Warner, both CEOs, Case and Levin, developed a strategic vision of the future merged company, that is, altering boundaries of AOL and Time Warner to become a new firm with the boundaries of content creation and delivery. For AOL, Case's vision was to vertically integrate AOL from media service delivery back into media content creation. Acquiring the media-content creation businesses of Time Warner would change AOL's future business capabilities. For TimeWarner, Levins' vision was to merge TimeWarner into a major e-commerce business Vision results from the intuitive cognitive function of the mind—vision is a synthetic view of a totality—a gestalt. How to facilitate intuition in a group setting is a difficult problem. For now, theimportant point is to emphasize that the procedures for strategic plan need to create a strategic vision arising from the team interactions of constructing a planning scenario and a strategic business model.

Strategic and Operational Plan

The final steps in constructing the procedures for a strategy process in a large organization is to translate the strategic vision of the future into strategic plans that can be implemented beginning as near-term operational plans by adding the following procedures:

- Construct an analytical long-term strategic plan.
- Construct short-term operational plans in the direction of the strategic plan.

What we have sketched are the key elements in strategic thinking as an organizational process in Figure. The strategic planning process begins with bidirectional views on the future of the company—top-down strategic thinking about changes in the environments of the firm and bottom-up strategic thinking about changes in the businesses of the firm.

The interactions of these two perspectives should create a strategic vision about the directions the company should go in the future; and the concrete steps to do so constitutes a strategic plan for the company.

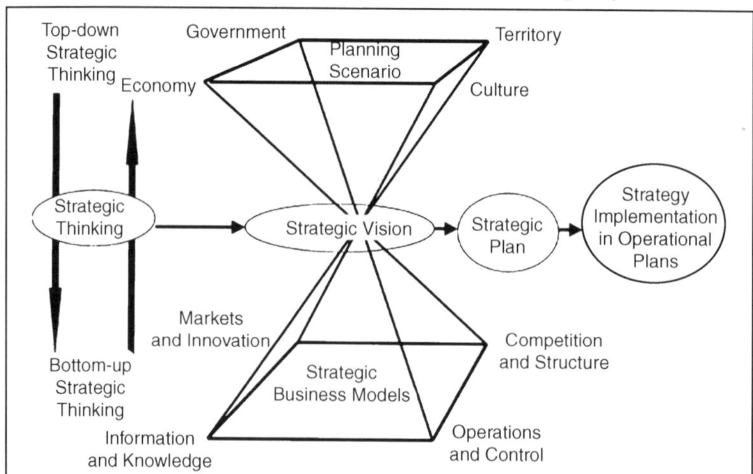

The top-down view arises from the construction of a planning scenario, which anticipates the kinds of changes in the environments that will be relevant to the businesses of the firm in the future. The bottom-up view arises from the construction of a strategic business model for each business of the firm.

This model anticipates the kinds of changes desired and needed to prepare the firm and its businesses for a competitive and successful future.

Multi-Business Firm Strategy

The strategy process depicted in Figure assumes a company is a singlebusiness firm, yet most large corporations are multi-business firms.

Strategy changes dramatically at the different levels of a multi-business corporation. For example, Lowell Steele emphasized the perspective differences in strategy between single and multiple business companies:

- One must distinguish between single-business companies and multi-business companies. Strategic planning at the corporate level for a multi-business enterprise cannot be the same for a company with a single line or closely related product lines."

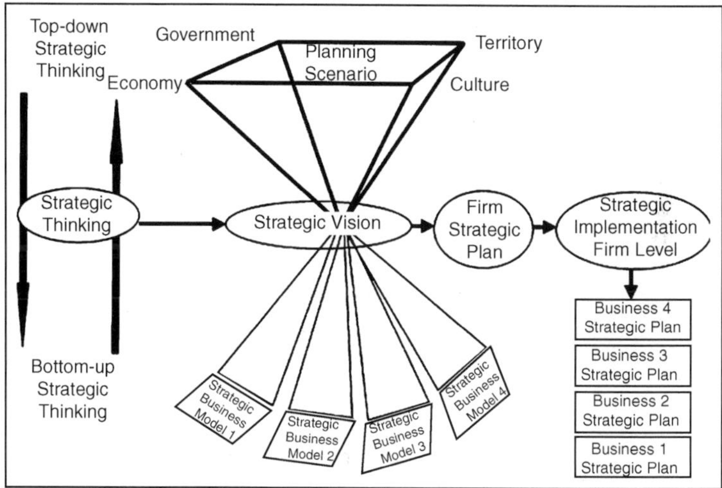

Fig. Strategy Process—Multibusiness Firm

The strategic differences arise from the kinds of competition each kind of company,—single-business or diversified-businesses—faces. The single business company finds its principle competition in the marketplace—face-to-face with customers and competitors also directly in contact with customers:

- Competition for a single-business entity is in the market place, offering superior value to customers. If it does that effectively, its performance will be satisfactory— provided that its markets permit an acceptable rate of return.

Accordingly, competitive strategy for the single business company must focus primarily upon its products and services—product, production, and marketing strategies. Strategy needs to be focused upon the variables that directly add value to customers, such as product attributes, quality, cost, safety, differentiation, distribution channels, advertising, and so on. In contrast, the multiple-business company is primarily a financial holder of businesses, so that it performance is not in the customer market but in the financial market:

- Competition for the multi-business enterprise is in the capital markets: Does its present portfolio of businesses and mode of management produce a competitive rate of return... ? Multi-business strategy focuses first and foremost on portfolio optimization— what mix of sources of revenue is desired and what allocation of resources will best bring about this preferred mix.

Multi-business company strategy must focus principally upon variables that directly impact the rate-of-return of capital, such as business portfolio, position of a business in its industry, business investments, business leadership, business acquisitions and divestitures, and so on. Accordingly, the strategy process for a multi-business firm needs to be modified as shown in Figure. Therein a common planning scenario is still appropriate for the entire firm and a common strategic vision. But each separate business in the firm needs to create a strategic business model appropriate to its business.

In a multibusiness firm, the strategy process will result in a:

- Firm strategic plan
- Strategic business models and strategic plans for each business and strategic business plans and operational plans for each business

NEW PRODUCT DEVELOPMENT

The dynamics of markets, technology, and competition have brought changes to virtually every market sector and have made new product development one of the most powerful business activities. The monumental changes that constantly impact commerce have forced companies to innovate with increasing speed, efficiency, and quality. In turn, this has made new product development one of the most complex and difficult business functions. However, firms must innovate in order to survive. The power of innovation is revealed in numerous studies, which show that companies leading their industries attribute about half of their revenues to products developed in the most recent five years. By comparison, companies at the bottom of their industries achieve approximately one-tenth of their sales from new products.

A firm's new product development efforts are shaped by its size, as well as the nature of the industry in which it operates. New products may be defined as any product, service, or idea not currently made or marketed by a company, or which the consumer may perceive as new.

Many types of new products exist, from never-seen-before products like Apple's personal communicator, to repositioned standards like Sears' shift to Sears Brand Central. Various studies suggest that between 50 and 80 per cent of new products fail—the greater the rate of new product development, the higher the failure rate. New Product News predicts that more than 36,000 new products will be brought to market in 2005. Although there are numerous reasons why new products fail, faulty management and planning are at the core of most failures. Therefore, managing the new product development process is a key to a healthy organization.

HISTORY

The history of product innovation can be divided into three stages, beginning with the product-oriented or technology-pushed stage. In the post-World War II era Americans were coming off wartime shortages and were in the mood to buy the many goods that manufacturers produced.

Engineers, who were more product-oriented than consumer oriented, designed new products that might or might not find places in consumers' hearts and minds. This was a product-oriented process in which the market was considered the receptacle for products that emerged from the firm's research and development efforts.

However, competition escalated and consumers became more skeptical and selective about the types of products they purchased. Marketers found it increasingly difficult to rely on persuasive sales techniques to move products. Retailers grew restless when these products did not move off shelves as quickly as planned. Companies had to know more about their target markets. What were the wants and needs of the people who were buying their products? How could their firm satisfy these wants and needs?

The second stage was marked by the emergence of the market as the driver of innovation. Instead of being technology-driven, new product development evolved into a market-led process in which new products emerged from well-researched customer needs. The new product development process was placed in the hands of marketers who knew consumers' wants and needs. Customer demand "pulled" the product through the development process. Modern new product development is a blending of these two orientations into a "dual-drive" approach to innovation. Companies recognize that innovation is a complex process that requires sound investment in research and development, as well as significant marketing expertise that focuses on satisfying consumers' wants and needs.

The rapid pace of change that engulfed businesses towards the end of the twentieth century put an even greater burden on companies to build adaptive capabilities into their organizations. Global competition means there are more competitors capable of world-class performance.

This has made competition more intense, rigorous, and aggressive than ever before. Fragmenting and more sophisticated markets mean that consumers demand more from products in terms of quality, differentiation, and "meaningfulness." New technologies have had two important outcomes in regards to innovation. First, new technologies are responsible for this new market sophistication in which consumers have more choices and are thus more demanding. Secondly, new technology has increased manufacturers' capabilities for rapid response to shifting market needs.

Finally, product life cycles have become more compressed as the skills required for developing new products increase in complexity. For example, consider the development of a new type of computer software. The expertise needed to develop the software from conception to commercialization might take years. The product's life cycle in such a competitive and turbulent environment might last only a few months.

Therefore, companies have embraced the view that new products are transient, whereas the skills and expertise needed to develop these products are a much more persistent requirement for success. Instead of the mono-approach, in which technology or markets drive innovation, new product development now requires a convergence of technology, marketing, product design, engineering, and manufacturing capabilities.

Speed, efficiency, and quality in product development are the challenges that new product development faces in today's intense competitive environment.

TYPES AND SOURCES OF NEW PRODUCTS

There are five categories of new products. New-to-the-world products or services are new inventions like in-line skates and health maintenance organizations. New category entries, such as sport utility vehicles, are products or services that are new to a firm. Additions to product lines add products or services to a firm's current markets. For example, when a powder laundry detergent offers a liquid version it is considered a line extension. Product improvements are another type of new product and are common to every product category. Repositionings target products to new markets or for new uses.

Firms can obtain new products internally or externally. External sourcing means the company acquires the product or service, or obtains the rights to market the product or service, from another organization. Internal development means the firm develops the new product itself. This is riskier than external development because the company bears all of the costs associated with new product development and implementation. Collaborations, which include strategic partnerships, strategic alliances, joint ventures, and licensing agreements, occur when two or more firms work together on developing new products.

NEW PRODUCT DEVELOPMENT PROCESS

Historically, the new product development process has been conceived in discreet terms with a beginning and an end. Different companies and different industries may alter this seven-step process for different products, or the steps themselves may become blurred as companies become engaged in several stages at the same time.

The process begins with idea generation. For every successful new product, many new product ideas are conceived and discarded. Therefore, companies usually generate a large number of ideas from which successful new products emerge.

Idea screening, the second step, considers all new product ideas in the idea pool and eliminates ones that are perceived to be the least likely to succeed. Not only should the firm's manufacturing, technology, and marketing capabilities be evaluated at this stage, but also how the new idea fits with the company's vision and strategic objectives.

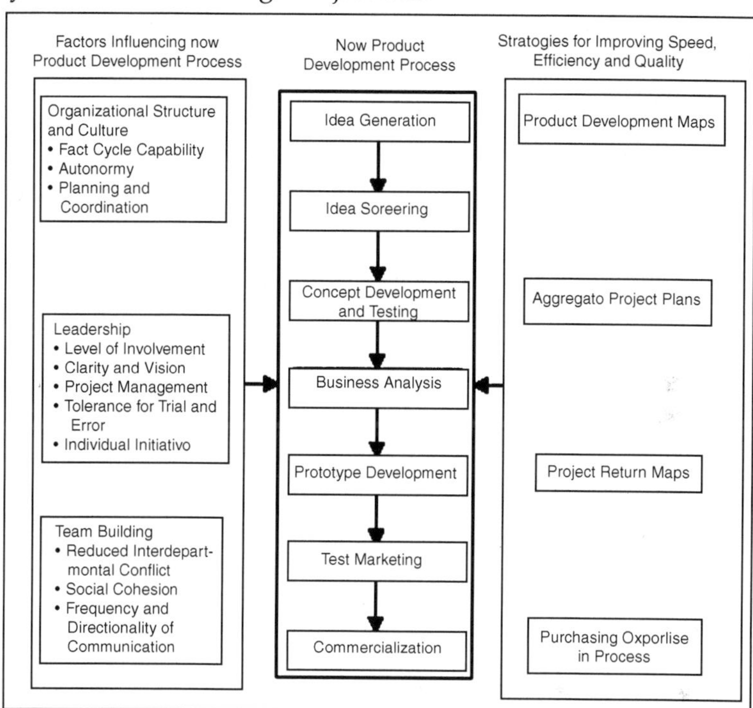

Fig. New Product Development Process, Factors and Strategies.

The third stage, concept development and testing, requires formal evaluations of the product concept by consumers, usually through some form of marketing research. New product ideas with low concept test scores are discarded or revised. While the Internet is making it easier to gather consumer data, there are limitations. As people get deluged with an increasing number of surveys and solicitations, it is possible that they will grow tired of helping marketers.

The business analysis stage is next. At this point the new product idea is analysed for its marketability and costs. After passing the first three stages an idea may be discarded once marketing and manufacturing costs are analysed, due to limited potential for profitability or commercial success. Throughout these four stages, the new idea has remained on document with a relatively small investment required.

The fifth stage, prototype development, is the first stage where new product costs begin to escalate. Because of this, many companies have placed greater emphasis on the first four stages and reduced the proportion of new products that reach the prototype stage from about 50 per cent to around 20 per cent. At this stage the concept is converted into an actual product. A customer value perspective during this phase means the product is designed to satisfy the needs expressed by consumers. Firms may use quality function deployment as they develop the prototype. QFD links specific consumer requirements such as versatility, durability, and low maintenance with specific product characteristics. The customer value perspective requires the new product to satisfy customer needs and meet desired quality levels at specified production costs.

Test marketing tests the prototype and marketing strategy in simulated or actual market situations. Because of the expense and risks associated with actual test markets, marketers use them with caution. Products that test poorly are pulled back and reconceptualized or discarded.

Commercialization, the final stage, is when the product is introduced full scale. The level of investment and risk are highest at this stage. Consumer adoption rates, timing decisions for introduction, and coordinating efforts with production, distribution, and marketing should be considered.

FACTORS INFLUENCING NEW PRODUCT DEVELOPMENT

The seven-step process assumes a definite beginning and end. However, studies suggest that what goes on before and after new products are introduced is as important as the process itself. Organizational structure, leadership, and team building influence the speed and efficiency with which new products are introduced. Structure influences efficiency, autonomy, and coordination. New product innovation requires structure that optimizes direction and guidance. Structure that facilitates internal information exchange, decision making, and materials flow is essential. A "fast-cycle" structure allows more time for planning and implementing activities to gain competitive advantage. This type of structure also cuts costs because production materials and information collect less overhead and do not accumulate as work-in-process inventory. Autonomy refers to the amount of decision making allowed at lower levels of management. The coordination of the engineering, product design, manufacturing, and marketing functions in the new product development process is vital.

Leadership influences strategy, culture, and the firm's overall ability to undertake new product development. Top management can demonstrate involvement in the development process by providing career advancement for entrepreneurial skills and encouraging broad employee participation. Clarity and vision are crucial to ensuring that new product ideas are good strategic fits for the company. The degree to which leadership allows trial and error and promotes individual initiative positively influences the development of new products. This acceptance of risk and support for an entrepreneurial spirit within the organization are crucial in order for innovation to flourish. New products emerge in a variety of ways and their development does not always proceed in rational and consistent manners. It is necessary for leadership to view the process as iterative and dynamic, and to foster adaptation and flexibility. Management flexibility and responsiveness to change also are needed. This type of leadership is particularly important to the project manager who must coordinate and integrate the various parts of the new product development process so that a coherent system emerges that produces a product with compelling value. Initiative encourages creativity and problem-solving skills. Teams provide mechanisms for breaking down functional biases created by a strict adherence to structure. The amount of interdepartmental conflict in the organization, the social cohesion among team members, and the frequency and directionality of interdepartmental communication influence team building. Through shared understanding of the objectives and purposes of the project, as well as the tasks required in the development process, teams can shape the project and influence how work gets done in the organization.

IMPROVING SPEED, EFFICIENCY, AND QUALITY

New products often fail because of unanticipated market shifts that result in missed opportunities and misused channels of distribution. Failures also occur because companies miscalculate their own technological strengths or the product's technological challenges. These potential problems often crop up in the latter stages and result in delays, redesigns, or poor quality products.

Companies are constantly seeking ways to avoid these pitfalls. One solution is new product development maps that chart the evolution of a company's product lines. This historical perspective helps the firm to identify and analyse functional capabilities in a systematic, repetitive fashion that allows for the development of linkages and the identification of resources for new endeavors. These maps can direct the firm to new market opportunities and point out technological challenges.

Aggregate plans for projects offer another solution. Rather than viewing each new product development project individually, they consider all of the new product development projects under consideration by the firm. This is particularly important in firms with hundreds of new product development projects going on at the same time. Projects are categorized according to resources required and contribution to the firm's bottom line. Aggregate project plans enable management to improve the management of new product development by providing greater control over resource allocation and utilization. These plans help to point out where capabilities need to be improved, how sequencing projects may help, and how projects fit with the firm's development strategies.

Return maps graphically represent the contributions of all team members to product success in terms of time and money. Their focus is on the point at which product sales generate sufficient profit so that the firm's initial investment in development is returned. Return maps show team members the time and money needed to complete their tasks in the development process so that they may estimate and re-estimate their investment in the process. In doing this return maps show the impact of their actions on the project's overall success.

Another way to improve the speed and efficiency with which new products are introduced is to involve purchasing in the development process. When purchasing expertise is introduced into the development project team, quality may increase, time to market entry may decrease, investment in inventory may diminish, and costs may significantly decrease.

Technology continues to change and create new opportunities and threats. Customer requirements and expectations continue to shift and create new demands. Old channels of distribution are becoming obsolete and new channels are opening new opportunities. Some competitors are falling by the wayside while others are surging to the forefront by making new and unexpected moves to gain advantage. The very structure of industry is changing. A key to success in this tumultuous environment will continue to be the ability to sustain a competitive advantage through innovation. However, speed, efficiency, and quality in product development will be paramount. Building capabilities in all aspects of product creation and implementation, overcoming uncertainty and facilitating decision-making, ensuring these innovations are strategically linked to the firm's vision, and doing this on a continuous basis is the challenge of new product development in the next century.

NEW PRODUCT FAILURE

In this era of tight competition from domestic and global firms the firm who don't come out with new products are putting themselves at great risk Because their existing products are prone to changing customer needs, shorter product life cycles, new technologies and increased competition. Despite years of research and huge capital being pumped in to understanding the consumer, making a launch successful is still a difficult task. The new product largely depends on the product quality and the marketing tactics of the firm, there are many occasions were the product failed miserably even after using the best technology and quality the reason is that the new product is not worth for the customers. The prime factor for the new product success is - customer value. Value is what the customer thinks is value. The major reasons for product failure are

FAULTY PRODUCT IDEA

The product often fail because faulty of product idea. A good idea can revolutionize the market but a bad idea may prove bitter to the firm or it may backfire Eg: Polar industries in 1991 launched "COOL CATS" fan - decorated with cartoon characters meant primarily for children. The fan was priced at premium; the idea was that children's were increasingly becoming influensors in purchase decisions and to attract the kids with the cartoon creatures and to position the product exclusively for kids. The product failed miserably inspite of its huge advertising budget because when the fan was put on it didn't have any colour effect and the customer did not justify its premium price.

DISTRIBUTION RELATED PROBLEMS

The new product fails if the product is unable to meet the channel requirements. While developing the product the channel requirements must be given adequate consideration. Eg: when NESTLE launched its new chocolates the product and promotion was ok but the product failed in the distribution side because the company stipulated the product to be stored in refrigerators.

The product faced two problems in the distribution side because it meant excluding a number of retail outlets as they didn't have this facility and secondly the chocolate was not picked by the customers as it was not seen upfront in the retail shops. Finally Nestle had to reformulate the product according to channel requirements.

POOR TIMING OF LAUNCH

Too early or late entry into the market is a common cause of failure. Kinetic Merlin was launched in pune in 1991.It was a 3 in 1 set consisting of a colour television, a stereo with detachable speakers and a home computer. The product was targeted at the Indian consumers who are fond of sophisticated gadgets to immediately adopt such an innovative idea but in reality the idea was too advanced for the customers to digest at that time because they were not exposed to such type of products before.

IMPROPER POSITIONING

Positioning means putting the product into the predetermined orbit. Improper positioning may affect the product success. Eg: Titan Tanishq introduced their 18 carat jewellery and the product was positioned at elite segment but there was a contradiction as to why these elite segment should go in for a low carat gold because the norms for gold in India at that time was 22 carat. The product failed miserably in retrospect Titan had to introduce 22-carat jewellery.

Some other reasons for product failure are:

- Lack of differential advantage
- Poor planning
- Technical problems in the product

- Competitors fighting back harder than expected
- Poor market research

These are some problems causing new product failure. The watchwords for new product success are right product to the right customer at right time.

TEN REASONS WHY NEW PRODUCTS & SERVICES FAIL

Why do fewer than 10% of all new products/services produce enough return on the company's investment to survive past the third year?

Here's our top 10 list of reasons new products and services fail:

1. Marketers assess the marketing climate inadequately.
2. The wrong group is targeted.
3. A weak positioning strategy is used.
4. A less-than-optimal "configuration" of product or service attributes and benefits is selected.
5. A questionable pricing strategy is implemented.
6. The advertising campaign generates an insufficient level of new product/new service awareness.
7. Cannibalization depresses corporate profits.
8. Over-optimism about the marketing plan leads to a forecast that cannot be sustained in the real world.
9. The marketing plan for the new product or service is not well implemented in the real world.
10. The marketer believes that the new product and its marketing plan has died and cannot be revived, when, in fact there is the potential for resurrection.

What can marketers do to improve the likelihood of new product success in an age of promotion and unprecedented competitive response? Testing the product before launch is one solution. Typically, if a company decides to do a test market before launching the product, managers run a test market. Traditional test markets are fraught with problems, starting with how companies select them—often because they are easy to manage rather than because they represent the actual markets a company wants to reach.

Traditional test markets are expensive and competitors can steal ideas and sabotage results. A well-done simulated test market, on the other hand, reduces the risks of launching a flop by collecting data a company needs to forecast the likelihood of success, more securely and more efficiently than a traditional test market.

STRATEGIES OVER PRODUCT LIFE CYCLE

Product life cycle management is the succession of strategies used by business management as a product goes through its life cycle. The conditions in which a product is sold changes over time and must be managed as it moves through its succession of stages.

PRODUCT LIFE CYCLE (PLC)

Like human beings, products also have their own life-cycle. From birth to death human beings pass through various stages e.g. birth, growth, maturity, decline and death. A similar life-cycle is seen in the case of products. The product life cycle goes through multiple phases, involves many professional disciplines, and requires many skills, tools and processes. Product life cycle has to do with the life of a product in the market with respect to business/commercial costs and sales measures.

To say that a product has a life cycle is to assert four things:

1. That products have a limited life,
2. Product sales pass through distinct stages, each posing different challenges, opportunities, and problems to the seller,
3. Profits rise and fall at different stages of product life cycle, and
4. Products require different marketing, financial, manufacturing, purchasing, and human resource strategies in each life cycle stage.

The four main stages of a product's life cycle and the accompanying characteristics are:

Stage	Characteristics
1. Market introduction stage	1. Costs are high 2. Slow sales volumes to start 3. Little or no competition 4. Demand has to be created 5. Customers have to be prompted to try the product 6. Makes no money at this stage
2. Growth stage	1. Costs reduced due to economies of scale 2. Sales volume increases significantly 3. Profitability begins to rise 4. Public awareness increases 5. Competition begins to increase with a few new players in establishing market 6. Increased competition leads to price decreases
3. Maturity stage	1. Costs are lowered as a result of production volumes increasing and experience curve effects 2. Sales volume peaks and market saturation is reached 3. Increase in competitors entering the market 4. Prices tend to drop due to the proliferation

	of competing products 5. Brand differentiation and feature diversification is emphasized to maintain or increase market share 6. Industrial profits go down
4. Saturation and decline stage	1. Costs become counter-optimal 2. Sales volume decline or stabilize 3. Prices, profitability diminish 4. Profit becomes more a challenge of production/distribution efficiency than increased sales

Request for Deviation

In the process of building a product following defined procedure, an RFD is a request for authorization, granted prior to the manufacture of an item, to depart from a particular performance or design requirement of a specification, drawing or other document, for a specific number of units or a specific period of time.

Market Identification

Termination is not always the end of the cycle; it can be the end of a micro-entrant within the grander scope of a macro-environment. The auto industry, fast-food industry, petro-chemical industry, are just a few that demonstrate a macro-environment that overall has not terminated even while micro-entrants over time have come and gone.

SESSIONS OF THE PRODUCT LIFE CYCLE (PLC)

It is claimed that every product has a life period, it is launched, it grows, and at some point, may die. A fair comment is that - at least in the short term - not all products or services die. Jeans may die, but clothes probably will not. Legal services or medical services may die, but depending on the social and political climate, probably will not.

Even though its validity is questionable, it can offer a useful 'model' for managers to keep at the back of their mind. Indeed, if their products are in the introductory or growth phases, or in that of decline, it perhaps should be at the front of their mind; for the predominant features of these phases may be those revolving around such life and death. Between these two extremes, it is salutary for them to have that vision of mortality in front of them. However, the most important aspect of product life-cycles is that, even under normal conditions, to all practical intents and purposes they often do not exist. In most markets the majority of the major brands have held their position for at least two decades. The dominant product life-cycle, that of the brand leaders which almost monopolize many markets, is therefore one of continuity.

In the criticism of the product life cycle, Dhalla & Yuspeh state:

- ...clearly, the PLC is a dependent variable which is determined by market actions; it is not an independent variable to which companies should adapt their marketing programmes. Marketing management itself can alter the shape and duration of a brand's life cycle.

Thus, the life cycle may be useful as a description, but not as a predictor; and usually should be firmly under the control of the marketer. The important point is that in many markets the product or brand life cycle is significantly longer than the planning cycle of the organisations involved. Thus, it offers little practical value for most marketers. Even if the PLC exists for them, their plans will be based just upon that piece of the curve where they currently reside; and their view of that part of it will almost certainly be 'linear', and will not encompass the whole range from growth to decline. Product life cycle means how a product run through out all of his life.

It have four stages which are:

1. Introduction stage
2. Growth stage
3. Maturity
4. Decline

LIMITATIONS

The PLC model is of some degree of usefulness to marketing managers, in that it is based on factual assumptions. Nevertheless, it is difficult for marketing management to gauge accurately where a product is on its PLC graph. A rise in sales per se is not necessarily evidence of growth. A fall in sales per se does not typify decline. Furthermore, some products do not experienced a decline. Coca Cola and Pepsi are examples of two products that have existed for many decades, but are still popular products all over the world. Both modes of cola have been in maturity for some years.

Another factor is that differing products would possess different PLC "shapes". A fad product would hold a steep sloped growth stage, a short maturity stage, and a steep sloped decline stage. A product such as Coca Cola and Pepsi would experience growth, but also a constant level of sales over a number of decades. It can probably be said that a given product may hold a unique PLC shape, and the typical PLC model can only be used as a rough guide for marketing management. This is why its called the product life cycle. The duration of PLC stages is unpredictable. It is not possible to predict when maturity or decline will begin. Strict adherence to PLC can lead a company to misleading objectives and strategy prescriptions.

INTERNATIONAL MARKETING AS A STRATEGY

International marketing or global marketing refers to marketing carried out by companies overseas or across national borderlines. This strategy uses an extension of the techniques used in the home country of a firm. It refers to the firm-level marketing practices across the border including market identification and targeting, entry mode selection, marketing mix, and strategic decisions to compete in international markets.

According to the American Marketing Association "international marketing is the multinational process of planning and executing the conception, pricing, promotion and distribution of ideas, goods, and services to create exchanges that satisfy individual and organizational objectives." In contrast to the definition of marketing only the word multinational has been added. In simple words international marketing is the application of marketing principles to across national boundaries. However, there is a crossover between what is commonly expressed as international marketing and global marketing, which is a similar term.

The intersection is the result of the process of internationalization. Many American and European authors see international marketing as a simple extension of exporting, whereby the marketing mix 4P's is simply adapted in some way to take into account differences in consumers and segments. It then follows that global marketing takes a more standardised approach to world markets and focuses upon sameness, in other words the similarities in consumers and segments.

FURTHER DEFINITIONS

Cateora and Ghauri International Marketing is the performance of business activities that direct the flow of a company's goods and services to consumers or users in more than one nation for a profit.

International marketing is often not as simple as marketing your product to more than one nation. Companies must consider language barriers, ideals, and customs in the market they are approaching. Tailoring your marketing strategies to attract the specific group of people you are attempting to sell to is highly important and can serve the number one cause of failure or success.

As with other elements of marketing, there is no single definition of international marketing. Furthermore some authors define international marketing and global marketing differently. It can be distinguished between different levels of international marketing: "At its simplest level, international marketing involves the firm in making one or more marketing mix decisions across national boundaries. At its most complex level, it involves the firm in establishing manufacturing facilities overseas and coordinating marketing strategies across the globe."

Another definition sees international marketing as the international involvement of business activities: "International marketing is the performance of business activities that direct the flow of a company's goods and services to consumers or users in more than one nation for a profit." It can be also defined as "the application of marketing orientation and marketing capabilities to international business."

"The international market goes beyond the export marketer and becomes more involved in the marketing environment in the countries in which it is doing business."

Some definition refer to the term global marketing: "Global/transnational marketing focuses upon leveraging a company's assets, experience and products globally and upon adapting to what is truly unique and different in each country." "Global marketing refers to marketing activities coordinated and integrated across multiple country markets."

TOPICS COVERING THE MICRO-CONTEXT OF INTERNATIONAL MARKETING

According to Kotabe, the following topics covers the micro-context of international marketing.

Organisational and consumer behaviour:

- Organisational buying behaviour;
- International negotiations;
- Consumer behaviour;
- Country of origin.

Marketing entry decisions:

- Initial mode of entry
- Specific modes of entry
- Exporting;
- Joint ventures.

Local market expansaion: marketing mix decisions:

- Global standardisation vs. local responsiveness
- Marketing mix:
- Product policy;
- Advertising;
- Pricing;
- Distribution.

Global strategy:

- Competitive strategy:
- Conceptual development;
- Competitive advantage vs. competitive positioning;
- Sources of competitive advantage and performance implications.
- Strategic alliances:
- Learning and trust;
- Recipes for alliance success;
- Performance of different types of alliance.
- Global sourcing:
- Global sourcing in a service context;
- Benefits of global sourcing;
- Country of origin issues in global sourcing.

- Multinational performance:
- Determinants of performance;
- A different interpretation of performance.

Analytical techniques in cross-national research:

- Measuerment issues;
- Reliability and validity issues.

DIFFERENCES BETWEEN DOMESTIC MARKETING AND INTERNATIONAL MARKETING

There are various differences between domestic marketing and international marketing. Due to a language barrier it is more difficult to obtain and interpret research data in international marketing. Promotional messages needs to consider numerous cultural differences between different countries. This includes the differences in languages, expressions, habits, gestures, ideologies and more. For example, in the United States the round O sign made with thumb and first finger means "okay" while in Mediterranean countries the same gesture means "zero" or "the worst". In Tunisia it is understood as "I'll kill you" meanwhile for a Japan consumer it implies "money".

MODE OF ENGAGEMENT IN FOREIGN MARKETS

After the decision to invest has been made, the exact mode of operation has to be determined. The risks concerning operating in foreign markets is often dependent on the level of control a firm has, coupled with the level of capital expenditure outlayed.

The principal modes of engagement are listed below:

- Exporting
- Joint ventures
- Direct investment

Exporting

Direct exporting involves a firm shipping goods directly to a foreign market. A firm employing indirect exporting would utilise a channel/ intermediary, who in turn would disseminate the product in the foreign market. From a company's standpoint, exporting consists of the least risk. This is so since no capital expenditure, or outlay of company finances on new non-current assets, has necessarily taken place. Thus, the likelihood of sunk costs, or general barriers to exit, is slim. Conversely, a company may possess less control when exporting into a foreign market, due to not control the supply of the good within the foreign market.

Joint Ventures

A joint venture is a combined effort between two or more business entities, with the aim of mutual benefit from a given economic activity. Some countries often mandate that all foreign investment within it should be via joint ventures. By comparison with exporting, more control is exerted, however the level of risk is also increased.

Direct Investment

In this mode of engagement, a company would directly construct a fixed/ non-current asset within a foreign country, with the aim of manufacturing a product within the overseas market. Assembly denotes the literal assembly of completed parts, to build a completed product. An example of this is the Dell Corporation.

Dell possesses plants in countries external to the United States of America, however it assembles personal computers and does not manufacture them from scratch. In other words, it attains parts from other firms, and assembles a personal computer's constituent parts within its factories. Manufacturing concerns the actual forging of a product from scratch. Car manufacturers often construct all parts within their plants. Direct investment has the most control and the most risk attached. As with any capital expenditure, the return on investment has to be ascertained, in addition to appreciating any related sunk costs with the capital expenditure.

5

Marketing Communication

AN OVERVIEW

As the term suggests, marketing communication functions within a marketing framework. Traditionally known as the promotional element of the four Ps of marketing, the primary goal of marketing communication is to reach a defined audience to affect its behaviour by informing, persuading, and reminding. Marketing communication acquires new customers for brands by building awareness and encouraging trial. Marketing communication also maintains a brand's current customer base by reinforcing their purchase behaviour by providing additional information about the brand's benefits. A secondary goal of marketing communication is building and reinforcing relationships with customers, prospects, retailers, and other important stakeholders.

Successful marketing communication relies on a combination of options called the promotional mix. These options include advertising, sales promotion, public relations, direct marketing, and personal selling. The Internet has also become a powerful tool for reaching certain important audiences. The role each element takes in a marketing communication programme relies in part on whether a company employs a push strategy or a pull strategy.

A pull strategy relies more on consumer demand than personal selling for the product to travel from the manufacturer to the end user. The demand generated by advertising, public relations, and sales promotion "pulls" the good or service through the channels of distribution. A push strategy, on the other hand, emphasizes personal selling to push the product through these channels.

For marketing communication to be successful, however, sound management decisions must be made in the other three areas of the marketing mix: the product, service or idea itself; the price at which the brand will be offered; and the places at or through which customers may purchase the brand. The best promotion cannot overcome poor product quality, inordinately high prices, or insufficient retail distribution.

Fig. Elements of Marketing Cpmmunication

Likewise, successful marketing communication relies on sound management decisions regarding the coordination of the various elements of the promotional mix. To this end, a new way of viewing marketing communication emerged in the 1990s. Called integrated marketing communication, this perspective seeks to orchestrate the use of all forms of the promotional mix to reach customers at different levels in new and better ways.

INTEGRATED MARKETING COMMUNICATION

The evolution of this new perspective has two origins. Marketers began to realise that advertising, public relations, and sales were often at odds regarding responsibilities, budgets, management input and myriad other decisions affecting the successful marketing of a brand. Executives in each area competed with the others for resources and a voice in decision making. The outcome was inconsistent promotional efforts, wasted money, counterproductive management decisions, and, perhaps worst of all, confusion among consumers.

Secondly, the marketing perspective itself began to shift from being market oriented to market driven. Marketing communication was traditionally viewed as an inside-out way of presenting the company's messages. Advertising was the dominant element in the promotional mix because the mass media could effectively deliver a sales message to a mass audience. But then the mass market began to fragment.

Consumers became better educated and more skeptical about advertising. A variety of sources, both controlled by the marketer and uncontrolled, became important to consumers. News reports, word-of-mouth, experts' opinions, and financial reports were just some of the"brand contacts" consumers began to use to learn about and form attitudes and opinions about a brand or company, or make purchase decisions. Advertising began to lose some of its luster in terms of its ability to deliver huge homogeneous audiences. Companies began to seek new ways to coordinate the multiplicity of product and company messages being issued and used by consumers and others.

Thus, two ideas permeate integrated marketing communication: relationship building and synergy. Rather than the traditional inside-out view, IMC is seen as an outside-in perspective. Customers are viewed not as targets but as partners in an ongoing relationship. Customers, prospects, and others encounter the brand and company through a host of sources and create from these various contacts ideas about the brand and company.

By knowing the media habits and lifestyles of important consumer segments, marketers can tailor messages through media that are most likely to reach these segments at times when these segments are most likely to be receptive to these messages, thus optimizing the marketing communication effort. Ideally, IMC is implemented by developing comprehensive databases on customers and prospects, segmenting these current and potential customers into groups with certain common awareness levels, predispositions, and behaviours, and developing messages and media strategies that guide the communication tactics to meet marketing objectives. In doing this, IMC builds and reinforces mutually profitable relationships with customers and other important stakeholders and generates synergy by coordinating all elements in the promotional mix into a programme that possesses clarity, consistency, and maximum impact.

Practitioners and academics alike, however, have noted the difficulty of effectively implementing IMC. Defining exactly what IMC is has been difficult. For example, merely coordinating messages so that speaking"with one clear voice" in all promotional efforts does not fully capture the meaning of IMC. Also, changing the organization to accommodate the integrated approach has challenged the command and control structure of many organizations. However, studies suggest that IMC is viewed by a vast majority of marketing executives as having the greatest potential impact on their company's marketing strategies, more so than the economy, pricing, and globalization.

ADVERTISING

Advertising has four characteristics: it is persuasive in nature; it is non-personal; it is paid for by an identified sponsor; and it is disseminated through mass channels of communication. Advertising messages may promote the adoption of goods, services, persons, or ideas. Because the sales message is disseminated through the mass media—as opposed to personal selling—it is viewed as a much cheaper way of reaching consumers. However, its non-personal nature means it lacks the ability to tailor the sales message to the message recipient and, more importantly, actually get the sale.

Therefore, advertising effects are best measured in terms of increasing awareness and changing attitudes and opinions, not creating sales. Advertising's contribution to sales is difficult to isolate because many factors influence sales. The contribution advertising makes to sales are best viewed over the long run. The exception to this thinking is within the internet arena. While banner ads, pop-ups and interstitials should still be viewed as brand promoting and not necessarily sales drivers, technology provides the ability to track how many of a website's visitors click the banner, investigate a product, request more information, and ultimately make a purchase.

Through the use of symbols and images advertising can help differentiate products and services that are otherwise similar. Advertising also helps create and maintain brand equity. Brand equity is an intangible asset that results from a favourable image, impressions of differentiation, or consumer attachment to the company, brand, or trademark. This equity translates into greater sales volume, and/or higher margins, thus greater competitive advantage. Brand equity is established and maintained through advertising that focuses on image, product attributes, service, or other features of the company and its products or services.

Cost is the greatest disadvantage of advertising. The average cost for a 30-second spot on network television increased fivefold between 1980 and 2005. Plus, the average cost of producing a 30-second ad for network television is quite expensive. It is not uncommon for a national advertiser to spend in the millions of dollars for one 30-second commercial to be produced. Add more millions on top of that if celebrity talent is utilized.

Credibility and clutter are other disadvantages. Consumers have become increasingly skeptical about advertising messages and tend to resent advertisers' attempt to persuade. Advertising is everywhere, from network television, to daily newspapers, to roadside billboards, to golf course signs, to stickers on fruit in grocery stores. Clutter encourages consumers to ignore many advertising messages. New media are emerging, such as DVRs which allow consumers to record programmes and then skip commercials, and satellite radio which provides a majority of its channels advertising free.

PUBLIC RELATIONS

Public relations is defined as a management function which identifies, establishes, and maintains mutually beneficial relationships between an organization and the publics upon which its success or failure depends. Whereas advertising is a one-way communication from sender to the receiver, public relations considers multiple audiences and uses two-way communication to monitor feedback and adjust both its message and the organization's actions for maximum benefit. A primary tool used by public relations practitioners is publicity. Publicity capitalizes on the news value of a product, service, idea, person or event so that the information can be disseminated through the news media. This third party "endorsement" by the news media provides a vital boost to the marketing communication message: credibility.

In the media are perceived as being more objective than advertisements, and their messages are more likely to be absorbed and believed. For example, after the CBS newsmagazine 60 Minutes reported in the early 1990s that drinking moderate amounts of red wine could prevent heart attacks by lowering cholesterol, red wine sales in the United States increased 50 per cent. Another benefit publicity offers is that it is free, not considering the great amount of effort it can require to get out-bound publicity noticed and picked up by media sources.

Public relations' role in the promotional mix is becoming more important because of what Philip Kotler describes as an "over communicated society." Consumers develop "communication-avoidance routines" where they are likely to tune out commercial messages. As advertising loses some of its cost-effectiveness, marketers are turning to news coverage, events, and community programmes to help disseminate their product and company messages.

Some consumers may also base their purchase decisions on the image of the company, for example, how environmentally responsible the company is. In this regard, public relations plays an important role in presenting, through news reports, sponsorships, "advertorials" and other forms of communication, what the company stands for.

DIRECT MARKETING AND DATABASE MARKETING

Direct Marketing

Direct marketing, the oldest form of marketing, is the process of communicating directly with target customers to encourage response by telephone, mail, electronic means, or personal visit. Users of direct marketing include retailers, wholesalers, manufacturers, and service providers, and they use a variety of methods including direct mail, telemarketing, direct-response advertising, online computer shopping services, cable shopping networks, and infomercials.

Traditionally not viewed as an element in the promotional mix, direct marketing represents one of the most profound changes in marketing and promotion in the last 25 years. Aspects of direct marketing, which includes direct response advertising and direct mail advertising as well as the various research and support activities necessary for their implementation, have been adopted by virtually all companies engaged in marketing products, services, ideas, or persons. Direct marketing has become an important part of many marketing communication programmes for three reasons. First, the number of two-income households has increased dramatically. About six in every ten women in the United States work outside the home. This has reduced the amount of time families have for shopping trips. Secondly, more shoppers than ever before rely on credit cards for payment of goods and services. These cashless transactions make products easier and faster to purchase. Finally, technological advances in telecommunications and computers allow consumers to make purchases from their homes via telephone, television, or computer with ease and safety. These three factors have dramatically altered the purchasing habits of American consumers and made direct marketing a growing field worldwide.

Direct marketing allows a company to target more precisely a segment of customers and prospects with a sales message tailored to their specific needs and characteristics. Unlike advertising and public relations, whose connections to actual sales are tenuous or nebulous at best, direct marketing offers accountability by providing tangible results. The economics of direct marketing have also improved over the years as more information is gathered about customers and prospects. By identifying those consumers they can serve more effectively and profitably, companies may be more efficient in their marketing efforts. Whereas network television in the past offered opportunities to reach huge groups of consumers at a low cost per thousand, direct marketing can reach individual consumers and develop a relationship with each of them. Research indicates that brands with strong brand equity are more successful in direct marketing efforts than little-known brands. Direct marketing, then, works best when other marketing communication such as traditional media advertising supports the direct marketing effort.

Direct marketing has its drawbacks also. Just as consumers built resistance to the persuasive nature of advertising, so have they with direct marketing efforts. Direct marketers have responded by being less sales oriented and more relationship oriented. Also, just as consumers grew weary of advertising clutter, so have they with the direct marketing efforts. Consumers are bombarded with mail, infomercials, and telemarketing pitches daily. Some direct marketers have responded by regarding privacy as a customer service benefit. Direct marketers must also overcome consumer mistrust of direct marketing efforts due to incidents of illegal behaviour by companies and individuals using direct marketing.

The U.S. Postal Service, the Federal Trade Commission, and other federal and state agencies may prosecute criminal acts. The industry then risks legislation regulating the behaviour of direct marketers if it is not successful in self-regulation. The Direct Marketing Association, the leading trade organization for direct marketing, works with companies and government agencies to initiate self-regulation. In March of 2003 the National Do Not Call Registry went into affect whereby consumers added their names to a list that telemarketers had to eliminate from their out-bound call database.

Database Marketing

Database marketing is a form of direct marketing that attempts to gain and reinforce sales transactions while at the same time being customer driven. Successful database marketing continually updates lists of prospects and customers by identifying who they are, what they are like, and what they are purchasing now or may be purchasing in the future.

By using database marketing, marketers can develop products and/or product packages to meet their customers' needs or develop creative and media strategies that match their tastes, values, and lifestyles. Like IMC, database marketing is viewed by many marketers as supplanting traditional marketing strategies and is a major component of most IMC programmes.

At the core of database marketing is the idea that market segments are constantly shifting and changing. People who may be considered current customers, potential customers, and former customers and people who are likely never to be customers are constantly changing. By identifying these various segments and developing a working knowledge of their wants, needs, and characteristics, marketers can reduce the cost of reaching non-prospects and build customer loyalty. Perhaps the most important role of database marketing is its ability to retain customers. The cumulative profit for a five-year loyal customer is between seven and eight times the first-year profit.

Since database marketing is expensive to develop and complex to implement effectively, companies considering database marketing should consider three important questions. First, do relatively frequent purchasers or high dollar volume purchasers for the brand exist? Secondly, is the market diverse enough so that segmenting into subgroups would be beneficial? Finally, are there customers that represent opportunities for higher volume purchases?

SALES PROMOTION/SPONSORSHIPS/EXHIBITIONS

Sales Promotion

Sales promotions are direct inducements that offer extra incentives to enhance or accelerate the product's movement from producer to consumer. Sales promotions may be directed at the consumer or the trade. Consumer promotions such as coupons, sampling, premiums, sweepstakes, price packs, low-cost financing deals, and rebates are purchase incentives in that they induce product trial and encourage repurchase.

Consumer promotions may also include incentives to visit a retail establishment or request additional information. Trade promotions include slotting allowances, allowances for featuring the brand in retail advertising, display and merchandising allowances, buying allowances, bill back allowances, incentives to salespeople, and other tactics to encourage retailers to carry the item and to push the brand.

Two perspectives may be found among marketers regarding sales promotion. First, sales promotion is supplemental to advertising in that it binds the role of advertising with personal selling. This view regards sales promotion as a minor player in the marketing communication programme. A second view regards sales promotion and advertising as distinct functions with objectives and strategies very different from each other. Sales promotion in this sense is equal to or even more important than advertising. Some companies allocate as much as 75 per cent of their advertising/promotion dollars to sales promotion and just 25 per cent to advertising. Finding the right balance is often a difficult task. The main purpose of sales promotion is to spur action. Advertising sets up the deal by developing a brand reputation and building market value. Sales promotion helps close the deal by providing incentives that build market volume.

Sales promotions can motivate customers to select a particular brand, especially when brands appear to be equal, and they can produce more immediate and measurable results than advertising. However, too heavy a reliance on sales promotions results in "deal-prone" consumers with little brand loyalty and too much price sensitivity. Sales promotions can also force competitors to offer similar inducements, with sales and profits suffering for everyone.

Sponsorships

Sponsorships, or event marketing, combine advertising and sales promotions with public relations. Sponsorships increase awareness of a company or product, build loyalty with a specific target audience, help differentiate a product from its competitors, provide merchandising opportunities, demonstrate commitment to a community or ethnic group, or impact the bottom line.

Like advertising, sponsorships are initiated to build long-term associations. Organizations sometimes compare sponsorships with advertising by using gross impressions or cost-per-thousand measurements.

However, the value of sponsorships can be very difficult to measure. Companies considering sponsorships should consider the short-term public relations value of sponsorships and the long-term goals of the organization. Sports sponsorships make up about two-thirds of all sponsorships.

Exhibits

Exhibits, or trade shows, are hybrid forms of promotion between business-to-business advertising and personal selling. Trade shows provide opportunities for face-to-face contact with prospects, enable new companies to create a viable customer base in a short period of time, and allow small and midsize companies that may not be visited on a regular basis by salespeople to become familiar with suppliers and vendors.

Because many trade shows generate media attention, they have also become popular venues for introducing new products and providing a stage for executives to gain visibility.

PERSONAL SELLING

Personal selling includes all person-to-person contact with customers with the purpose of introducing the product to the customer, convincing him or her of the product's value, and closing the sale. The role of personal selling varies from organization to organization, depending on the nature and size of the company, the industry, and the products or services it is marketing. Many marketing executives realise that both sales and non-sales employees act as salespeople for their organization in one way or another.

One study that perhaps supports this contention found that marketing executives predicted greater emphasis being placed on sales management and personal selling in their organization than on any other promotional mix element. These organizations have launched training sessions that show employees how they act as salespeople for the organization and how they can improve their interpersonal skills with clients, customers, and prospects. Employee reward programmes now reward employees for their efforts in this regard.

Personal selling is the most effective way to make a sale because of the interpersonal communication between the salesperson and the prospect. Messages can be tailored to particular situations, immediate feedback can be processed, and message strategies can be changed to accommodate the feedback. However, personal selling is the most expensive way to make a sale, with the average cost per sales call ranging from $235 to $332 and the average number of sales calls needed to close a deal being between three and six personal calls.

Sales and marketing management classifies salespersons into one of three groups: creative selling, order taking, and missionary sales reps. Creative selling jobs require the most skills and preparation. They are the "point person" for the sales function. They prospect for customers, analyse situations, determine how their company can satisfy wants and needs of prospects, and, most importantly, get an order. Order takers take over after the initial order is received. They handle repeat purchases and modified rebuys. Missionary sales reps service accounts by introducing new products, promotions, and other programmes. Orders are taken by order takers or by distributors.

INTERNET MARKETING

Just as direct marketing has become a prominent player in the promotional mix, so too has the Internet. Virtually unheard of in the 1980s, the 1990s saw this new medium explode onto the scene, being adopted by families, businesses and other organizations more quickly than any other medium in history. Web sites provide a new way of transmitting information, entertainment, and advertising, and have generated a new dimension in marketing: electronic commerce. E-commerce is the term used to describe the act of selling goods and services over the Internet.

In other words, the Internet has become more that a communication channel; it is a marketing channel itself with companies, CDNow, eBay, and others selling goods via the Internet to individuals around the globe. In less than 10 years advertising expenditures on the Internet will rival those for radio and outdoor. Public relations practitioners realise the value that web sites offer in establishing and maintaining relationships with important publics. For example, company and product information can be posted on the company's site for news reporters researching stories and for current and potential customers seeking information. Political candidates have web sites that provide information about their background and their political experience.

The interactivity of the Internet is perhaps its greatest asset. By communicating with customers, prospects, and others one-on-one, firms can build databases that help them meet specific needs of individuals, thus building a loyal customer base. Because the cost of entry is negligible, the Internet is cluttered with web sites. However, this clutter does not present the same kind of problem that advertising clutter does.

Advertising and most other forms of promotion assume a passive audience that will be exposed to marketing communication messages via the mass media or mail regardless of their receptivity. Web sites require audiences who are active in the information-seeking process to purposely visit the site. Therefore, the quality and freshness of content is vital for the success of the web site.

THE FUTURE OF MARKETING COMMUNICATION

Marketing communication has become an integral part of the social and economic system in the United States. Consumers rely on the information from marketing communication to make wise purchase decisions. Businesses, ranging from multinational corporations to small retailers, depend on marketing communication to sell their goods and services.

Marketing communication has also become an important player in the life of a business. Marketing communication helps move products, services, and ideas from manufacturers to end users and builds and maintains relationships with customers, prospects, and other important stakeholders in the company. Advertising and sales promotion will continue to play important roles in marketing communication mix. However, marketing strategies that stress relationship building in addition to producing sales will force marketers to consider all the elements in the marketing communication mix.

In the future new information gathering techniques will help marketers target more precisely customers and prospects using direct marketing strategies. New media technologies will provide businesses and consumers new ways to establish and reinforce relationships that are important for the success of the firm and important for consumers as they make purchase decisions. The Internet will become a major force in how organizations communicate with a variety of constituents, customers, clients, and other interested parties.

IMPORTANCE OF MARKETING COMMUNICATION

Marketing communication is done in different ways like some marketers do marketing with the help of print media like Flyer's, banners, brochures, billboard etc and mostly do with the help of electronic media like Tv commercial, radio advertisements and so on. Every medium has its own importance but the goal is same which is to capture the market and to brand name. Marketing helps the marketers to create the brand image. Like by repeating the commercial again and again on the TV, on the back of people mind, when ever people want to buy soap then commercial which is repeated the most will hit there mind and they will go for that brand. So This is one way that marketing helps the marketers to promote their product.

MEDIA MANAGEMENT

Media management is a term used for several related tasks throughout post-production. In general, any task that relates to processing your media is considered to be media management, such as capturing, compressing, copying, moving, or deleting media files. However, media management also refers to keeping track of your media files via clip properties such as log notes, comments, scene number, shot/take number, and so on. The flexibility and power of media management in Final Cut Pro stems from one simple fact: a clip and its media file are treated independently. In Final Cut Pro, a more accurate description of media management would be clip and media management. What makes the separation of clips and media files so powerful?

Here are a few examples:

- *Reconnecting clips to new media files*: You can create new media files for your project at any time, and reconnect the clips in your project to the new media files.
- *Direct access to your media files*: You can directly access your QuickTime media files in the Finder at any time. You can also easily create clips by dragging media files directly into your project via the Browser. In fact, you can even edit by dragging media files from the Finder directly into the Timeline or Canvas.
- *Logging clip information without media*: You can modify clip properties such as log notes, comments, labels, and even In and Out points without the associated media files. This means you can organize your clips and sequences even though your current editing system may not have the media files.

- *Trading projects without media files*: A Final Cut Pro project file contains clips and sequences, but not media files. Because a project file is so small, you can e-mail or post your project file online. Anyone who has the corresponding media files can open the project file and reconnect the clips to the local media files.

Making a movie is a tremendous logistical undertaking. It's the execution of the details that ultimately determines the quality of the finished product. What does it matter how good the lead actress's performance was in the third take of scene 2 if you can't find it among a thousand other shots? And what use is a week of fine-tune editing, frame by frame, if the final sequence is improperly assembled by the negative cutter because of a faulty edit decision list that you provided?

Final Cut Pro has incredibly versatile media management options, allowing you to customise your workflow to fit the needs of your project.

REASONS TO USE MEDIA MANAGEMENT

Computers are very effective for sorting and organizing information, much more so than scraps of document and handwritten notes. This isn't to say you should dispense with these basic tools—most editors still use them prolifically. However, mastering management of your media, clips, and notes in Final Cut Pro is critical for an efficient editing workflow.

- *Browser*: A virtual media database for sorting, categorizing, and commenting on clips.
- *Find command*: Allows you to quickly search a sequence or project for any clip based on any criterion.
- *Media Manager*: A powerful clip and media file processor for duplicating, removing, and recompressing media files, as well as clips and sequences in your project.
- *Recapturing and reconnecting*: You can recapture or reconnect clips to new media files at any time you want. The connection between clips and media files is easy to change, making Final Cut Pro one of the most flexible media editing systems available.
- *Finder*: You can sort, view, and archive media files directly in the Finder because Final Cut Pro works directly with QuickTime media files.

WHAT YOU NEED TO KNOW TO MANAGE YOUR MEDIA

To effectively keep track of or manage your media, you must have a good understanding of the following:

- The distinction between a clip and a media file, as well as the relationship between the two
- The relationship between master and affiliate clips in a Final Cut Pro project

- How timecode works, providing a bridge between footage on tape or film to media files on hard disk to clips in your project
- How to effectively sort and search large amounts of data, such as clips in the Browser or in a sequence
- How to name files concisely and descriptively
- The fundamental nature of your media: frame size, aspect ratio, frame rate, codec, colour bit depth, colour space, and audio sample rate and bit depth

STRATEGIES FOR MEDIA MANAGEMENT

It's a good idea to pick a strategy for media management before you begin your project. Some important things to consider as part of your strategy are reel name conventions, clip name conventions, working with full-resolution media versus offline media, working with multiple editing workstations, and using a storage area network.

Reel Name Conventions

This issue affects recapturing in Final Cut Pro or any other editing system. Reel numbers must be correct so that Final Cut Pro asks for the proper tape when you recapture media. Some Edit Decision List formats have strict rules for reel names, so be conservative with your reel names if there is even a slight chance you will export an EDL for your project.

Clip Name Conventions

Clips can get their names in several ways. If you log clips individually, a clip name is derived from a combination of the description, shot/take, scene, and angle properties of a clip. However, if you create clips by importing a batch list, EDL, or Final Cut Pro XML, you may name the clips independently of these other properties. In either case, choose a fairly concise but descriptive name. If you are working on a narrative, scene name and take number may be sufficient because the shooting script provides the information you need to order your shots. However, unplanned footage for news or documentaries requires more descriptive names. Try to avoid special characters in clip names. This is especially important if you happen to use the Media Manager to create new media files based on clip names. Remember that clips in Final Cut Pro have many properties besides the Name field where descriptive information can be added. Log notes, comments, the Mark Good property, labels, and markers within clips can be used to describe your clips more accurately.

Media Filename Conventions

Avoid special characters for filenames. If you are logging clips in the Log and Capture window, the name of your clip determines the name of the file, so this means you should avoid special characters in clip names too. Don't change media filenames directly in the Finder, or your clips will go offline.

Working with Full-Resolution Media

You can capture and edit your media at full resolution, or you can use an offline/online workflow where you capture and edit at low-resolution, and then recapture at full resolution for your final edit.

Working with Multiple Editing Workstations and Trading Project Files

If you are working on the same project on multiple editing systems, you need multiple copies of your media files. All systems can have identical copies of full-resolution media, or some can have low-resolution media while others use full-resolution files. Project files can be transferred from one system to another and clips are reconnected to local media files.

Using Multiple Workstations with a Storage Area Network

Storage area networks allow you to connect multiple computers to a centralized media storage device, so everyone is working with exactly the same media files instead of multiple copies. You can build a SAN using Xserve RAIDs, Apple Xsan software, and a fibre channel card installed in each computer.

Using Another Linear or Nonlinear System

If you plan to do final colour correction, effects, and broadcast specifications on a non–Final Cut Pro system, consider how you will deliver your sequence and media. You need to pick a project interchange format that the online editing system recognizes. For example, many Avid and ProTools systems recognize AAF and OMF files; other post-production tools recognize the Final Cut Pro XML Interchange Format; and linear tape-to-tape edit suites use EDL files. Media can be delivered on tape for recapturing into a nonlinear system, or for editing onto the master tape in a tape-to-tape suite. In many cases it is faster to recapture tapes than to transcode digital files from a Final Cut Pro-compatible codec to a format the online system recognizes.

MEDIA SELECTION

MEDIA SELECTION PROCESS

Understanding the Market

To determine which medium we should use to advertise our product we must first understand our target market.

This includes the following:

- *Knowing who they are*: Are they consumers, Fortune 100, small business, etc. If they are all consumers, or a large part of the population, we can use mass market medium such as network TV, radio or general publications. If they are Fortune 100 or small business we might use specific trade publications that target our same markets.

- *Their buying process*: Is the sale simple, or complex—requiring numerous complex presentations and layers of approvals.
- Who are the final decision makers, along with the primary and secondary influencers. For example, for a sales force automation decision, the final say may be the VP of Sales. However, the primary influencers may be the sales people and sales managers, plus the IT department. The secondary influencers may be the president, the CFO, and the secretary.
- The percentage weight of influence of each person in the decision chain helps determine which medium and publications we may target. The VP of Sales may travel. The Regional Sales Manager may be trying to move up. The IT department may need integration support, etc.
- I typically create a matrix showing the key decision and influencers within the market and have the most market—knowledgeable internal team members come to a consensus as to which percentage weight we should assign to each group. This process is subjective, but usually yields fairly accurate results—when the numbers come in.
- *Where they buy*: If the target buys from retail, we may use "Run of Press" ads. If the target buys from VARs or Integrators, we may use VARBusiness to recruit more VARs. If they buy on-line—we may run direct response ads with an on-line or 800# call to action.
- *How they buy*: If the customer buys on terms, our ads may mention financing options.
- *What the competition is doing*: We might use services such as AdScope to compile a 12-month history of our competitor's campaigns so we can see their media targets and either apply a blocking campaign, were we match a competitor's campaign, or use a separatist campaign, where we fish in a different pond entirely. Or we may choose to do some of both.
- *What has worked for us in the past*: This is one of the most difficult steps since most companies do not capture this information. If nothing is in place, then you must extrapolate the data from whatever sources you have. You must also fix this problem immediately and setup a complete tracking system—or you will not have the managerial information you need to determine which medium is working best TV, Radio, Publications —i.e., are you fishing in the right pond, nor will you know which ad format and message is working best.

Understanding your customer and being able to answer each of the previous questions is the hard part. Finding media that targets our same prospect is actually the easy part.

Selecting The Correct Media

The next step is to determine which medium type will reach your desired targets and generate the greatest ROI. It may be multiple types—if so, you should put a% weight value on each and consider your budget accordingly. In the high-tech market, the most widely used advertising medium is print. Within the print medium, the most common for high-tech is trade publications. Trade publications might include PC Magazine, Network Computing, Videomaker, Gaming, etc.

The key is to find the right publication that contains the most of your preferred target.

Fortunately, there are several publications that can help you determine the demographics of various media and publications. For example, the Nielson Rating can tell you the audience demographics and ratings for specific network and cable stations and specific television shows. Other services like those from IAG Research can measure the performance of every ad. However, they often only measure recall within the channel, by brand, and the fit. Based on these criteria, they rate as "most effective" those ads that are recalled by the most people. However, a more important indicator is not the recall scores, but the ads that actually sell and cause a change in brand preference.

You can find a fairly comprehensive on-line listing of TV, radio, newspapers, on-line, and trade magazines at Media Post. Registration is free and they even include a free on-line media scheduling tool.

If you are moving into a new market and don't know the most popular trade publications, then you will have to use media books, internet resources, get help from alliances, and clients, or from a media buying company. If you are fairly certain of the publications you want to use, you can go to their web site and get rates, demographics, circulation, frequency, etc.

If you talk to a rep, be cautions not to place too much merit when they say they cater to your market. The Editor in Chief understands the publication's target best since he/she must create content to appease that audience. This is one of the reason's I usually get PRs assistance in the media selection—they know who covers your space by the type and number of objects produced for your desired target. The PR group also has the editorial schedule that helps identify the target audience.

PRINT MEDIA EFFECTIVENESS

In the era of desktop computers, laptops, BlackBerries and iPhones, advertising and news media has seen a shift to advertising on the Internet and television. While Internet media has its place, the use of print media, such as newspapers, magazines, brochures, press packets and other printed material, has not disappeared and can still be used in a very effective manner—and even has advantages over advertising with other types of media.

KEEPSAKE MEMORABILIA

Print media is great for special events or occasions that a person may want to remember. For instance, newspaper sales skyrocketed the day after tragedy struck the U.S. on September 11, 2001, as many people just wanted to have the document as a keepsake of that day in history. The same concept applies to events such as a wedding, an anniversary, the death of a legend like Michael Jackson, the inauguration of the nation's first black president, and other momentous times in history or in an individual's life.

Ultimately, with print media, people can collect memories from magazines or newspapers, keep them in a special place and look back on them years later.

CONVENIENCE

People always find themselves waiting, whether it's for a table at a restaurant, at the doctor's office or in line at the grocery store. Waiting is a part of life, and that's the perfect time to pick up a magazine, newspaper or brochure and start reading through it. Computers and televisions don't line the grocery store checkout area, but newspapers and magazines do.

CLEAN DESIGN

Depending upon the site, reading information on a web page can be distracting at times, as there is often a jumble of ads and other graphics competing for your attention. On the other hand, print media offers an easier to read design that doesn't disappear.

VARIETY

So many people work on a computer as part of their daily job that it's the last thing they want to stare at when they get home. This is also where print media can be effective, as it gives people a welcome alternative to on-screen stimuli. There is nothing like lying down and relaxing while reading a document or magazine, which is not such an easy feat with a computer.

RELIABILITY

Although it might not happen often, occasionally a cable line needs repair and television reception and Internet access are lost. Once printed media is dispersed to the public it is there for a while.

DEVELOPING AN EFFECTIVE MEDIA PLAN

At no time has the need for knowledgeable, professionally-trained media planners been greater. After all, costs for space and time have risen dramatically to the point that budgetary controls are more critical than ever. And how do you know you are reaching the right people when there are literally hundreds of television and radio stations, thousands of newspapers and magazines and a host of direct mail and outdoor advertising options from which to choose?

Because of this huge selection, today's media planners must have broader knowledge of marketing goals, advertising objectives, audience profiles and media characteristics... All with the goal of reaching the largest number of prospects at the lowest possible cost, and in an editorial or programming environment suitable for the particular product or service.

THINGS TO CONSIDER

Target Audience

Who are the present and potential prospects for the product or service? In recent years, media has been evaluated on its ability to maximize target-audience exposures. As a result, most agencies use some sort of weighted or demographic cost per thousand to determine a medium's efficiency at reaching a specific audience.

Geography/Seasonality

Where is the product distributed? Where are the heaviest concentrations of prospects? Are there times of the year when sales are strongest? Answers to these questions help narrow media selection, determine the timing of a schedule and budget allocations per geographic area.

Creative Considerations

Are we effectively using the communicative strengths of the various media? Sometimes the very nature of the product may indicate the most appropriate media. Are demonstrations key to selling the product? Is a coupon involved? How much detail is necessary?

Reach/Frequency

There are often trade-offs that must be considered between reach and frequency. Is it more important to advertise to fewer people more often, or a broader base less frequently? Few budgets can stress both.

What about "Interactive" Media?

This rapidly unfolding media realm is opening up a whole new world of opportunity for advertisers. We'd be happy to review the basics with you and explore how you can best prepare your organization for interactive messages.

Competition

Virtually every aspect of advertising is measured against the competition. Ad budgets typically take into account what competitors spend. Product success is measured in terms of market share. Often, in order to gain market share, you must be willing to outspend your competition. If that's not possible, the media planner must look for appropriate areas where the competition is weaker. Remember, a good media plan systematically excludes non-prospects from the mix and includes methods for evaluating overall communications effectiveness. Since media usually represents the largest expenditure of an ad budget, it's no wonder advertisers are paying more attention to it.

STEPS FOR DEVELOPING A MEDIA PLAN

- Decide which outlets are most influential to your target audience.
  - For example, if you're working on a campaign to get your campus to buy renewable energy, your target audience is probably going to be the administration first, then students. Therefore, the school-sponsored document would probably be the best place to get coverage to get them to notice it.
  - Whereas if you were trying to educate lots of students about how to properly use the recycling system on campus, you might decide that public service announcements on the radio station was a better idea b/c more people listen to it.
  - If you are working on a campaign to get the city your school is in to adopt a Renewable Portfolio Standard, your target audience is going to be people in the city, not just campus, so you would put much more attention on getting covered in city-wide outlets than on-campus outlets.
- Decide the best way to get those outlets to cover the campaign
  - For example, if you were trying to get the campus document to cover renewable energy, you might do a big event that lots of people would see and wonder about so the document would want to cover it.
  - If you were trying to get the city-wide document to cover you, you might do a press conference with local experts and alumni.
- Make sure that you have a media plan for all of your campaign events
- Put your ideas and events on a timeline

ROLE OF A MEDIA MANAGER

There are actually two types of Media Managers. One for Communications Services and one for Media Services.

COMMUNICATION SERVICES

The main objective for the Media Manager is to promote media visibility and present their company in the best possible light. Serves as the company's primary media spokesperson by executing external public relations initiatives. Builds and maintains professional working relationships with key media people in local and/or national media outlets. Often supervises projects with outside PR agencies and/or in-house media relations team. Writes and edits copy for press releases, press kits, fact sheets and white documents.

MEDIA SERVICES

Media managers decide which media to use for advertising campaigns. Working from a brief about the product or service to be advertised, they devise strategic plans appropriate to the target audience and available budget. They base plans on industry statistics such as National Readership Surveys, viewing figures from BARB and the Target Group Index directory. Because precise targeting is essential, additional research may also be commissioned. Media managers then present a media and cost schedule to the client, recommending which type of media to use, where, and when to advertise the product or service. When the client agrees to this, it is used to brief the media buyer. In some agencies the roles of planner and media buyer are combined.

ADVERTISING CAMPAIGN APPROACH

An advertising campaign is a series of advertisement messages that share a single idea and theme which make up an integrated marketing communication. Advertising campaigns appear in different media across a specific time frame. The critical part of making an advertising campaign is determining a champion theme as it sets the tone for the individual advertisements and other forms of marketing communications that will be used. The campaign theme is the central message that will be communicated in the promotional activities. The campaign themes are usually developed with the intention of being used for a substantial period but many of them are short lived due to factors such as being ineffective or market conditions and/or competition in the marketplace and marketing mix.

TIPS FOR AN EFFECTIVE ADVERTISING CAMPAIGN

The goal of advertising is to cost-effectively reach a large audience and attract customers. If done correctly, advertising can enhance the success of your business.

Here are 10 advertising tips to pay attention to:

1. *Go after your target audience*: An advertising campaign should be geared to your niche market. It is a common mistake to create generic ads that do not speak the language or grab the attention of your potential customers.
2. *Highlight your competitive advantage*: One of the keys to all advertising is to accentuate the pros of your company, those factors that give

you your competitive edge. Too many ads are clever but fail to sell the benefits of the product or service.

3. *Establish an image*: You can recognize the McDonald's arches while whizzing by on the highway. Likewise, there are plenty of products that you recognize by their packaging or logo. Image counts when it comes to advertising and promoting your business. Too many advertisers do not work to build a consistent image. Check out Three Brand Identity Myths That Will Bring Your Business Down for additional issues to avoid.
4. *You have to spend money to make money*: There are ways to save money, but typically advertising is not the place to cut corners. It will affect sales, and that affects the bottom line. Successful advertising may cost some money, but that is because it works. Check out More Bang for Your Advertising Buck for cost-cutting tips that won't cut your goals.
5. *Advertise in the right places*: *Your* favourite magazine, radio station, or even television programme might not be a favourite of your audience. Know what they read, watch, and listen to, and advertise in media that reaches your target market.
6. Don't allow your budget to run your advertising campaign. If you budget $5,000 per month for advertising, you've made it very easy from a bookkeeping perspective. However, if like most businesses you have seasonal highs and lows, you are spending too much money advertising during down times and not enough when you want to attract customers. Too many entrepreneurs do not budget according to their seasonal advertising needs.
7. *Diversify*: It is all too common for business owners to choose the best place to advertise based on price and potential rate of returns and then stop. As is the case with investing, you do not want to put all of your eggs in one basket. Spread your advertising dollars around.
8. *Don't try to be everything to everyone*: No product or service will appeal to everyone. Many business owners, including corporate executives, try to come up with ways to reach every market. Typically, this does not work. It can spell disaster for small businesses, who cannot afford to spread themselves too thin. Therefore, find your market and be everything you can be to that audience.
9. *Test your ads in advance*: If you have the time or money to invest in focus groups, you should test your ads on other people. Do they understand and accept the message that you are trying to convey? For further information, read Focus Groups: How They Can Work for Your Small Business. There are other less-expensive ways to test your ads as well: questionnaires, for example.

NEW TRENDS IN MARKETING COMMUNICATION

In 2010 is poised to be an exciting year for marketers; trends that have been taking shape over the course of the past decade are creating new opportunities for business owners. The first 10 years of the 21st century brought economic problems, corporate collapses and environmental disasters, but it was also a decade defined by a shift in communications from traditional media to a worldwide conversation that flows faster and farther than anyone could have imagined. Thanks to the tools of the social web, such as Twitter, Facebook, blogs, online video and so on, news and information travels instantaneously, and that means marketers have new and exciting opportunities to reach consumers.

With those economic, cultural, political and environmental events, as well as the advances in technology and the global online conversation in mind, following are 10 trends that affect all areas of marketing, from advertising to branding and everything in between, and will shape marketing strategy throughout 2010 and beyond.

- Transparency and trust are paramount.
- Consumers have lived through a variety of negative events throughout the past decade, and they're no longer willing to accept anything businesses tell them. Brands that embrace the loss of naïveté and make a concentrated effort to be honest and open in their marketing communications will generate positive consumer responses, which can lead to brand loyalty and brand advocacy. Building trust is the most important thing in 2010, and once you've earned it, you need to make sure you keep it. In other words, transparency and trust are not a one-time thing. They're an ongoing effort.
- Less interruption, more enhancement and value-add.
- The days when ads and marketing messages were developed for the sole purpose of getting the attention of consumers are over. People expect more from businesses and brands. Give them more by ensuring your marketing communications and efforts deliver useful and meaningful value.
- Speaking of value...
- The economic downturn that occurred in the latter part of the past decade stopped many consumers in their tracks. Rather than spending money frivolously, consumers began seeking out deals, using coupons and actively looking for the biggest bang for their buck. When the economy recovers, that behaviour will not disappear immediately. Be prepared for the consumer focus on value to continue well beyond 2010, and build marketing campaigns with that consumer demand in mind.
- Show it, don't tell it.

- Consumers don't believe everything they hear. Indeed, consumers are more skeptical than ever, and you need to prove your marketing claims. Don't just tell consumers about your product, business or services, show them what's in it for them if they pull out their hard-earned money and buy from you.
- Social media is not going away, and engagement is critical.
- Twitter, Facebook, blogs, YouTube, and other tools of the online social community are not going anywhere. Instead, these tools are being adopted by more and more people around the world. If you thought you could avoid joining the bandwagon, you were wrong. In 2010, it's critical that your business joins the social web conversation, and you must engage consumers on the social networking sites. Give them amazing content and interact with them to fully leverage the power of the social media.
- Peace-of-mind messages prevail.
- Consumers have lived through a wide variety of negative events over the past several years, from economic turmoil to environmental disasters and more. They're actively seeking marketing messages that give them a feeling of peace of mind. Try to communicate a feeling of security in your marketing efforts to meet this need.
- Relationships rule.
- With the growth of web-based social networks and a desire for transparency, trust and peace-of-mind messages, it shouldn't be surprising that relationships rule in 2010 and beyond. Leverage the social web to interact with people around the world and build relationships that wouldn't have been possible a decade ago. When you build relationships with consumers, you also build a band of brand loyalists that can become your most powerful source of word-of-mouth marketing, brand advocacy and brand guardianship.
- Online video and mobile marketing are hot.
- Both online video and mobile marketing are set to explode, and we'll really start to see that happen in 2010. You can create your own online video content or mobile content, or you can invest in online video or mobile advertising. The choice is yours, but there is no better time to jump in than right now!
- Focus, focus, focus!
- Don't try to be everything to everyone in 2010. The strongest brands are focused brands. As the first decade of the 21st century unfolded, marketers and social media professionals began using the term *niche* more and more to identify highly focused products, websites, blogs and so on. Today, that strategy is even more important. Build your core and keep it as strong as possible before you try to extend your brand and branch out into new areas.

- Integrated marketing trumps stand-alone tactics.
- It is absolutely essential that you surround consumers with your marketing messages in 2010. The number of marketing communications that people see each day is overwhelming, so it's important that your messages don't get lost in the clutter. You can make your brand, your business and your messages stand out by surrounding consumers with branded experiences and allowing them to choose which of those experiences they want to consume. For example, use online advertising, online video, custom content, point-of-sale collateral, and ads with consistent messaging to engage consumers in different parts of their lives. If you're consistent and persistent, your messages are more likely to connect with your target audience—raising brand awareness, recognition, purchases and loyalty.

6

Foreign Market Entry Strategies

FOREIGN DIRECT INVESTMENT (FDI)

Economists usually advocate a free flow of capital across national borders because capital can then seek out the highest rate of return. Owners of capital can diversify their investment, while governments will be less able to pursue bad economic policies. In addition, a global integration of capital markets spreads best practices in corporate governance, accounting rules, and legal traditions. However, some critics point out that free capital flows are driven by speculative and short-term considerations. For some reason, one noticeable feature of FDI flows is that their share in total inflows is higher in countries where the quality of institutions is lower. In other words, a high share of FDI in a country's total capital inflows may reflect its institutions' weakness instead of its strengths. However, empirical evidence indicates that FDI benefits developing host countries both the largest recipients and sources of FDI.

The phenomenon is dominated by the triad of the European Union, the USA, and Japan, accounting for 71 per cent of inward flows and 82 per cent of outward flows. Certain countries have managed to attract large amounts of FDI. In the case of Africa, to attract FDI, African countries have relied on their natural resources, locational advantages, and targeted policies. The countries that are successful in attracting FDI have certain traits: political and macroeconomic stability and structural reforms. "Strong, pro-democracy political leadership that has embraced policies to overcome social and political strife and a firm commitment to economic reform are key factors linked with sizable FDI inflows." Therefore, even those countries that lack natural resources or location advantages still can attract foreign investors by adopting sound economic policies within an open political environment. Corruption has a negative impact on FDI. From the ethics standpoint, foreign investors generally avoid corruption because it is morally wrong. From the economic standpoint, investors prefer not to have to manage such costly risks.

EXPORTING

Exporting is a strategy in which a company, without any marketing or production organization overseas, exports a product from its home base. Often, the exported product is fundamentally the same as the one marketed in the home market. The main advantage of an exporting strategy is the ease in implementing the strategy. Risks are minimal because the company simply exports its excess production capacity when it receives orders from abroad. As a result, its international marketing effort is casual at best.

This is very likely the most common overseas entry approach for small firms. Many companies employ this entry strategy when they first become involved with international business and may continue to use it on a more or less permanent basis. R.R. Donnelley Japan K.K., for example, has issued American Showcase/Japan which is a "catalog of catalogs." This marketing programme involves several American catalogers, and allows Japanese consumers to request American catalogs and order merchandise.

The problem with using an exporting strategy is that it is not always an optimal strategy. A desire to keep international activities simple, together with a lack of product modification, make a company's marketing strategy inflexible and unresponsive. The exporting strategy functions poorly when the company's home country currency is strong. In the 1970s, the Swiss franc was so strong that Swiss companies found it exceedingly difficult to export and sell products in the US market. Swiss companies had to resort to investing abroad in order to reduce the effects of the strong franc. During the first term of the Reagan administration, the US dollar had also gained an extremely strong position.

US firms not only found it extremely difficult to export US products but they also had to contend with a flood of inexpensive imports that became even more inexpensive as the dollar became stronger. A currency can remain strong over a stretch of several years, creating prolonged difficulties for the country's exports.

Continuing the long-term trend, the Japanese yen surged 20 per cent against the US dollar in early 1995 and greatly harmed Japanese exporters. Austria represents a small but open economy that requires international exchange. Based on a study of the effects of determinants on export performance, the most promising predictors of export performance are firm size, management's motives to internationalize, and use of the differentiation strategy. Another study of small and medium-sized exporters found that decision makers' cosmopolitanism influenced export initiation.

These decision makers often learned of foreign opportunities through their existing social ties–rather than formal scanning and market research. The findings were consistent across different industrial settings. One study measured the export-entrepreneurial orientation construct so as to derive a high versus low export-entrepreneurial taxonomy.

While Nigerian firms in the study perceive domestic environmental problems, high export-entrepreneurial firms appear to be better able to adapt and subsequently exhibit a higher tendency to initiate exporting. In addition, high export-entrepreneurial firms are more proactive and innovative in developing exporting while being less averse to exporting risks.

It should be noted that research in international exchange tends to focus on the perspective of exporters. A more complete understanding requires an inclusion of the perspective of importers in the dyad. Based on a study of thirty-six exporter– importer dyads operating in four countries, the best performing dyads exhibited a maintenance of close relationships by people on either side.

LICENSING

When a company finds exporting ineffective but is hesitant to have direct investment abroad, licensing can be a reasonable compromise. Licensing is an agreement that permits a foreign company to use industrial property, technical know-how and skills, architectural and engineering designs, or any combination of these in a foreign market. Essentially, a licensor allows a foreign company to manufacture a product for sale in the licensee's country and sometimes in other specified markets.

Examples of licensing abound. Some 50 per cent of the drugs sold in Japan are made under license from European and US companies. *Playboy* used to take licensed materials from France's *Lui* for its *Oui* magazine, which was distributed in the US market. *Playboy*'s more common role, however, is that of a licensor, resulting in nine *Playboy* foreign editions. *Penthouse* magazine, likewise, has Japanese and Brazilian versions under license in addition to those in Spain, Australia, and Italy.

German-speaking countries account for *Penthouse*'s largest overseas edition. Licensing is not only restricted to tangible products; a service can be licensed as well. Chicago Mercantile Exchange's attempt to internationalize the futures market led it to obtain licensing rights to the Nikkei stock index. The exchange then sublicensed the Nikkei index to the SIMEX for trade in Singapore in 1986. In spite of a general belief that foreign direct investment is generally more profitable and thus the preferred scheme, licensing offers several advantages. It allows a company to spread out its research and development and investment costs, while enabling it to receive incremental income with only negligible expenses. In addition, granting a license protects the company's patent and/or trademark against cancellation for nonuse.

This protection is especially crucial for a firm that, after investing in production and marketing facilities in a foreign country, decides to leave the market either temporarily or permanently. The situation is especially common in Central and South America, where high inflation and devaluation drastically push up operating costs. There are other reasons why licensing should be used. Trade barriers may be one such reason. A manufacturer should consider licensing when capital is scarce, when import restrictions discourage direct entry, and when a country is sensitive to foreign ownership. The method is very flexible because it allows a quick and easy way to enter the market. Licensing also works well when transportation cost is high, especially relative to product value. Although Japan banned all direct investment and restricted commercial loans in South Africa, Japan's success there was due to licensing agreements with local distributors. A company can avoid substantial risks and other difficulties with licensing. Most French designers, for example, use licensing to avoid having to invest in a business.

In another example, Disney obtains all of its royalties virtually risk-free from the $500 million Tokyo Disneyland theme park owned by Keisei Electric Railway and Mitsui. The licensing and royalty fees as arranged are very attractive: Disney receives 10 per cent of the gate revenue and 5 per cent of sales of all food and merchandise. Moreover, Disney, with its policy of using low-paid young adults as park employees, does not have to deal with the Japanese policy of lifetime employment.

An owner of a valuable brand name can benefit greatly from brand licensing. In addition to receiving royalties from sales of merchandise bearing its name or image, the trademark owner receives an intangible benefit of free advertising which reinforces the brand's image. Another benefit is that the brand is extended into new product categories in which the trademark owner has no expertise. Coca- Cola, for example, has licensed its brand name to more than 3000 products which are marketed by 200 licensees in thirty countries. Nevertheless, licensing has its negative aspects. With reduced risk generally comes reduced profit. In fact, licensing may be the least profitable of all entry strategies. It is necessary to consider the long-term perspective. By granting a license to a foreign firm, a manufacturer may be nurturing a competitor in the future–someone who is gaining technological and product knowledge.

At some point, the licensee may refuse to renew the licensing contract. To complicate the matter further, it is anything but easy to prevent the licensee from using the process learned and acquired while working under license. Texas Instruments had to sue several Japanese manufacturers to force them to continue paying royalties on its patents on memory chips.

Another problem often develops when the licensee performs poorly. To attempt to terminate the contract may be easier said than done. Once licensing is in place, the agreements can also prevent the licensor from entering that market directly. Japanese laws give a licensee virtual control over the licensed product, and such laws present a monumental obstacle for an investor wishing to regain the rights to manufacture and sell the investor's own product. Inconsistent product quality across countries caused by licensees' lax quality control can injure the reputation of a product on a worldwide basis.

This possibility explains why McDonald's goes to extremes in supervising operations, thus ensuring product quality and consistency. McDonald's was successful in court in preventing a franchisee from operating the franchises in France because the franchisee's quality was substandard. Anheuser- Busch, likewise, requires all licensees to meet the company's standards. The licensees must agree to import such ingredients as yeast from the USA. Even when exact product formulations are followed, licensing can still sometimes damage a product's image–that is, psychologically. Many imported products enjoy a certain degree of prestige or mystique that can disappear rapidly when the product is made locally under license. The Miller brewery became aware of this perception problem when it started brewing Lowenbrau, a German brand, in Texas. In some cases, a manufacturer has no choice at all about licensing. Many developing countries force patent holders to license their products to other manufacturers or distributors for a royalty fee that may or may not be fair. Canada, owing to consumer activism, is the only industrialized nation requiring compulsory licensing for drugs.

Licensing, in spite of certain limitations, is a sound strategy that can be quite effective under certain circumstances. Licensing terms must be carefully negotiated and explicitly treated. In general, a license contract should include these basic elements: product and territorial coverage, length of contract, quality control, grant back and cross licensing, royalty rate and structure, choice of currency, and choice of law. When licenses are to be granted to European firms, a firm must consider the antitrust rules of the EU, specifically Article 85 of the Rome Treaty.

This article prohibits those licensing terms that are likely to adversely affect trade between EU countries. Such arrangements as price fixing, territorial restrictions, and tie-in agreements are void. A prudent licensor does not "assign" a trademark to a licensee. It is far better to specify the conditions under which the mark can or cannot be used by the licensee. From the licensee's standpoint, the licensor's trademark is valuable in marketing the licensed product only if the product is popular.

Otherwise, the licensee would be better served by creating a new trademark to protect the marketing position in the event that the basic license is not renewed. Licensing should be considered a two-way street because a license also allows the original licensor to gain access to the licensee's technology and product. This is important because the licensee may be able to build on the information supplied by the licensor. Unlike American firms, European licensors are very interested in grant-backs and will even lower the royalty rate in return for product improvements and potentially profitable new products. Thus an intelligent practice is always to stipulate in a contract that license for new patents or products covered by the return grant are to be made available at reasonable royalties.

Finally, the licensor should try not to undermine a product by over licensing it. For example, Pierre Cardin diluted the value of his name by allowing some 800 products to use the name under license. Subsequently, he created Maxim's as the second brand for restaurants, hotels, and food items. Similarly, fashion legend Yves Saint Laurent put his name on numerous products ranging from baseball caps to plastic shoes. A luxury brand can lose its cachet when it has too much exposure. Gucci Group paid $1 billion for YSL's ready-to-wear and perfume businesses and quickly moved to restore the brand's image. Production, marketing, and distribution were overhauled. Even though YSL's licensing agreements contributed 65 per cent of YSL's revenues, Gucci Group decided to walk away from revenues for the sake of the brand's luxury image.

In three months, eleven franchised stores were bought back, and a ready-to-wear factory in Tours was sold. Overall, Gucci terminated 152 of 167 licenses to stop the brand's slide in quality and reputation. Some critics felt that Gucci paid too much for YSL by underestimating how far the brand has fallen. Neither extreme of over-licensing nor under-licensing is desirable. Under-licensing results in potential profit being lost, whereas over-licensing leads to a weakened market through overexposure. Over-licensing can increase income in the short run, but in the long run it may mean killing the goose that laid the golden egg. Some of the risks associated with licensing are suboptimal choice, opportunism, quality, production, payment, contract enforcement, and marketing control. The methods to manage such risks include planning, licensee selection, compensation choices, ongoing relationship, contract specification, and organization of the licensing function.

MANAGEMENT CONTRACT

In some cases, government pressure and restrictions force a foreign company either to sell its domestic operations or to relinquish control. In other cases, the company may prefer not to have any FDI. Under such circumstances, the company may have to formulate another way to generate the revenue given up. One way to generate revenue is to sign a management contract with the government or the new owner in order to manage the business for the new owner. The new owner may lack technical and managerial expertise and may need the former owner to manage the investment until local employees are trained to manage the facility. Management contracts may be used as a sound strategy for entering a market with a minimum investment and minimum political risks.

Club Med, a leader in international resort vacations, is frequently wooed by developing countries with attractive financing options because these countries want tourism. Club Med's strategy involves having either minority ownership or none at all, even though the firm manages all the resorts. Its rationale is that, with management contracts, Club Med is unlikely to be asked to leave a country where it has a resort. Management contract is a common strategy in the hotel business. Accor SA, a French hotel giant, for example, has purchased a large stake in Zenith Hotels International. Zenith itself manages nine hotels in China and one hotel in Thailand without owning them, and most of its hotels do not carry the Zenith name. Accor's acquisition is an attempt to catch up in China with Bass PLC, the parent of Holiday Inn. It hopes to use Zenith's connections and experience to land more management contracts. Accor's Sofitel brand also has a hotel in China. In the USA, the Motel 6 chain is also operated by Accor.

JOINT VENTURE

The joint venture is another alternative a firm may consider as a way of entering an overseas market. A joint venture is simply a partnership at corporate level, and it may be either domestic or international. For the discussion here, an international joint venture is one in which the partners are from more than one country. Much like a partnership formed by two or more individuals, a joint venture is an enterprise formed for a specific business purpose by two or more investors sharing ownership and control. Time Warner Entertainment and Taiwan Pan Asia Investment Company, for instance, have formed a joint venture in Taiwan called Tai Hua International Enterprise Co., Ltd. for the purpose of providing products and services to Taiwan's emerging cable TV industry.

The US-based McDonald's owns 50 per cent of McDonald's Holdings in Japan. One recent joint venture involves Advanced Micro Devices and Fujitsu to replace a previous joint venture. The previous joint venture allowed the partners to jointly develop flash memory chips. The arrangement was for them to have separate sales forces and geographic territories while competing against each other in selling these jointly developed chips in Europe. Unlike the previous 50–50 joint venture, AMD owns 60 per cent of the new company, while Fujitsu owns the rest. The three manufacturing plants in Japan, owned by the former joint venture, are folded into the new venture. With the new joint venture, both partners combine all sales, research, engineering, and marketing.

Joint ventures, like licensing, involve certain risks as well as certain advantages over other forms of entry into a foreign market. In most cases, company resources, circumstances, and the reasons for wanting to do business overseas will determine if a joint venture is the most reasonable way to enter the overseas market. Firms tend to use joint ventures when they enter markets that are characterized by high legal restrictions or high levels of investment risks. Marketers consider joint ventures to be dynamic because of the possibility of a parent firm's change in mission or power. There are two separate overseas investment processes that describe how joint ventures tend to evolve. The first is the "natural," non-political investment process.

In this case, a technology- supplying firm gains a foothold in an unfamiliar market by acquiring a partner that can contribute local knowledge and marketing skills. Technology tends to provide dominance to the technology-supplying firm. As the technology partner becomes more familiar with the market, it buys up more or all equity in the venture or leaves the venture entirely. A contributor of technology, however, is not likely to reduce its share in a joint venture while remaining active in it. The second investment process occurs when the local firm's "political" leverage, through government persuasion, halts or reverses the "natural" economic process.

The foreign, technology-supplying partner remains engaged in the venture without strengthening its ownership position, the consequence being a gradual takeover by the local parties. Partners' commitment to a joint venture is a function of the perceived benefits of the relationship.

Conflict, on the other hand, reduces efficiency and thus adversely affects satisfaction. There are several reasons why joint ventures enjoy certain advantages and should be used. One benefit is that a joint venture substantially reduces the amount of resources that each partner must contribute. Frequently, the joint venture strategy is the only way, other than through licensing, that a firm can enter a foreign market. This is especially true when wholly owned activities are prohibited in a country. Centrally planned economies, in particular, usually limit foreign firms' entry to some sort of cooperative arrangement. China has made it quite clear that only those car makers with long-term commitments will be allowed to assemble foreign models with local partners.

Foreign manufacturers must agree to have less than 50 per cent control of the joint ventures. Sometimes *social* rather than legal circumstances require a joint venture to be formed. When Pillsbury planned to market is products in Japan, it considered a number of options, ranging from exporting and licensing to the outright purchase of a Japanese company. Although foreign ownership laws had been relaxed, Pillsbury decided to follow traditional business custom in Japan by seeking a good partner. It thus got together with Snow Brand to form Snow–Brand/Pillsbury. Joint ventures often have social implications. The familial and tightly knit relationship between suppliers and middlemen is prevalent in many countries. In Japan, this relationship is known as *keiretsu,* which means that family-like business groups are linked by cross-ownership of equity.

Such customs and business relationships make it difficult for a new supplier to gain entry. Even in the event that the new supplier is able to secure some orders, those orders may be terminated as soon as a member of the family is able to supply the product in question. A joint venture thus provides an opportunity for the foreign supplier to secure business orders through the back door.

A joint venture can also simultaneously work to satisfy social, economic, and political circumstances since these concerns are highly related. In any kind of international business undertaking political risks always exist, and a joint venture can reduce such risks while it increases market opportunities. In this sense, a joint venture can make a difference between securely entering a foreign market or not entering it at all. Many American firms seek Saudi partners to establish joint ventures so that they can deal effectively with Saudi Arabia's political demands.

Joint ventures are not without their shortcomings and limitations. First, if the partners to the joint venture have not established clear-cut decision-making policy and must consult with each other on all decisions, the *decision-making process* may delay a necessary action when speed is essential. Whenever two individuals or organizations work together, there are bound to be *conflicts* because of cultural problems, divergent goals, disagreements over production and marketing strategies, and weak contributions by one or the other partner. Although the goals may be compatible at the outset, goals and objectives may diverge over time, even when joint ventures are successful. Dow–Badische was set up in the USA with BASF providing the technology to make chemical raw materials and fibers and Dow supplying the marketing expertise.

A split eventually occurred despite good profits when BASF wanted to expand the fibre business–Dow felt that the venture was moving away from Dow's mainstream chemical business. BASF ultimately bought out Dow and made the business its wholly owned subsidiary. Another potential problem is the matter of *control*. By definition, a joint venture must deal with double management. If a partner holds less than 50 per cent ownership, that partner must in effect allow the majority partner to make decisions. If the board of directors has a 50–50 split, it is difficult for the board to make a decision quickly or at all. Dow's experience with its Korea Pacific Chemical joint venture illustrates this point. When prices plunged, the joint venture lost $60 million. To stem the loss, Dow wanted to improve efficiency but was opposed by its Korean partner.

The government-appointed directors boycotted board meetings and a decision could not be reached. Both sides eventually ended up bringing lawsuits against each other. There are several factors that may determine whether a company wants to take equity ownership in international joint ventures. These source country factors are exchange rate, cost of borrowing, export capability, and management orientation. Based on a study of 8078 international joint ventures in China, parent firms are more likely to take equity ownership when they are from a source country with a strong currency, low cost of borrowing, strong export capability, and high uncertainty avoidance. It is interesting to note that, while cultural differences indeed affect international joint venture performance, culture distance stems more from differences in organizational culture than from differences in national cultures. A survey of Indian executives and their partners from other countries confirmed this relationship.

MANUFACTURING

The manufacturing process may be employed as a strategy involving all or some manufacturing in a foreign country. IBM, for example, has sixteen plants in the USA and eighteen more in other countries. One kind of manufacturing procedure, known as sourcing, involves manufacturing operations in a host country, not so much to sell there but for the purpose of exporting from that company's home country to other countries.

This stage is concerned more with another manufacturing objective: the goal of a manufacturing strategy may be to set up a production base inside a target market country as a means of invading it. There are several variations on this method, ranging from complete manufacturing to contract manufacturing and partial manufacturing. From the perspective of the host countries, it is obvious as to why they want to attract foreign capital.

Although job creation is the main reason, there are several other benefits for the host country as well. Foreign direct investment, unlike other forms of capital inflows, almost always brings additional resources that are very desirable to developing economies.

These resources include technology, management expertise, and access to export markets. There are several reasons why a company chooses to invest in manufacturing facilities abroad. One reason may involve gaining access either to raw materials or to take advantage of resources for its manufacturing operations. As such, this process is known as *backward vertical integration*. Another reason may be to take advantage of lower labour costs or other abundant factors of production. Hoover was able to cut its high British manufacturing costs by shifting some of its production to France. The strategy may further reduce another kind of cost–transportation.

British publishing firms have begun to print more books abroad because they can save 25 to 40 per cent in production and shipping costs. Manufacturing in a host country can make the company's product more price competitive because the company can avoid or minimize high import taxes, as well as other trade barriers. Honda, with 68 per cent of its car sales coming from exports and 43 per cent from the US market, has a good reason to be sensitive to trade barriers. In order to avoid future problems of this nature, it set up plants in Ohio. A manufacturer interested in manufacturing abroad should consider a number of significant factors. One study investigated the incentive preferences of MNCs and found absence of restrictions on inter-company payments to be the most important determinant.

The other important incentives include: no controls on dividend remittances, import duty concessions, guarantees against expropriation, and tax holidays. From the marketing standpoint, *product image* deserves attention. Although Winston cigarettes are made in Venezuela with the same tobaccos and formula as the Winston cigarettes in the USA, Venezuelans still prefer the more expensive US made Winston. Philip Morris and R.J. Reynolds face this same problem in Russia when setting up manufacturing plants there. Unilever had a similar problem when it began manufacturing locally in Nepal where people prefer Indian-made products.

Competition is an important factor, since to a great extent competition determines potential profit. Another factor is resources of various countries, which should be compared to determine each country's comparative advantage.

The comparison should also include production considerations, including production facilities, raw materials, equipment, real estate, water, power, and transport. Human resources, an integral part of the production factor, must be available at reasonable cost. Manufacturers should pay attention to absolute as well as relative changes in *labour costs*. A particular country is more attractive as a plant's location if the wages there increase more slowly than those in other countries. The increase in labour costs in Germany led GM's Opel to switch its production facilities to Japan and led Rollei to move its production to Singapore.

Several Japanese firms have been attracted by the $1 hourly wage rate in Mexico, a rate even lower than the hourly pay in Singapore and South Korea. A manufacturer must keep in mind, however, that labour costs are determined not only by compensation but also by productivity and exchange rates. Mexico's labour costs, already absolutely low, become even lower because of the country's falling exchange rate, but this advantage is offset somewhat because Mexican workers are relatively unskilled and thus produce more defective products. The *type of product* made is another factor that determines whether foreign manufacturing is an economical and effective venture. A manufacturer must weigh the economies of exporting a standardized product against the flexibility of having a local manufacturing plant that is capable of tailoring the product for local preferences.

Taxation is another important consideration. Countries commonly offer tax advantages, among other incentives, to lure foreign investment. Puerto Rico does well on this score. In addition, there are no exchange problems since the currency is the US dollar. Just as important as other factors is the *investment climate* for foreign capital.

The investment climate is determined by geographic and climatic conditions, market size, and growth potential, as well as by the political atmosphere. Political, economic, and social motives are highly related, and it is hardly surprising that countries, states, and cities compete fiercely to attract foreign investment and manufacturing plants. Multinational corporations have been investing more and more overseas, with Asia and Latin America as their prime targets. It should be pointed out that the importance of cheap, unskilled labour in attracting manufacturing investment has diminished in recent years and is likely to continue. Because of technology development in products and processes, there is a greater need for human skill in product manufacturing. Therefore, developing countries that can successfully influence plant location decisions will be those that have more highly skilled labour at relatively low wages.

ASSEMBLY OPERATIONS

An assembly operation is a variation on a manufacturing strategy. "Assembly means the fitting or joining together of fabricated components." The methods used to join or fit together solid components may be welding, soldering, riveting, gluing, laminating, and sewing. In this strategy, parts or components are produced in various countries in order to gain each country's comparative advantage. Capital-intensive parts may be produced in advanced nations, and labour-intensive assemblies may be produced in a less developed country, where labour is abundant and labour costs low. This strategy is common among manufacturers of consumer electronics. When a product becomes mature and faces intense price competition, it may be necessary to shift all of the labour-intensive operations to less developed countries.

An assembly operation also allows a company to be price-competitive against cheap imports, and this is a defence strategy employed by US apparel makers against such imports. As far as pattern design and fabric cutting are concerned, a US firm can compete by using automated machines, but sewing is another matter altogether, since sewing is labour-intensive and the least automated aspect of making the product.

To solve this problem, precut fabrics can be shipped to a low-wage country for sewing before bringing them back for finishing and packaging. Warnaco and Interco save on aggregate labour costs by cutting fabrics in the USA and shipping them to plants in Costa Rica and Honduras to be sewn. The duties collected on finished products brought back are low. Assembly operations also allow a company's product to enter many markets without being subject to tariffs and quotas.

The extent of freedom and flexibility, however, is limited by local product-content laws. South American countries usually require that 50–95 per cent of components used in products be produced domestically. Note that as the percentage of required local content increases, the company's flexibility declines and the price advantage is eroded. This is so because domestic products can be sheltered behind tariff walls, and higher prices must be expected for products with a low percentage of local content. In general, a host country objects to the establishment of a screwdriver assembly that merely assembles imported parts. If a product's local content is less than half of all the components used, the product may be viewed as imported, subjected to tariffs and quota restrictions.

The Japanese, even with joint ventures and assembly operations in Europe, keep local content in foreign production facilities to a minimum while maximizing the use of low-cost Japanese components. British Leyland's Triumph Acclaim is one such example. Made in the United Kingdom under license from Honda, Acclaim contained over 55 per cent Japanese parts. Italy considered Acclaim as a Japanese, not a European, car. Since the EU's rule of thumb seemed to be at least 45 per cent local content, Italy asked the European

Commission to decide what percentage of local content a product must have to be considered "made in Europe." An assembly manufacturing operator must therefore carefully evaluate the trade-off between low-cost production and the process of circumventing trade barriers.

TURNKEY OPERATIONS

A turnkey operation is an agreement by the seller to supply a buyer with a facility fully equipped and ready to be operated by the buyer's personnel, who will be trained by the seller. The term is sometimes used in fast-food franchising when a franchisor agrees to select a store site, build the store, equip it, train the franchisee and employees, and sometimes arrange for the financing.

In international marketing, the term is usually associated with giant projects that are sold to governments or government- run companies. Large-scale plants requiring technology and large-scale construction processes unavailable in local markets commonly use this strategy. Such large-scale projects include building steel mills; cement, fertilizer, and chemical plants; and those related to such advanced technologies as telecommunications.

Owing to the magnitude of a giant turnkey project, the winner of the contract can expect to reap huge rewards. Thus it is important that the turnkey construction package offered to a buyer is an attractive one. Such a package involves more than just offering the latest technology, since there are many other factors important to less developed countries in deciding on a particular turnkey project.

Financing is crucial, and this is one area in which US firms are lacking. European and Japanese firms are much more prepared to secure attractive financing from their governments for buyers. Another factor for consideration involves an agreement to build a local plant. All equipment must be installed and tested to make certain that it functions as intended. Local personnel must be trained to run the operation, and after-sales services should be contracted for and made available for the future maintenance of the plant.

ACQUISITION

When a manufacturer wants to enter a foreign market rapidly and yet retain maximum control, direct investment through acquisition should be considered. The reasons for wanting to acquire a foreign company include product/geographical diversification, acquisition of expertise and rapid entry.

For example, Renault acquired a controlling interest in American Motors in order to gain the sales organization and distribution network that would otherwise have been very expensive and time-consuming to build from the ground up. After being outbid in 1994 when Forstmann Little & Co. bought Ziff- Davis Publishing, a company well known for its *PC Magazine* and other computer-related publications, Japan's Softbank Corp. was able finally to acquire the publisher a year later, albeit at a much higher price. The deal made the Japanese software company the world's largest computer magazine publisher and the largest operator of computer trade shows including Comdex. Acquisition is viewed in a different light from other kinds of foreign direct investment. A government generally welcomes foreign investment that starts up a new enterprise, since that investment increases employment and enlarges the tax base. An acquisition, however, fails to do this since it displaces and replaces domestic ownership.

Therefore, acquisition is very likely to be perceived as exploitation or a blow to national pride–on this basis, it stands a good chance of being turned down. There was a heated debate before the United Kingdom allowed Sikorsky, a US firm, to acquire Westland, a failing British manufacturer of military helicopters. That episode caused the Thatcher government to halt its negotiation with Ford concerning the acquisition of British Leyland's Austin–Rover passenger-car division. A greenfield project, while embraced by the host country, implies gradual market entry. A special case of acquisition is the brownfield entry mode. This mode happens when an investor's transferred resources dominate those provided by an acquired firm. In addition, this hybrid mode of entry requires the investor to extensively restructure the acquired company so as to assure fit between the two organizations. This is not uncommon in emerging markets, and the extensive restructuring may yield a new operation that resembles a greenfield investment. As such, integration costs can be high. However, brownfield is a worthwhile strategy to consider when neither pure acquisition nor greenfield is feasible. Due to the sensitive nature of acquisition, there are more legal hurdles to surmount.

In Germany, the Federal Cartel Office may prohibit or require divestiture of those mergers and acquisitions that could strengthen or create market domination. Nestlé, in a space of three months, completed three major deals. First it paid $10.3 billion in cash for Ralston Purina Co., a pet-food powerhouse. Second, it paid over $2.6 billion in stock for a controlling stake in Dreyer's Grand Ice Cream Inc., the largest US maker of ice cream. Another $2.6 billion deal followed for Chef America Inc. Nestlé spent almost a year convincing American regulators to allow it to acquire Dreyer's Grand Ice Cream. The US Federal Trade Commission blocked the proposed deal because the takeover would eliminate brand and price competition for such premium brands as Häagen-Dazs and Godiva. Nestlé, Dreyers, and Unilever control 98 per cent of superpremium ice cream sales in the USA. There does not appear to be any sign that mergers and acquisitions are abating.

Anheuser- Busch has negotiated in 2003 to increase its stake in Tsingtao Brewery, China's biggest brewer, from 4.5 per cent to 27 per cent over seven years at the cost of $182 million. Several of Ford Motor Co.'s premium brands are a result of acquisitions, and they include Volvo, Jaguar, and Aston Martin. A 2000 acquisition was a payment of nearly $3 billion to BMW Group for the

Britishborn Land Rover line of sport-utility vehicles. BMW acquired Rover Group Ltd. in 1995 and lost $1.25 billion on this investment over five years. To cut the loss, BMW sold Rover Group's Rover and MG brands to a British investment group and Land Rover to Ford. The value of a currency may either reduce or increase the costs of an acquisition. A buyer whose home currency is getting weaker will see its costs go up but will benefit if its currency becomes stronger. As in the case of Hoechst, a German chemical giant, it bid $7.2 billion for the US-based Marion Merrell Dow Inc. and was able to save at least $250 million because the value of the dollar plunged in the meantime.

International mergers and acquisitions are complex, expensive, and risky. The problems are numerous: finding a suitable company, determining a fair price, acquisition debt, merging two management teams, language and cultural differences, employee resentment, geographic distance, and so on. Acquirers thus must exercise due diligence.

Sometimes, it may be better to walk away from a deal. The reasons for exiting from a deal include: high price, no agreement on governance issues, no synergies, poor quality of management, environmental issues, ethical reasons, no strategic fit, detection of significant unrecorded/undisclosed liability, potential problems with antitrust laws, and uncertainty about legal/ tax aspects. Quite often, the future synergies due to vertical integration are elusive. Unicord PLC, a large fish processor located in Thailand, paid $280 million to acquire Bumble Bee Seafood Inc., a San Diego tuna canner.

The acquisition was a failure, and the founder of Unicord committed suicide in 1995 as lenders sought payment. Japan's Bridgestone Corp. paid $2.6 billion to acquire money-losing Firestone Tire and Rubber Co. and lost $1 billion in the first five years after the acquisition while enduring a bitter and lengthy strike. Overall, foreign acquirers pay almost twice as much as would domestic buyers. The US market in particular, due to its size, tends to force foreign acquirers to pay a premium price. When judged by stock performance in relation to Standard and Poor's industry indexes, about half of the 150 deals harmed shareholder wealth, while another one-third hardly contributed anything. Yet, in spite of the high failure rate for cross-border acquisitions, more and more international deals may be expected.

A follow-up study showed that transatlantic mergers had a better chance to succeed–far better than the usual success ratio of American domestic or intra-European deals. One contributing factor is that such deals tended to expand geographic reach, reducing the need to cut costs by disruptively merging overlapping operations. In addition, because of the hassles of having to pass the scrutiny of antitrust regulators on both sides of the ocean, companies choose to pursue only the most promising prospects.

STRATEGIC ALLIANCES

As discussed, to gain access to new markets and technologies while achieving economies of scale, international marketers have a number of organization forms to choose from: licensing, partially owned or wholly owned subsidiaries, joint ventures, and acquisitions. A relatively new organizational form of market entry and competitive cooperation is strategic alliance. This form of corporate cooperation has been receiving a great deal of attention as large multinational firms still find it necessary to find strategic partners to penetrate a market.

There is no clear and precise definition of strategic alliance. There is no one way to form a strategic alliance. Strategic alliances may be the result of mergers, acquisitions, joint ventures, and licensing agreements. Joint ventures are naturally strategic alliances, but not all strategic alliances are joint ventures. Unlike joint ventures which require two or more partners to create a separate entity, a strategic alliance does not necessarily require a new legal entity.

As such, it may not require partners to make arrangements to share equity. Instead of being an equity-based investment, a strategic alliance may be more of a contractual arrangement whereby two or more partners agree to cooperate with each other and use each partner's resources and expertise to penetrate a particular market. America Online is a good example of strategic alliances. In 2000,America Online and Bertelsmann AG formed a global alliance to expand the distribution of Bertelsmann's media content and electronic commerce properties over America Online's interactive brands worldwide. Earlier, a strategic alliance between America Online and Sun Microsystems, Inc. involved a joint development of a comprehensive suite of easy-to-deploy, end-to-end solutions to assist companies and Internet service providers in entering the electronic commerce market and scale their electronic commerce operations.

America Online has committed to buy systems and services worth approximately $400 million from Sun. In return, in 2000, America Online received $123 million in licensing, marketing and advertising fees, and about $317 million in minimum revenue commitments. Airlines are a good example of the international nature of strategic alliances. Almost all major airlines have joined one of the three strategic groups: Star, SkyTeam, and Oneworld. The SkyTeam group consists of Delta, Air France, Aeromexico, Alitalia, Czech Airlines, and Korean Air.

Oneworld comprises American, British Airways, Aer Lingus, Cathay Pacific, Finnair, Iberia, LanChile, and Qantas. The Star alliance, the largest group, comprises United, Air Canada, Air New Zealand, ANA, Austrian, British Midland, Lauda, Lufthansa, Mexicana, Scandinavian, Singapore, Thai, Tyrolean, and Varig. While the alliances vary in size and degree of integration, most have code sharing by offering seats on a partner's flights. In addition, passengers earn frequent- flier points on their home carrier when flying with the alliance members. These members also provide reciprocal access to their airport lounges.

Companies enter into alliance relationships for a variety of reasons. Those in the emerging Latin American economies are similar to their counterparts in many other nations in terms of their motivations. In general, through alliances with foreign partners, they seek resource acquisition, competitive posturing, and risk/cost reduction. While companies have paid attention to the hard side of alliance management, the soft side also requires attention. The soft side has to do with the management of relationship capital in an alliance. Relationship capital focuses on the socio-psychological aspects of the alliance, and the two important areas of relationship capital are mutual trust and commitment. There are at least three types of strategic alliances: shared distribution, licensed manufacturing, and research and development alliances. Examples of shared distribution include Chrysler's distribution of Mitsubishi cars in the USA and the shared routes of SAS, KLM, Austrian Air, and Swiss Air. Matshushita's manufacturing of IBM PCs is an example of licensed manufacturing, enabling the partners to fill unused capacity while avoiding an investment in a new plant and equipment. In the case of R&D alliances, one recent example is an alliance between Sony and Philips which competed with another alliance led by Toshiba in developing DVDs.

ANALYSIS OF ENTRY STRATEGIES

To enter a foreign market, a manufacturer has a number of strategic options, each with its own strengths and weaknesses. Many companies employ multiple strategies. IBM has employed strategies ranging from licensing, joint ventures, and strategic alliances on the one hand to local manufacturing and subsidiaries on the other hand. Likewise, McDonald's uses joint ventures in the Far East while licensing its name without putting up equity capital in the Mideast.

Walt Disney Co. has a 39 per cent stake in Euro Disney while collecting management and royalty fees which amount to $70 million a year. One would be naive to believe that a single entry strategy is suitable for all products or in all countries. For example, a significant change in the investment climate can make a particular strategy ineffective even though it worked well in the past. There are a number of characteristics that determine the appropriateness of entry strategies, and many variables affect which strategy is chosen. These characteristics include political risks, regulations, type of country, type of product, and other competitive and market characteristics.

The impact of culture on FDI is somewhat ambiguous. One study found no support for the belief that foreign direct investments first took place in foreign markets close to the home country before spreading to more culturally distant markets. Another study involved service multinational firms and found that their foreign investments were negatively related to the cultural distance between the home and host countries. Interestingly, multinational corporations with social knowledge have less need to resort to ownership for control purposes. Viacom Inc. appears to take culture into account in deciding on entry strategies. In the case of its MTV channel, the company generally does not have partners, but in the case of its Nickelodeon channel, the firm has made an effort to have local partners. It is difficult to tell Europeans that they should have the same cultural underpinnings inherent in American children's programming. Although children may watch programming from other countries, they are more inclined to watch their own programmes.

Markets are far from being homogeneous, and the type of country chosen dictates the entry strategy to be used. One way of classifying countries is by the *degree of control exerted on the economy by the government,* with capitalism at one extreme and communism at the other. Other systems are classified somewhere in between depending on the freedom allowed to private citizens in conducting their business activities. In free-enterprise economies, an MNC can choose any entry strategy it deems appropriate. In controlled economies, the options are limited. Until recently, the most frequent trade entry activity in controlled economies was exporting, followed by licensing for Eastern Europe. Market entry strategies are also influenced by *product type.* A product that must be customised or that requires some services before and after the sale cannot be exported easily to another country.

In fact, a service or product whose value is determined largely by an accompanied service cannot be distributed practically outside of the producing country. Any portion of the product that is service oriented must be created at the place of consumption. As a result, service-intensive products require particular modes of market entry. The options include management contract to sell service to a foreign customer, licensing so that another local company may be trained to provide that service, and local manufacturing by establishing a permanent branch or subsidiary there. A product that is basically a *commodity* may require local production in order to reduce labour and shipping costs.

For a *value-added or differentiated product,* a firm can depend on the exporting mode because of the higher profit margin. Furthermore, local manufacturing may destroy the product's mystique and thus diminish a previously existing market. A study of foreign direct investment entries in the USA found that 65 per cent entered the USA through acquisitions and that joint ventures and greenfields accounted for 9 per cent and 26 per cent respectively. Foreign acquisitions of American firms were more likely to fail than foreign greenfield investments. Foreign-controlled firms failed less often than domestically owned firms. There may be a relationship between ownership entry modes and performance.

One study of 321 Japanese firms entering the North American market, new ventures outperform joint ventures, and joint ventures outperform acquisitions. There are two schools of thought that explain how multinational corporations select ownership structures for subsidiaries. The first has to do with what the firm wants, and MNCs want structures that minimize the transaction costs of doing business abroad. Factors affecting what the firm wants include the capabilities of the firm, its strategic needs, and the transaction costs of different ways of transferring capabilities.

The second school of thought, related to what the firm can get, explains that what it wants may differ from what it can get. In this case, ownership structures are determined by negotiations, whose outcomes depend on the relative bargaining power of the firm and that of the host government. The statistical analysis supports the bargaining school, in that attractive domestic markets increase the relative power of host governments. However, there is no support for the prediction that firms in marketing- and R&D-intensive industries have more bargaining power than others.

MNCs prefer whole ownership when they have a lot of experience in an industry or a country, when intrasystem sales of the subsidiary are high, or when the subsidiary is located in a market-intensive industry. The joint venture is the preferred mode when MNCs rely on local inputs of raw materials and skills. In practice, American manufacturers prefer joint ventures in the Far East because of legal and cultural barriers.

Regarding how American manufacturers want to enter the European Union market, the preferred methods of entry are: joint venture (26 per cent), sales representative (21 per cent), branch/subsidiary (19 per cent), distribution facility (17 per cent), increasing exports (9 per cent), and expanding existing facilities (8 per cent).Their preferred European locations are: Britain (30 per cent), Germany (24 per cent), France (9 per cent), Italy (9 per cent), the Netherlands (8 per cent), Belgium (8 per cent), Ireland (5 per cent), Spain (5 per cent), and Denmark (3 per cent). A company's entry choice of joint ventures versus wholly owned subsidiaries may be influenced by its competitive capabilities as well as market barriers.

In the case of Japanese investors entering the US market, they choose joint ventures when facing high market barriers. However, they prefer to establish wholly owned subsidiaries when they possess competitive capabilities. These ownership decisions are influenced more by marketing variables than by technological factors. One caveat: the results vary across industries and products. The costs of organizing a business in transition economies influence entry mode choice. Host country institutions have an impact because underdeveloped institutions drive up costs of establishing wholly owned ventures.

Institutional isomorphism seems to exist as later entrants often use the entry mode patterns established by earlier entrants. In addition, this behaviour exists within a firm as companies exhibit consistency in their entry mode choices across time. In the case of China, a company's timing of entry is associated with non-equity modes, competitors' behaviour, and lower levels of country risk. Firms cannot delay their entry when the competitors are moving in. In addition, a firm's entry is accelerated if a non-equity mode of entry is chosen. Favorable risk conditions, likewise, accelerate entry timing. In addition, corporate size facilitates early entry.A firm of good size is able to muster resources, extend support among the related products sectors, and capitalize on economies of scale.

This is consistent with the resource-based arguments that early entrants differ from late entrants in terms of resources and capabilities. One study focuses on conflicting results which show that cultural distance is associated with wholly owned modes in some studies and with joint ventures in other studies. The evidence shows that, for Western firms investing in Central and Eastern Europe, investment risk moderates the relationship between cultural distance and entry mode selection.

Firms entering culturally distant markets that are low in investment risk preferred cooperative modes of entry. However, if such culturally distant markets pose high investment risk, wholly owned modes of entry are preferred. However, although cultural distance is routinely used as an independent variable which supposedly influences performance and entry mode choice, it is conceivable that the relationship may be reversed. A case can be made that cultural distance is a dependent variable because entry mode and performance may affect the perceived distance.

FOREIGN TRADE ZONES (FTZS)

When entering a market, a company should go beyond an investigation of market entry modes. Another question that should be asked is whether a foreign trade zone is involved and needs consideration. The decisions concerning market entry and FTZs are somewhat independent. An FTZ may be used regardless of whether the entry strategy is exporting or local manufacturing. An FTZ is a secured domestic area in international commerce, considered to be legally outside a country's customs territory. It is an area designated by a government for the duty-free entry of goods. It is also a location where imports may be handled with few regulations, and little or no customs duties and excise taxes are collected. As such, goods enter the area without any duty being payable.

The duty would be paid only when goods enter customs territory of the country where an FTZ is located. Variations among FTZs include freeports, tarifffree trade zones, airport duty-free arcades, export processing zones, and other foreign grade zones. FTZs are usually established in countries for the convenience of foreign traders. The zones may be run by the host government or by private entities. FTZs vary in size from a few acres to several square miles. They may be located at airports, in harbor areas, or within the interior of a country. In addition to the FTZs, there are also subzones throughout the USA. Subzones are special-purpose facilities for companies unable to operate effectively at public zone sites.

One popular misconception about FTZs is that they are used basically for warehousing. Although goods may be stored for an unlimited length of time in an FTZ, any gain from doing so is small when compared to the alternative of a bonded warehouse, which allows temporary storage without duty. Actually, the future of FTZs lies in manufacturing, not storing. FTZs offer several important benefits, both for the country and for companies using them. One benefit is job retention and creation. When better facilities and grants are provided to attract MNCs, FTZs can generate foreign investment and jobs. For example, in Buffalo, New York, FTZ was able to attract a Canadian automobile assembly operation and a Japanese camera importer to establish operations there.

China has set up Special Economic Zones for manufacturing, banking, exporting and importing, and foreign investment. These SEZs provide a more liberal environment than that of the rest of the country. SEZs, when compared to the rest of China, are unique in the sense that they enjoy considerable administrative autonomy and they offer numerous economic incentives.

Some countries, due to political reasons, are not able to open up their economies completely. Instead they have set up export processing zones, a special type of FTZ, in order to attract foreign capital for manufacturing for export. However, for export processing zones to be effective, exporters should not be isolated from other firms. There is evidence that manufacturers take free trade zones into account when selecting a site for their foreign operations.

Plant location is related positively to size of free trade zones, per capita GNP, exchange rate devaluation, length of income tax holidays, political stability, and manufacturing concentration. On the other hand, the location of export-oriented manufacturing investment is related negatively to wage rate, inflation rate, transportation cost, and profit repatriation restrictions.

The benefits of FTZ use are numerous. Some of these benefits are country-specific in the sense that some countries offer superior facilities for lower costs. Other benefits are zone-specific in that certain zones may be better than others within the same country in terms of tax and transportation facilities. Finally, there are zone-related benefits that constitute general advantages in using an FTZ. Some of the zone-related benefits are: lower theft rate, lower insurance costs, delay of tax payment, and reduction of inventory in transit. FTZs provide a means to facilitate imports.

Imported merchandise can be sent into FTZs without formal customs entry and duty payment until some later date. Both foreign and domestic goods may be moved into FTZs and remain there for storage, assembling, manufacturing, packaging, and other processing operations. Goods that were improperly marked or cannot meet standards for clearance can be remarked and salvaged. Moreover, goods can be cleaned, mixed, and used in the manufacturing of other products. One Swiss cosmetics company imports in bulk and employs US labour to repackage its goods for retailing. In fact, importers can even display and exhibit merchandise and take orders in FTZs without securing a bond. For retailers, benefits derived by using FTZs include the sorting, labeling, and storing of imports. FTZs not only facilitate imports but also facilitate export and re-export, though the gain from this practice is small when compared to the alternatives of duty drawback and temporary import bond. However, domestic goods can be taken into an FTZ and are then returned free of quotas and duty, even when they have been combined with other articles while inside the zone. Sears uses the New Orleans FTZ to inspect foreign cameras it subsequently ships to Latin America. Seiko Time Corporation of America opened a 200,000-square-foot facility in the New Jersey FTZ to store and ship watches to Canada and Latin America. One European medical supply firm that makes kidney dialysis machines uses German raw materials and American labour in a US FTZ for assembly purposes, and then exports 30 per cent of the finished product to Scandinavia.

CONCLUSION

If a company wants to avoid foreign direct investment when marketing in foreign markets, it has a number of options. It can export its product from its home base, or it can grant a license permitting another company to manufacture and market its product in a foreign market. Another option is to sign a contract to sell its expertise by managing the business for a foreign owner. If the firm is interested in making foreign direct investment, it can either start its business from the ground up or acquire another company. The acquisition, however, may receive a less than enthusiastic response from the foreign government. If the company decides to start a new business overseas, it must consider whether a sole venture or joint venture will best suit the objective. Sole ventures provide a company with better control and profit, whereas joint ventures reduce risk and exploit the strengths of a local partner.

Regardless of whether a sole venture or joint venture is used, the company must still decide whether local production is going to be complete or partial. Finally, foreign sales to governments often take the form of giant turnkey projects that require the company to provide a complete package, including financing, construction, and training.

Once a particular market is chosen, management needs to decide on the market entry strategy. In addition, the company should consider the feasibility of operating all or some of its international business in a free trade zone, since such a zone can complement many of the market penetration options. Each market entry strategy has its own unique strengths and weaknesses. In most circumstances the strategies are not mutually exclusive. A manufacturer may use multiple strategies in different markets as well as within the same market. No single market penetration is ideal for all markets or all circumstances. The appropriateness of a strategic option depends on corporate objectives, market conditions, and political realities.

7

Currencies and Foreign Exchange

MONEY

Money is so simple that most users take it for granted. Actually, it is one of the great innovations in history. Being so simple, useful, and common, money facilitates the exchange of goods and services. In the USA, numerous currencies circulated during the late 1700s and throughout most of the 1800s.

It took nearly 140 years after becoming one nation for the USA to have a successful central bank in 1914. A hard currency is hard because of the solid trust that people have in the currency and not because of its gold backing. Businesspeople must have faith that the country issuing the currency will fulfill its obligations. For money to function as a store of value, there must exist something of value to store. Even though Russia has gold and oil, people still have doubts about the ruble as a store of value. An Act of Parliament does not make a currency hard or international.

Currencies become internationalized only because they meet the needs of official institutions and private parties more effectively than do other financial assets. The Federal Reserve Board, nearly two-thirds of the $300 billion of US currency in circulation is outside of the USA. Ex-communist economies and South America's inflation-wracked countries demand US dollars in their attempt to seek economic stability. Panama and Liberia have long used the US dollar as their official currencies. Honduras, Hong Kong, and several Asian countries have pegged their money to the dollar. While it is true that the US dollar now comprises only half of official foreign exchange reserves, the dollar is still the world's most instantly and easily recognized international currency.

Due to historical reasons, the former Soviet economies were hesitant to accept the German mark. Japan, on the other hand, is reluctant to allow the yen to become an international transaction currency. An international currency fulfills three basic functions in the global monetary system: it serves as a medium of exchange, a unit of account, and a store of value. As a *medium of exchange,* private parties use an international currency in foreign trade and international capital transactions, whereas official agents use it for balance-of-payments financing and to intervene in foreign exchange markets. As a *unit of account,* private parties use an international currency for invoicing merchandise trade and for denominating financial transactions, whereas official agents use it to define exchange rate parities.

As a *store of value,* international currencies are held by private agents as financial assets and by official agents as reserve assets. For a currency to be used internationally, two sets of factors are essential. First, there must be confidence in the value of the currency and in the political stability of the issuing country. Second, a country should possess financial markets that are substantially free of controls. These markets should be broad and deep. The country should also possess financial institutions that are sophisticated and competitive in overseas financial centers.

FOREIGN EXCHANGE

Foreign exchange transactions involve the purchase or sale of one national currency against another. The easiest way to understand this type of transaction is to view money as just another product that customers are willing to buy and sell. Like other products, money can be branded, and the US dollar, Swiss franc, Japanese yen, and so on are simply some of the brand names for a money "product." Some of these brand names carry more prestige and are more desirable than others, much like brand names of consumer products. People often wonder why it is necessary to have so many different currencies. Obviously, it would be preferable to have only one worldwide currency that could be used anywhere on Earth, similar to the US dollar's being used and accepted in all fifty states. But a global currency is currently impossible due to two uncontrollable factors–national sovereignty and inflation.

Under normal circumstances, it is very rare for a country to adopt another country's currency as its own. One exception is Liechtenstein, which signed a customs treaty with Switzerland in 1923, making the Swiss franc its official currency. Moreover, Liechtenstein's customs affairs are administered by Switzerland.

Many Americans, knowing that the dollar is widely accepted, do not understand why the US dollar cannot become a global currency and why other nations resist replacing their national currencies with the US dollar. The resistance may perhaps be better understood if one imagines the tables being turned. Would the American public be willing to abandon the dollar and replace it with a new global currency? The fact that the USA is so unwilling to embrace the metric system in spite of its demonstrated superiority underscores this point clearly. Because of *national pride,* no nation wants to give up its identity and sovereignty, and this includes its national currency.

National pride may also explain Great Britain's reluctance to allow the pound to join the European Monetary System, especially since the British believe that the pound has a more important role in the international financial world. Great Britain withdrew the pound from the EMS in 1992 and has so far refused to switch to the euro. A less emotional but often uncontrollable issue is *inflation,* which reduces the value of money. Since it is impossible for all nations to have an identical inflation rate, the effect of inflation on the value of various currencies is uneven. In Argentina, the inflation rate was greater than 400 per cent in 1984, and it subsequently accelerated to more than 800 per cent, forcing the government to adopt the austral as its new currency in 1985.

Inflation in the USA at the same time was running in single digits. In China during the 1940s, the currency had so little value that the Chinese had to cart their money around in wheelbarrows. After World War I, the value of the German mark stood at 4 trillion marks to a dollar. These examples should make clear that it is impractical for any single currency to be used on a worldwide basis while maintaining constant value in all countries.

FOREIGN EXCHANGE MARKET

Firms needing to make payment for foreign business transactions never seem to have enough currency on hand, and it is cumbersome for them to seek out those with adequate amounts to sell. There is thus a need for a foreign exchange market to suit all individuals and institutions in order that they may contact one another for this purpose. The foreign exchange market as it exists has no central trading floor where buyers and sellers meet. Most trades are completed by banks and foreign exchange dealers using telephones, cables, and mail. As a worldwide market, the foreign exchange market operates twenty-four hours a day.

The foreign exchange market facilitates financial transactions in three different ways. First, it provides *credit* or *financing* for firms engaged in international business. This can be achieved through a variety of means, such as letter of credit, time draft, forward contract, and so on. Second, it performs a *clearing* function similar to a domestic bank's clearing process for checking-account customers.

Clearing is a process by which a financial transaction between two parties involving intermediation between banks is "settled." In the case of international clearing, the funds are transferred on paper from a commercial customer to its local bank, from there to a New York bank, and finally to a foreign bank abroad. The process allows payments to be made for foreign goods without a physical transfer or movement of money across countries. Third, the market furnishes facilities for *hedging* so that businesses can cover or reduce their foreign exchange risks. Hedging is an activity that is used as a temporary substitute purchase or sale for the actual currency. This temporary transaction allows users to protect the price they secure from fluctuations because it establishes equal and opposite positions in the market. The rationale for hedging lies in the exchange rate fluctuation, which can move significantly and erratically, even within a short time. For example, due to inflation and instability, the Russian ruble lost 27 per cent of its value against the US dollar in a single day in 1994.

The panic started when the central bank stopped supporting the declining ruble. The ruble tumbled from 3081 to the dollar to 3926, and it was a record fall. In just three months, the ruble lost half its value. Consumers, to hedge against price increases, bought merchandise as much as they could, while merchants sharply marked up prices. Since it is common for a customer to take some time in accepting the quoted price, placing an order, and making payments, financial loss caused by exchange rate movement can easily occur.

Without a hedge, an American exporter selling to an Italian customer will suffer financially when the euro declines in value because the euros paid, after conversion, will yield fewer dollars than first expected. Some observers may conclude that, though the danger of the falling euro to the US exporter is real and serious, there is an equal opportunity for the euro to gain in value instead. Under this scenario, the exporter can increase the expected profit– once from the sale of the goods and again from the exchange gain. Based on this contention, the exporter would miss the windfall profit if the exporter had hedged. The problem with this idea, however, is that the exporter is in reality a mere amateur as far as the speculation game is concerned. He or she may be an expert in and have wide knowledge of the manufacturing and selling of products.

However, the exporter is not in the business of making windfall profits and should concentrate on familiar trading operations rather than attempting to be a gambler in the unfamiliar and risky game of currency speculation. The caution applies to the Italian importer as well, especially when payment is to be made in dollars instead of euro. As demonstrated by Shell Sekiyu, a Japanese-Dutch oil refiner and distributor, its finance department lost more than $1 billion by making a bad bet in the futures market that the dollar would rise in 1993.

The foreign exchange market provides a hedging mechanism needed to protect corporate profits against undesirable changes in the exchange rate that may occur in the future. For this purpose, the market has two submarkets– spot and forward. The two differ with respect to the time of currency delivery.

The spot market is a *cash* market where foreign exchange is available for immediate delivery. In practice, delivery of major currencies occurs within one or two business days of the transaction, whereas other currencies may take slightly longer. A US firm holding foreign currency can go to its bank for immediate conversion into dollars based on the spot rate for that day. Exporters should also consider doing some hedging well before the arrival of foreign funds, and this is where the forward market becomes significant.

Companies can protect themselves by selling their expected foreign exchange forward. A forward contract is a commitment to buy or sell currencies at some specified time in the future at a specified rate. By signing a forward contract of, say, forty-five days, a company has locked in a certain rate of exchange and knows precisely how many dollars, after conversion, it will get–even though payment, conversion, and delivery will not be made until later. It should be understood that the exchange rate specified in the forty-five-day forward contract is not necessarily the same rate as the forward rate of the next day or the spot rate of forty-five days later. Both rates change constantly, fluctuating from day to day and even from minute to minute. The only rate that will stay unchanged is the one agreed on by the bank and the hedger as stipulated in the signed forward contract, even though subsequent forward and spot rates may move drastically the day after the signing of that contract.

An exporter should realise that, in most cases, the spot rate is irrelevant for the preparation of price quotations and the determination of operational costs, since foreign currency as payment is not received until a later date. Since there is no immediate conversion, the forward rate is the more appropriate one. The expectation in terms of interest rate inflation has already been factored into the agreed-on forward rate.

It is not uncommon for companies to limit their exposure to foreign currency fluctuations by requiring payments in US dollars or other currencies corresponding to the currency in which costs are incurred. They may use forward exchange contracts to hedge foreign currency transactions. These contracts allow the companies to exchange, say, US dollars for foreign currencies at maturity at rates agreed to at inception of the contracts.

FOREIGN EXCHANGE RATE

The foreign exchange rate is simply a *price*–the price of one national currency as expressed by the value of another. This exchange price, once established, allows currencies to be exchanged one for another.

The exchange rate, however, is more than just a price of a currency. It affects the cost of imported goods and exported goods; the country's rate of inflation; and a firm's profit, output, and employment. Much like the price of any other product, the price of a currency is determined by the demand and supply of that currency. When the currency is in demand, its price increases, but if a currency's supply increases without any corresponding increase in demand, its value declines.

With excess imports comes an excess supply of money because a large volume of money must be generated to pay for all the imports. With excess money in circulation, the business community, as well as the general population, begins having doubts about its value, making the currency appear overvalued.

In contrast, excess export results in too much demand for the exporting nation's currency, since foreign buyers require large amounts to pay for goods.

The currency then becomes expensive due to its scarcity, and its real value increases. The demand of a currency is determined by several factors.

Some of these include the following:

- Domestic and foreign prices of goods and services.
- Trading opportunities within a country.
- International capital movement as affected by the country's stability, inflation, money supply, and interest, as well as by speculators' perceptions and anticipations of such conditions.
- The country's export and import performance.

During the first term of the Reagan administration, the demand for dollars was extraordinarily strong because of cheap land, huge markets, economic growth, low inflation, and a relatively high interest rate in the US market. The perception that the USA was the most stable country was bolstered further by investors' confidence in former President Reagan.

These favorable factors, operating in conjunction, were more than enough to push the dollar sky-high despite the huge trade deficits of the USA at the time. Inflation discourages lending but encourages borrowing, because a loan when due can be repaid with less expensive money. A country with high inflation tends to have a weak currency, which is usually accompanied by high interest rates. The higher interest costs do not necessarily make it an undesirable place to take out loans.

CURRENCY EQUILIBRIUM

A nation's currency is in equilibrium when its rate creates no net change in the country's reserve of international means of payment. The equilibrium rate operates to keep the nation's balance of payments in proper perspective over an interval of time by making imports equal to exports. When in equilibrium, the foreign exchange rate is stable, perhaps fluctuating slightly before returning to its parity position.

Despite most nations' desire to maintain currency equilibrium, currency has a tendency to get out of balance. The equilibrium is affected by the intensity of such fundamental problems as inflation and excess import. Both inflation and excess import are negatively related to the subsequent price of the currency. In theory, neither persistent trade surpluses nor deficits are desirable. Persistent trade surpluses are unwelcome because they make the surplus nation's currency too cheap and imported products too expensive, resulting in a loss of local consumers' buying power. More serious than the surplus problem is the problem of persistent trade deficits.

When this occurs, an adjustment of the disequilibrium is necessary to restore the equality of demand and supply. The adjustment may be achieved through several techniques. For instance, the disequilibrium within limits can be temporarily financed while waiting for the disequilibrium to reverse itself. Persistent deficits cannot be financed for long periods because the country would soon exhaust its reserves and credits in the effort to pay for imports. The country may opt to choose to control its money supply in order to correct the situation. Trade deficits eventually cause a country to take steps to tighten its money supply.

By buying up excess supplies of money, the government makes money less available for imports, and the economy ultimately slows down. There are other methods that can help in restoring equilibrium by shifting demand away from foreign goods. Trade restrictions such as tariffs and foreign exchange controls achieve this purpose by making imports more expensive. If all else fails, the government may resort to changing its exchange rate in order to alter the price relationship of goods traded between two countries. The new rate would reflect a new equilibrium, which would be reinforced by an increase in the cost of imported goods.

EFFECT OF DEVALUATION

Devaluation is a reduction in the price of one currency in terms of other currencies. As in the case of Russia before its economic crisis in August 1999, it gave up 6.7 rubles for each dollar. Then the crisis hit, and the exchange rate jumped to about 23 rubles per dollar by the end of the year. Turkey did not fare any better. In early 2001, the country's currency lost 28 per cent of its value in a single day. Turkey was forced to let its currency float freely to prevent capital flight and stabilize its stock market. To the layperson, devaluation carries negative connotations, but countries that wish to stimulate exports normally want to devalue their own currency. To understand the effect of devaluation, one might consider two possible exchange rates: assume that the Japanese yen is going to be devalued from 110 yen to the dollar to 120 yen to the dollar.

A question one might then ask is whether the new rate is better than the old rate as far as Japanese exporters are concerned. The answer is a definite yes. One dollar now receives 10 more yen, meaning that a dollar spent in US currency will purchase 120 yen-worth of Japanese goods rather than 110-yen worth.

In effect, it becomes attractive for others to buy from Japan because they essentially get 10 extra yen worth of merchandise for free. This effect helps to explain why Komatsu had a $20,000 price advantage at one time over Caterpillar on a $100,000 tractor. The explanation for the differential is that the dollar was too expensive in relation to the yen. Another question one might ask is what effect devaluation will have on Japanese importers. This time, the effect is unfavorable because Japanese importers are required to spend 10 more yen to get the same amount of goods for each dollar as before.

The yen devaluation has therefore made imported goods more expensive for Japanese importers and consumers. Likewise, if the USA elects to pursue the goal of full employment, the 110-yen rate is preferred because this rate makes it easier for Japan to import more American goods without having to spend a relatively larger amount of yen. This increase in demand in Japan is accompanied by a rise in employment in the USA.

However, if the US goal is to maximize consumer welfare, the 120-yen rate is better because American consumers can get more of the relatively inexpensive imported products without having to spend relatively more dollars for them. Yet this positive effect is countered by a negative one–the demand for imported goods reduces the demand for domestic products, and unemployment increases in the USA. How well does devaluation really work? Although devaluation is supposed to expand exports and reduce imports, in practice the actual impact is often not as great as one might expect, especially in the short term.

There are several reasons for this. Initially, the trade balance may worsen instead of improve. The country in difficulty often has a low marginal propensity to save, and buying habits and long-term contracts make it difficult in the short run to alter the physical trade volume. Devaluation, instead of correcting the problem, can aggravate inflation–the very thing it is intended to control. Workers, seeing imported goods are more expensive than before, often demand wage increases to compensate for their loss of buying power. To compound the problem, domestic industries usually take advantage of the situation by boosting their own domestic prices. This is the route frequently taken by the US steel and automobile industries whenever import prices are driven up by devaluation or other restrictive measures. Therefore, devaluation cannot work in the long run because if these effects continue to cycle and recycle, a collapse of the economy is the result.

In order to be effective, devaluation must be accompanied by a programme to urge local firms to exercise self-restraint and to encourage people to consume less and save more. In February 1989, the Sandinista government of Nicaragua devalued its currency and raised prices for petroleum products for the third time that year. The devaluation was designed to contain hyperinflation that had reached 20,000 per cent in 1988. One must also keep in mind that a substantial time lag occurs between the change in currency value and its impact on the physical flow of trade. The lag occurs because suppliers and buyers need time to adjust their habits and decisions before they start getting used to the new exchange rates. Furthermore, although devaluation makes imports more expensive, consumers may fail to curtail their purchases of those imports.

This phenomenon is known as the J curve because it takes quite a while for the economy to round the turn of the J. One should then expect a modest swelling of the trade deficit to occur after devaluation, before a sharp recovery can follow if the right steps have been taken. In general, economists believe that it takes about eighteen months before an increase in import prices can have significant impact on the volume of trade adjustment. If the economy is successful in expanding exports and reducing imports as intended, devaluation should increase the national income, which in turn will stimulate the volume of imports once again. Thus the initial effect of devaluation can be reversed in the long run. Moreover, any deliberate devaluation carried on will result in a beggar-my-neighbour policy, which will export domestic unemployment to other countries. The deliberate practice of devaluation can easily provoke other trading partners to retaliate by lowering their own money value. Because of these consequences, the net gain from devaluation in the longer run is not going to be as large as its initial gain.

EXCHANGE RATE SYSTEMS

There should be no doubt that an exchange rate can be quite volatile and that anyone who is unfortunate enough to make an incorrect decision about the rate's direction will pay for it dearly. Anyone having any doubts about the validity of this statement need only consider Argentina. In 1981, the Argentine peso plunged to only one-seventh of the value of what it had been at the beginning of the same year. The concern over such a severe reduction in value has led economists and government officials into a heated and continuing debate over the best exchange rate system. All existing systems have strengths as well as weaknesses, and there is probably no such thing as a perfect exchange rate system. The major exchange rate systems may be ranked in terms of increasing flexibility: fixed rate, semifixed and flexible or floating rate.

GOLD STANDARD

The gold standard was the start of modern exchange rate systems. Gold was first developed as the standard of international exchange in the United Kingdom in the late 1700s, and many other nations had followed suit by the mid-1800s. In the case of the USA, the US Coinage Act placed the dollar on the gold standard in 1873. Each country was required to link its currency value to gold by legally defining a *par value* based on a specified quantity of gold for its standard monetary unit. Thus, exchange rates had fixed par values as determined by the gold content of the national monetary links.

A modification of this system occurred at a later date, and it became known as the gold exchange standard. Created in 1922, the modified system allowed countries to use both gold and the US dollar for international settlement because the USA stood ready to redeem dollars in gold on demand.

In 1930, a dollar was defined as containing 23.22 grains of fine gold, whereas a British pound had 113 grains. In 1971, the gold content of the dollar was redefined from 0.888671 grams of gold to 0.73666 grams. The price of gold, being $20.67 per fine troy ounce in 1879, was later changed to $35 in 1933. The increase in gold price in effect devalued the dollar. Because each national currency had to be backed by gold, each country's money supply, in turn, was determined by its gold holdings. Because of this common denominator, all currencies' values were rigidly fixed.

Although the values were fixed by law, that does not mean that these exchange rates could not fluctuate to some small degree in accordance with the demand and supply of a currency. The fluctuation had to be within the limits set by the costs of interest, transport, insurance, and handling of gold from one country to another. The gold standard functioned to maintain equilibrium through the so-called *price-specie-flow mechanism* with specie meaning gold.

The mechanism was intended to restore the equilibrium automatically. When a country's currency inflated too fast, the currency lost competitiveness in the world market. The deteriorating trade balance resulting from imports being greater than exports led to a decline in the confidence of the currency.

As the exchange rate approached the gold export point, gold was withdrawn from reserves and shipped abroad to pay for imports. With less gold at home, the country was forced to reduce its money supply, a reduction accompanied by a slow-down in economic activity, high interest rates, recession, reduced national income, and increased unemployment.

The onset of hard times would pressure inflation to be reduced. As domestic prices declined, demand for domestic products increased, and demand for imports declined. Price deflation thus made domestic products attractive both at home and abroad.

The country's balance of payments improved, and gold started to flow into the country once again. The price-specie-flow mechanism also restored order in the case of trade surpluses by working in the opposite manner.

There are several reasons why the gold standard could not function well over the long term. Because gold is a scarce commodity, gold volume could not grow fast enough to allow adequate amounts of money to be created to finance the growth of world trade.

The problem was aggravated further by gold being taken out of reserve for art and industrial consumption, not to mention the desire of many people to own gold. The banning of gold hoarding and public exporting of gold bullion by President Franklin Roosevelt was not sufficient to remedy the problem. Another problem of the system was the unrealistic expectation that countries would subordinate their national economies to the dictates of gold as well as to external and monetary conditions.

In other worlds, a country with high inflation and/or trade deficit was required to reduce its money supply and consumption, resulting in recession and unemployment. This was a strict discipline that many nations could not force upon themselves or their population. Instead of having sufficient courage to use unemployment to discourage imports, importing countries simply insisted on intervention through tariffs and devaluations instead. Nations insisted on their rights to intervene and devalue domestic currencies in order to meet nationwide employment objectives. Because of the rigidity of the system, it was only a matter of time before major countries decided to abandon the gold standard, starting with the United Kingdom in 1931 in the midst of a worldwide recession. With a 12 per cent unemployment rate at the time, the United Kingdom chose to leave the gold standard rather than exacerbate the unemployment problem. Monetary chaos followed in many countries.

PAR VALUE

The need to restructure the international monetary system after World War II was the incentive for the delegates of forty-four countries to meet at Bretton Woods, New Hampshire, in 1994.The result of the meeting was the creation of the World Bank to finance development projects and the International Monetary Fund to promote monetary stability while facilitating world trade expansion.

The IMF system, also known as the par value, adjustable, or Bretton Woods system, was created to overcome the problems associated with the gold standard. The inadequacy of gold as an international currency was overcome by turning to the US dollar.

As the other international currency, the dollar provides added reserves for stability as well as liquidity for gold and currencies. The IMF required a fixed exchange ratio or par value. The agreement fixed the world's paper currencies in relation to the US dollar, which was fully convertible into gold. Regarding the dollar as the acceptable store of value, countries were willing to receive it in settlement for international balances.

Based on policies designed to avoid disruptive fluctuations and rate rigidity, members had to establish a par value for their currency, either directly in terms of gold, or indirectly by relating the par value to the gold content of the US dollar.

The IMF prohibits any unauthorized use of multiple exchange rates. A correction of the par of exchange was possible in the case of a fundamental disequilibrium. The IMF was required to concur with a change from the initial par value through a cumulative amount of up to 10 per cent. Any change in par value beyond this amount required the IMF's approval.

However, there was difficulty in determining:

- When a fundamental disequilibrium existed,
- Whether the currency was overvalued or undervalued, and
- The extent of the overvaluation or undervaluation.

To discourage speculation, the change in par value was kept infrequent, resulting in a late adjustment. Further, during a crisis, there was no time for mutual consultations as called for by the IMF's Articles of Agreement. In fact, mere rumors of pending consultations would probably be more than enough to encourage intense speculation. For instance, if the dollar sank in value to its lower limit but was not allowed to go further, no one would want to buy it at that point because its value was being kept artificially high. Its high price did not reflect its actual lower value. Speculators, knowing that devaluation had to follow soon and that the dollar had nowhere to go but down once devaluation took effect, would sell dollars first before buying them back at a new lower rate or price. With only sellers and no buyers, the resulting panic could force the financial markets to close.

One more problem with the par value system was the burden it placed on the dollar. The constant requirements for more and more dollars to finance the ever-expanding trade volume made foreign central banks and private holders nervous, weakening their confidence in the dollar and heightening speculation.

After starting strong, the dollar ended up being weak and unwanted, just as predicted by Gresham's law: Bad money drives out good money. An analogy may be used to explain this problem. A man of wealth and reputation is able to obtain credit to buy anything he desires, but as he begins to overextend himself or as he prints his own money, the confidence of creditors in him and his money would severely erode. This analogy may serve to explain why Japan does not want its yen to become a reserve currency. The consequent lack of confidence in the US dollar drove creditors to turn to gold once again as an alternative. As the gold price rose, a gold pool was created in 1961 to stabilize its market price. When the pool sold gold to bring its price down, it had a negative impact on the dollar because 59 per cent of the pool was a contribution from the USA. As the US gold reserve shrank from $24 billion to $12 billion in 1970, the gold price remained stubbornly high, and confidence in the dollar eroded further. The pool was finally dissolved, and a two-tier gold price came into being; that is, central banks agreed to continue to buy and sell gold at the official price of $35 an ounce, but the free market price was allowed to seek its own level.

To many people, the adjustable peg lacks the certainty of the gold system as well as the flexibility of the floating system. In spite of the periodic growth in world trade, low inflation, and low interest rates under the IMF system, the problems created for the dollar were so great that President Richard Nixon finally severed the link between the dollar and gold in August 1971, thus ending the Bretton Woods international monetary system. Citizens of the USA were once again allowed to own or trade gold on 31 December 1974, and the dollar was permitted to float to seek its own value.

CRAWLING PEG

A cross between a fixed rate system and a fully flexible system are the semifixed systems such as the crawling peg and the wide band. They differ from fixed rates because of their greater flexibility in terms of the exchange rate movement. However, they are not a floating system either because there is still a limit with regard to how far the exchange rate can move. Because the infrequent adjustment of the IMF's par value system necessitated a large devaluation at a later date, the crawling peg rate was developed. The idea is to adjust the rate slowly by small amounts at any point in time on a continuous basis to correct for any overvaluation and undervaluation. The continuous but small adjustment mechanism was designed to discourage speculation by setting an upper limit that speculators could gain from devaluation in one year.

The crawling peg system requires countries to have ample reserves for the prolonged process of adjustment. In addition, the minor adjustments may not correct the currency's overvaluation or undervaluation. Consider the case of Brazil, which has employed a form of a crawling peg to remedy its hyperinflation problem by devaluing its currency by a few percentage points each month. Usually, the devaluation of 2 per cent each week takes place on Thursdays, as if it were some kind of a supermarket special. However, even this annual adjustment total of more than 100 per cent is not enough, and from time to time the 2 per cent mini-devaluations must be supplemented by a maxi-devaluation.

In December 1979 and February 1983, for example, Brazil suddenly chopped the value of the cruzerio by 30 per cent and 24 per cent, respectively.

Similarly, Mexico has devalued the peso at a controlled rate that proved too small to reflect the peso's proper value. In the first part of 1985, the peso lost more than 85 per cent of its value against the dollar on the free market. In contrast to the official rate of 24 pesos to the dollar, the free market exchange houses charged 325 pesos, and the rates at the border were even higher. Considering that only a few years earlier the exchange rate was less than 100 pesos to the dollar, it may at first seem that the extent of the devaluation was dramatic. However, it was not enough.

In mid-1986, the peso plunged a great deal more, resulting in each US dollar fetching more than 700 pesos. Near the end of 1987, the peso lost as much as 59 per cent in value in only a few days and ended the year at the rate of 2200 pesos to a US dollar. Such large devaluations are exactly what speculators wait for.

In late 1994, *Business Week* magazine mentioned that Mexico's use of crawling peg to systematically devalue the peso had worked well in controlling inflation while boosting exports. Yet only a month later the peso was in full crisis. The collapse of the Mexican peso at the end of 1994 as well as the economic crisis which ensued in 1995 was a result of Mexico's attempt to keep the value of the peso artificially high, but when the government ran out of reserves to support the currency, the peso collapsed and savagely hit Mexican citizens.

WIDE BAND

The purpose of the wide band is to compensate for the rigidity of the fixed rate systems. Similar to and yet different from the adjustable peg system, the wide band allows the currency value to fluctuate, say, 5 per cent on each side of the par. Not being dedicated primarily to exchange rate changes, this system uses the more flexible movement to warn speculators of the adverse consequences when their guess about the direction of the exchange rate proves to be wrong. To pursue the elusive goal of exchange rate stability, the European Monetary system incorporated certain features in order to force member countries to make adjustments to correct their divergent economic conditions.

As a miniature Bretton Woods system, the EMS employed the socalled grid-parity system to link the members' currencies so tightly that they became almost a single currency. The EMS had a fixed exchange rate among members, and the participating currencies could fluctuate by up to 2.25 per cent on either side of their bilateral "central rates" against other members, with the exception of the volatile lira's 6 percent fluctuation on either side. The EMS created a currency bloc known as the European Currency Unit to provide a substitute as well as a complement to the US dollar. The ECU was a composite of several national currencies. The weights for each currency were based on the relative GNP of each country and each country's share in intra-European trade.

The weights were examined every five years or if the relative value of any currency changed by 25 per cent. Under the wide band scheme, a country pursuing more inflationary policies will find the prices of its international goods going up, necessitating a depreciation programme to correct the country's balance of payments in order to slow growth and curb inflation, while eventually risking recession. The country's exchange rate would then sink towards the floor under its par value. Once the fixed limit is reached, the country is back to the rigidity of the fixed rate all over gain. Moreover, if a wide band is desirable due to the increase in flexibility, a country may be better off with no limit for movement at all.

FLOATING (FLEXIBLE) SYSTEM

Under the fixed systems, excessive demand for gold developed and the USA was forced to suspend the sale of gold in 1968, except to official parties. However, taking this action did not help, and by the late 1960s the dollar came under increasing pressure due to the prolonged and steep deterioration in the balance of payments. A crisis of confidence developed and foreigners' reluctance to hold dollars resulted in a change in the dollar's historic value.

On August 15, 1971, the USA suspended the convertibility of the dollar into gold and other reserve assets altogether, and it floated the dollar to force a change in the parity as well as a review of the IMF. The subsequent Smithsonian Agreement resulted in a revaluation of other currencies and the devaluation of the dollar by 10.35 per cent. In February 1973, following a great deal of speculation against the dollar, the crisis renewed, and a second 10 per cent devaluation followed. The crisis forced the official foreign exchange markets to close in Europe and Japan for about two and a half weeks. When these markets reopened, all major currencies were allowed to float. After an initial period of remarkable stability, the dollar sank rapidly for seven weeks because of balance-of-payments deficits, Watergate revelations, renewed inflation in the USA, and a tightening of money abroad.

Had the fixed systems been in effect, a traditional crisis would have resulted. Foreign exchange markets would have been closed, and large-scale adjustment of parities would have been necessary. With the dollar free to float, however, the beneficial effect was that speculative pressures were reflected in a sharp drop in the exchange value of the dollar without a closing of the market. The resultant devaluation, in turn, helped the USA to improve its trade performance.

In October 1978, another crisis came along for the US dollar. Concerns over inflation in the USA prompted a panic selling of the dollar, and the stock market plunged. In spite of the risk of recession, the Carter administration was forced to take drastic measures. Among the measures taken were an increase in the Federal Reserve's discount rate, gold sale, and dollar buying. Initially, the magnitude of the action took the market by surprise. Gold prices dropped, and the bond market, stock market, and dollar all rose significantly. Yet by the end of the month, the strong anti-inflation policies themselves weakened confidence in the government, and chaos ensued.

Additional panic selling drove the dollar to record lows. Once again, by allowing the dollar to float, the traditional adverse consequences of market closings and official devaluation were averted. Under a flexible or floating system, the market force, based on demand and supply, determines a currency's value. A surplus in a country results in an appreciation of its currency, immediate higher prices, mass reserve, and opportunity costs. In addition, too much money on reserve leads to a loss of investment opportunities. On the other hand, a country's deficit will lower its currency value, making it easier to export more later.

In the absence of government intervention, the float is said to be *clean*. It becomes *dirty* when there is central bank intervention to influence exchange rates, which is a common action, especially by those with inflation and trade problems. A country experiencing inflation must reduce public spending and the money supply to cool its economy. However, due to the delayed impact of devaluation on trade improvement, such restrictive measures need time to achieve their intended purpose before inflationary pressures work themselves back into the economy through higher import prices. Therefore, the country must continuously monitor and defend its currency over the time that the changes are taking effect. Interventions are unlikely to change a market trend.

Central banks' combined resources are not adequate to reverse a fundamental trend in the foreign exchange market. The foreign exchange reserves held by central banks total only $1 trillion, about the average daily volume of currency trading. On June 24, 1994, the Federal Reserve Board and sixteen other central banks spent more than $3 billion to support the US dollar. Market forces, determined to send the dollar the other way, fought back. By the end of the day, the dollar was even worse off than it was before the intervention, proving an old rule in currency intervention. However, one recent study of the Institute for International Economics broke with the conventional wisdom by stating that intervention could serve an effective policy tool. The published study maintained that intervention on the foreign exchange market is useful to determine how the market perceives a country's macroeconomic policy.

OFFICIAL CLASSIFICATION OF EXCHANGE RATE REGIMES

The IMF has identified eight types of exchange rate regimes. These regimes may be divided into three broad groups: floating, intermediate, and hard peg. Floating exchange rate regimes include independently floating regimes and managed floating regimes with no predetermined path for the exchange rate.

Intermediate exchange rate regimes include soft pegs and tightly managed floating regimes. Hard peg regimes include currency boards and exchange rate regimes with no separate legal tender. It should be noted that a country's official classification of its exchange rate regimes may be more fiction than fact. The declared regime often differs from actual country practices. A study of 153 countries dating back to 1946 found that, in the 1950s, 1960s, and early 1970s, 45 per cent of the countries that officially claimed a pegged exchange rate actually had some variant of a float. In the 1980s and 1990s a new type of misclassification emerged: 53 per cent of the official "managed floats" turned out to be de facto pegs or crawling pegs.

These misclassifications may have led to a false conclusion that a freely floating exchange rate might be an unwise choice for policy makers. The countries with official floating exchange rates experienced an average annual inflation rate of 174 per cent while achieving a meager annual per capita growth rate of 0.5 per cent. However, after weeding out countries with de facto pegs or "freely falling" episodes, countries with true floats actually had annual inflation rates below 10 per cent and an annual per capita growth of 2.3 per cent. In practice, exchange rate regimes vary along a continuum. There is also evidence that countries have moved away from intermediate exchange rate regimes towards floating and, to a lesser extent, hard pegs. For countries that have integrated themselves closely with global capital markets, they need to choose between the two extremes–either a floating currency or a hard peg. Some economies have hardened their pegs by introducing currency boards. A monetary union provides even harder pegs.

EVALUATION OF FLOATING RATES

Given that a perfect system does not exist, how does one go about evaluating existing systems? A system is acceptable when, given a certain rate of inflation in a country, the value of that country's currency is reduced in the international exchange markets by the same extent, while the value of the currency in a country with no inflation holds steady or moves up accordingly. The system being used should not allow countries to manipulate their rates to gain an unfair advantage over rival trading partners. In essence, a good system promotes stability, certainty, and inflation control. The fixed rate and floating rate systems have diverse natures and characteristics. Therefore, both of the systems cannot meet the same goals of certainty, stability, and inflation control.

Advocates of the fixed rate plan believe that the certainty and rigidity of exchange rates can promote economic efficiency, public confidence, and inflation control. In recent years, several US public officials have been encouraging the return of some kind of gold standard. If this system could indeed work as intended, there would probably be no need to have more than one world currency. One book published in 1994 generated some interest by claiming that floating exchange rates would create catastrophes. The author advocated a return to the classical gold standard. However, the book provided little empirical evidence that the floating system has impeded economic growth, and the author's analysis was heavily criticized. Experience has shown that fixed rates do not work well for a prolonged period. For fixed rates to work, the gold price must remain fixed to control inflation–a difficult if not impossible requirement. In addition, making fiat money convertible into gold cannot guarantee the willingness to achieve long-term stability in the purchasing power of money. Furthermore, while gold prices and general prices tend to move together over long periods of time, short-term movements of gold prices have been much more erratic than movements in general prices. Other commodity indices provide better early warnings of fluctuations in inflation than gold. Therefore, there are better alternatives than a gold standard on which to base monetary policy.

Other problems associated with fixed rates include massive capital flows during a crisis and the closing of financial markets. Between 1976 and 1985, citizens of Mexico and Venezuela sent $53 billion and $30 billion, respectively, out of their countries. It is also unrealistic to believe that the USA wants its money supply to be backed by gold and to be at the mercy of major gold producers such as South Africa. Critics of floating exchange rates contend that the system causes uncertainty, which discourages trade while promoting speculation.

In fact, world exports climbed steadily for eight years after the float was put in place, and it is apparent that the system does not interfere with world exports. The claim that uncertainty encourages investors to speculate and destabilize exchange rates is probably invalid. The fixed rate system is more likely to encourage speculation by giving speculators a one-way, no-lose bet to make money, as the exchange rate can move in only one direction once the upper limit is reached. Whatever the fault of the floating rates, the fixed rate regime is subject to the same fault, probably to a greater magnitude. Because of a lack of the inherent discipline imposed by fixed rates, floating currencies are said to encourage inflation.

In reality, the flexible rate system makes the consequences of inflationary policies more readily apparent to the general public, labour, and employers in the form of a declining foreign value of the currency and an upward trend in domestic prices. This public awareness makes it easier to implement proper policies to correct the situation without reacting in a crisis atmosphere, as might otherwise occur. These countries are then able to pursue the mixture of unemployment and price objectives that they prefer and that are consistent with international equilibrium. The floating system should be accepted with reservation. One problem occurs due to a high degree of short-term volatility and the large medium-term swings in exchange rates.

In addition, floating rates do not work well during recessions or through a faltering economic recovery. The float may exacerbate inflationary problems by quickly feeding higher import costs into local wages and prices. When Mexico devalued its peso in 1976, labour unions won a 23 per cent wage increase, which served only to force the government to make a second devaluation just two months later.

The plunging value of the peso in late 1994 and 1995, on the other hand, created a great deal of unemployment and hardship in Mexico. A decade of floating exchange rates has shown that developing countries have realised more benefits than problems. Floating rates do not necessarily result in a currency's free fall, and they do not imply higher inflation or lower output. Of the twelve countries surveyed for the period 1985 to 1992, inflation declined in six countries following floating and accelerated in only one.

Regarding output, of the eleven countries surveyed, six experienced faster GDP growth; only Brazil and Paraguay showed decline in growth after floating. The financial crises experienced by many emerging market economies appeared to have one thing in common. These economies maintained soft pegs by pegging their exchange rates in value to either a particular currency or a basket of currencies.

As in the case of the Asian economic crisis, the five Asian economies were actively managing their exchange rates, partly to promote their competitiveness. To maintain soft pegs, the authorities were committed to defend it but would allow rate changes under a significant attack. However, the increased integration of their national capital markets and the international capital markets makes it almost impossible to sustain soft pegs over extended periods. The international capital markets simply will not allow domestic policy mistakes to go unnoticed and unpunished. In spite of some limitations, the floating system was able to carry the world through a number of economic crises quite smoothly. The floating system has proven itself through several periods of raging inflation, deep recession, and massive money movements. Many observers continue to find fault with it, but other systems have just as much, if not more, of the same flaws. At present, there does not appear to be a superior alternative that can be used.

FINANCIAL IMPLICATIONS AND STRATEGIES

It is extremely difficult to predict the movement of a currency. As an example, the US dollar depreciated by about 10 per cent against the German mark and the Japanese yen during the first half of 1994, even though the Federal Reserve Board pushed up the federal funds rate while the Bundesbank lowered its rates and the Japanese prime minister resigned. During the first few months of 1995, the dollar dropped by about 20 per cent more against the Japanese yen before beginning a surge of 25 per cent. The euro was introduced at $1.18 to the dollar on 1 January 1999, floated to below 83 cents in October 2000, and soared to a record high of $1.29 in early 2004; that is, down 31 per cent and back up more than 50 per cent in four years with no obvious economic fundamentals to explain gyrations.

EARLY WARNING SYSTEMS

While exchange rate movements are predictable at longer horizons based on the countries' varying interest rates, business firms have to find some practical ways to deal with short-term volatility. It may be worthwhile to consider some early warning systems. While some models have as many as twenty indicators, the IMF researchers have developed a simple five-variable macroeconomic model for an after the event analysis. The indicators are: degree of real exchange rate overvaluation, size of current account deficit as a share of GDP, growth rate of exports, rate of growth of reserves, and ratio of short-term external debt to reserves. The model worked reasonably well, producing results with relatively high warning signals for Korea, Thailand, Indonesia, and Malaysia, but not for the Philippines. Investment banks have been developing their own in-house models to predict currency crises. One such economic model is Deutsche Bank's Alarm Clock. While these models are certainly not perfect, they seem to be far superior to some of the alternative indicators often used by the markets and analysts. Even though there were many false alarms, the models were able to anticipate potentially dangerous pressures at work in foreign exchange markets. In addition, they are objective and mechanical, thus minimizing analysts' biases.

HEDGING

"Hedges protect yards from dogs and businesses from financial exposure." One study found a firm's size to have the most important effect on its risk management practices. The effect of size is in terms of the use of computer technology, the use of both physical and synthetic products, and the number of both short-term and long-term foreign funding activities employed. In practice, size is irrelevant because any prudent firm must manage foreign exchange risks.

One study focused on the extent to which industry actively manages rather than hedges foreign exchange risk. 70 per cent of firms trade their foreign exchange exposures, and some traders do so without internal foreign exchange dealing limits or controls on their position taking. The favored techniques of risk management are demonstrated by the extensive use of synthetic products in addition to the more usual physical products such as spot and forward transactions.

There are a number of hedging methods, and they include forward contracts, swaps, or options. One method involves the inter-bank market, which offers both spot and forward transactions. An importer or buyer may purchase foreign currency immediately on the spot market for future use. When the foreign exchange is not needed until sometime in the future, the seller can turn to the forward market, usually entering into a forward contract with a bank agreeing on the purchase and sale of currencies at a certain price at some future time. Smaller companies often have trouble obtaining forward contracts from their banks for two reasons. First, they are not well known. Second, their transaction sizes are too small to attract banks' interest.

Regardless of size, any company may use the futures market for hedging. The main difference between forward and futures contracts is the "standardized" sizes and delivery dates of the futures transactions. The standardization feature provides market liquidity, making it easy to enter and exit the market at any time, but this same feature excludes the likelihood of meeting individual needs exactly.

The most dominant futures market for foreign currencies is the International Monetary Market division of Chicago Mercantile Exchange in Chicago. These global commodities demand twenty-four-hour attention. To meet this need, the LIFFE and the SIMEX both patterned after the IMM, make twenty-four-hour trading a reality. Currency options, once illegal in the USA, provide another hedging alternative.

The most important characteristic of options is an option buyer's ability to limit the loss, if the buyer's guess is wrong, to the premium paid. A buyer of a currency option acquires the right either to buy or sell a fixed amount of foreign currency at a set price within a specified time period, and the buyer may exercise this right when it is profitable to do so. Both *futures* and *options on futures* significantly reduce risk. However, there are two key advantages of options on futures over futures. First, since a trader is able to take positions smaller than standard futures contracts, options on futures allow small businesses to hedge more effectively. Second, compared to futures, options on futures provide greater flexibility by allowing hedgers to cap their exposure. Although banks have been and still are the first choice of corporations seeking to manage foreign exchange risk, exchanges have devised new ways to attract firms or to get banks to work through exchanges.

Coca-Cola Co. hedges its foreign earnings by buying options. GAF Corp., a New Jersey specialty chemicals and building materials conglomerate with $1 billion in sales, works with either a bank or an exchange, depending on the dollar volume.

It uses exchanges for most of its options transactions when they fall in the range of $5 million to $25 million because exchanges are more competitive in transactions of that size. When the amounts exceed $25 million, GAF uses banks instead. One study found that it is not a common practice to adopt innovative foreign exchange risk management products.

In fact, the simple, first-generation product is still more popular among American corporations than the second-generation and third generation products. Hedging, like buying insurance, can be expensive.

It costs about $26 million to hedge $500 million worth of earnings. A forward contract costs half a percentage point per year of the revenue being hedged. This explains why Eastman Kodak Co. has decided to abandon hedging, believing that the ups and downs of currencies would simply even out in the long run. Multinationals, due to the nature of their operations, may be able to employ a natural hedge.

The technique involves matching revenues and costs in the same currency. One variation of the technique is to manufacture and buy supplies locally. By using locally earned revenues to pay for production of local goods, a company can minimize the earnings that must be translated or repatriated. Another variation of the method is to look at the net exposure. Coca-Cola manages most of its foreign currency exposures on a consolidated basis by using natural offsets to determine the net exposure.

In addition, the weakness in one currency is often offset by the strengths in others over time. It should be noted that a firm's ability to construct operational hedges has an impact on its exchange rate risk exposure. Those multinationals with greater breadth are less exposed to currency risk. In contrast, those with more highly concentrated networks are more exposed.

LEADING AND LAGGING

In order to deal with the complexity of international trade, two strategies should be considered: leading and lagging. For an MNC with a network of subsidiaries, several techniques may be used to reduce foreign exchange. Subsidiaries with strong currencies could delay or lag the remittances of dividends, royalties, and fees. Those in weak currency countries could try to lead, or pay promptly, their liabilities. It is important to recognize, however, that these strategies involve speculation since no one really knows the timing and extent of the movement of a currency.

INVOICING

The currency to be used for the purpose of invoicing should be considered carefully. Toyota Motor Corp. operates two factories in England. Since the United Kingdom has so far refused to give up the pound sterling for the euro, Toyota faces a risk of losing money when it converts its euro revenues into pounds to pay for British-made components. To solve the problem, Toyota has told its local suppliers to set prices in euros for any new business. Ideally, Toyota wants to eventually pay bills in Europe in euros as it expands operations in the region. When the buyer is in a soft currency but the seller is in a hard currency, the invoice should use the seller's currency. However, the buyer's currency should be used for invoicing when the buyer is in a hard currency but the seller is in a soft currency. When both the buyer and the seller are in soft currencies, they should consider a third currency as an alternative, but if both are in hard currencies, it may not matter much whether the buyer's currency or the seller's currency is employed. Note that these invoicing strategies apply also to an MNC's subsidiaries that trade with one another. Furthermore, when the volume justifies the cost, the MNC should coordinate the invoicing activities by setting up a reinvoicing center.

PASS-THROUGH COSTS

Domestic firms should not expect to improve their performance solely on the basis of foreign competitors' misfortunes. After all, foreign firms are still in a position to decide how much of the cost increase to pass on to buyers. Regarding the gap in percentage terms between the appreciation in the value of each country's currency measured in dollars and the price of its exports measured in dollars, Japan passed on far less of its currency-induced cost increases. Specifically, Japan passed on only 53 per cent of its currency-induced price increases and left a large 47 per cent gap between the increase in its dollar-measured costs and the dollar price of its exports.

In the case of the United Kingdom, it passed on more than the currency appreciation by 10 per cent and almost exactly its labour cost increases. Germany, in contract, passed on 100 per cent of its currency increases, resulting in a 0 per cent gap. However, Germany passed on 83 per cent of its labour cost increases, leaving a 17 per cent labour cost gap.

OTHER STRATEGIES

Hedging techniques are not adequate in managing long-term exposure for foreign exchange risk. Other production and marketing strategies should be considered. This is exactly what Oki Electric Industry Co. Ltd. did to cope with the yen's rapid appreciation in 1993.The company shifted production of high-export-ratio products overseas. It built another production plant in Thailand for printer components and also planned to increase overseas procurement.

Renault, a French car maker, believes that geographic diversification is a natural hedge. The assumption is that the many currencies will balance each other out. This assumption, however, may be occasionally debatable. Renault itself lost $108 million in one quarter in 1992 due partly to the sharp devaluations of the British and Italian currencies.

Globalization offers protection from currency fluctuations. One study confirmed that exchange rate uncertainty, while having a negative effect on capacity expansions by domestic companies, has no effect on investment by multinational firms. Evidently, multinational corporations can manage exchange rate uncertainty better than domestic firms because they are able to shift their production among different countries to minimize the effects of uncertainty. In the late 1980s, Komatsu was hit hard by the strong yen. To solve this problem, this Japanese firm established strategic alliances overseas to shift production abroad. Komatsu has a joint venture with Dresser Industries in the USA while being linked in Europe with Hanomag, which has 20 per cent of the German wheel-loader and bulldozer market. In addition to its ties with Korea's Samsung Shipbuilding and Heavy Industries, Komatsu imports sheet metal parts from its Indonesian joint venture and has a long-standing agreement with Robbins, a US firm, on underground machinery.

Japanese multinationals have demonstrated how they have been able to cope–painfully but successfully–with the strong yen. In the early 1980s, Japan's net foreign assets were only $25 billion. The overseas stake should exceed $1 trillion at the end of the century. These assets should earn Japan a large amount of profits, dividends, and interest. Japanese exporters have responded to the surging yen by sacrificing profit margins in order to hold the line on export prices in real terms. They have accelerated their direct investment in nearby Asia to capitalize on low cost labour. At the same time they have shifted production at home from commodity- type products to high-value quality products. In addition, geographic diversification has allowed Japanese firms to soften losses due to yen appreciations. Finally, it should be pointed out that an exporter's overvalued currency may still have some unintended benefits. Japanese firms have been able to use their overvalued yen to buy raw materials from abroad at a lower cost, thus reducing their manufacturing costs. Furthermore, the adverse currency movement may allow a company to show market commitment while gaining market share.

CONCLUSION

This stage, although somewhat technical in nature, has covered various financial circumstances related to international marketing. Borrowing money is one thing, but exchanging money is another matter altogether. There have been, there are, and there always will be dreadful accounts about how companies were caught short by the devaluation of a currency. For decades, authorities have debated the merits of the various competing currency exchange systems. Although no single system is able to eliminate completely the volatility of rate movements, there is at present no superior alternative to the system of managed floating rates. Regardless of the exchange rate system used, rate changes are almost always a certainty, and thus some degree of risk is inevitable. Because MNCs have no determination with regard to the exchange systems–fixed or floating rates–they must attempt to reduce their foreign exchange exposure. To hedge, multinationals may consider any one of the following markets: spot, forward, futures, options, and brokers' services.

Other alternatives may include using adjustable prices and billing in strong currencies. Due to the varying rates of inflation among countries, the impact of inflation on the value of the currency cannot be overlooked. For companies with assets in a high-inflation country, the value of their assets can be substantially and adversely affected. Yet MNCs can benefit from inflation if they know how to borrow money wisely. With regard to the timing of payment, money managers should lead in soft currencies and lag in stronger currencies. For an MNC with subsidiaries in many countries, reinvoicing is a well-advised strategy. In spite of an increasing number of techniques believed to minimize foreign exchange exposure, it is premature to expect that the methods discussed here are all the techniques that corporate managers can employ. With trends indicating movement towards further deregulation in an increasingly complex world of financial activities, it is just a matter of time before new strategies are created to manage exchange risks.

Index